CITY KIDS

The Rutgers Series in Childhood Studies

The Rutgers Series in Childhood Studies is dedicated to increasing our understanding of children and childhoods, past and present, throughout the world. Children's voices and experiences are central. Authors come from a variety of fields, including anthropology, criminal justice, history, literature, psychology, religion, and sociology. The books in this series are intended for students, scholars, practitioners, and those who formulate policies that affect children's everyday lives and futures.

Edited by Myra Bluebond-Langner, Board of Governors Professor of Anthropology, Rutgers University and True Colours Chair in Palliative Care for Children and Young People, University College London, Institute of Child Health.

Advisory Board

Perri Klass, New York University

Jill Korbin, Case Western Reserve University

Bambi Schieffelin, New York University

Enid Schildkraut, American Museum of Natural History and Museum for African Art

CITY KIDS

Transforming Racial Baggage

MARIA KROMIDAS

RUTGERS UNIVERSITY PRESS

New Brunswick, New Jersey, and London

Library of Congress Cataloging-in-Publication Data
Names: Kromidas, Maria, 1974– author.
Title: City kids : transforming racial baggage / Maria Kromidas.
Description: New Brunswick, New Jersey : Rutgers University Press, 2016. | Series:
Rutgers series in childhood studies | Includes bibliographical references and index.
Identifiers: LCCN 2016008281| ISBN 9780813584799 (hardcover : alk. paper) | ISBN
9780813584782 (pbk. : alk. paper) | ISBN 9780813584805 (e-book (epub)) | ISBN
9780813584812 (e-book (web pdf))
Subjects: LCSH: Ethnicity in children—New York (State)—New York—Case
studies. | Race awareness in children—New York (State)—New York—Case studies.
| Race—Study and teaching (Elementary)—New York (State)—New York—Case
studies. | Multiculturalism—Study and teaching (Elementary)—Case studies. |
United States—Race relations—Study and teaching (Elementary)—Case studies.
Classification: LCC GN495.6 .K76 2016 | DDC 305.8009747—dc23
LC record available at https://lccn.loc.gov/2016008281

A British Cataloging-in-Publication record for this book is available from
the British Library.

Visit our website: http://rutgerspress.rutgers.edu

Manufactured in the United States of America

For Markella

CONTENTS

ACKNOWLEDGMENTS

Although my name is on the cover, this book is a posse cut, and here those others get credit for the good things in it. First and foremost I salute my participants. This book is but an imperfect attempt to capture the joy of my encounter with the kids and their unruly spirits. They've been standing above me the whole time, making sure I properly represent. I thank the parents, teachers, and administrators at PS AV, residents of Augursville who participated in or enabled the research, as well as the gatekeepers at the NYC Department of Education. A special shout out to Ms. Lee for adopting an anthropologist, not a task for the meek.

I thank my William Paterson University crew for their support and encouragement through the long haul—Tom Gundling, Vidya Kalaramadam, Ruth Maher, Murli Natrajan, and Maria Villar. I give a special thanks to Murli for his critical eye on the book proposal and his repeated exhortations to finish! I am grateful for the inspiration provided at the very last stages by Jason Ambroise and Anna M. West. I thank Jim Hauser and the members of the Professional Writing Group at WPU for their comments on early drafts of the introduction and chapter 5. The university supported the writing of the book by granting release time from 2013 to 2015, and the Research Center for the Humanities and Social Sciences provided three small grants. The extraordinary staff at the Cheng Library greatly assisted this research, and their professionalism and speed prove once again that size is no match for skill.

This book is a product of an ongoing dialogue with my students at WPU and was implicitly written to them. Their questions, curiosity, own struggles with race, and desire for something else have helped me see the urgency of this project. I shout out Mario Benitez, Priscilla Cordero, Kierra Edmunds and Tierra Edmunds, Kelly Ginart, Shonté Jenkins, Belkis Kaplan, Siana Lita, and Dwayne Stubbs, and a special thanks to Meredith Fazzone for her comments on the conclusion.

I thank Marlie Wasserman for her enthusiasm and support from the beginning. It has been a delight to work with her and the staff at Rutgers University Press. A special thanks to the word surgeon Joseph Dahm for the thorough copyediting of the manuscript. I also thank the three anonymous reviewers for their comments and suggestions. I am particularly grateful to "Reviewer 2," whose generous comments greatly improved the manuscript and renewed my faith that academic labors of love still exist.

A portion of chapter 5 was previously published by Palgrave Macmillan in 2015 as "He's Cute for Her" in the volume *Children, Sexuality and Sexualization*, and a portion of my introduction was published by Sage in 2014 as "The 'Savage' Child and the Nature of Race" in *Anthropological Theory*. I thank the presses for permission to republish the material.

I am grateful for Jed Tucker's and Nadeen Thomas's critical insights and always humorous comments and engagement with various chapters. I thank Lambros Comitas for his generous read and comments on the manuscript and for his long-lasting and caring mentorship. For the latter, I also thank Nicholas De Genova for his continued support and inspiration and for the photo that graces the cover of this book.

I could not have written this book if my mind had not been at ease that my daughter was in the loving hands of my parents, Markella and John, and my sister Irene. I thank Irene and Mike for opening up their home on the regular and providing food and festivities for the family. I thank Daniel for sharing all of life's struggles and joys, especially those of parenting our daughter Markella. This book is dedicated to her—may the refusal and imagination at its core animate her journey to create a more human world.

TRANSCRIPTION CONVENTIONS

[	indicates simultaneous talk by two or more speakers
[…]	indicates deleted speech
/	indicates interrupted speech or speech that was quickly followed by the next speaker
((word))	indicates nonspeech actions such as laughter, nodding, movement, shift in gaze, and so on
[word]	indicates transcriber comment
word	indicates stressed word

CITY KIDS

INTRODUCTION
The Transformative Politics of Learning Race

In widely publicized experimental research, a team of psychologists found that white children believed that Black children felt less pain than white children.[1] The study extended the findings of previous research wherein both Black and white health care professionals exhibited this belief. The research was designed to find the point in development when children acquire this bias, and found it absent among five-year-olds, emerging at age seven, and "strong and reliable" by age ten. Framed differently, this study illustrates that by ten years of age, some white children fully inhabit our racial common sense, its core structure and logic. They have learned that they and all others belong to a hierarchy of human types, wherein some are less than human and others are more fully human. This highlights that our humanity is always at stake when race is the question. The indisputable fact that there are no natural types of human beings,[2] but at some point we just "see" these types as such, should inspire an awe-inspiring wonder that the question properly deserves: *how* does this happen? How does one learn to chop up humanity into different types, to consider oneself a type of human and encounter another as a different type that is more or less human? Can these processes possibly be smooth and unproblematic? Is race easy to learn?

This book addresses these questions and joins a group of scholars who insist they can be answered only by grounding them among particular children situated in specific places and times, amid the multiple, overlapping contexts, processes, and practices of their everyday lives.[3] Instead of presenting racial learning as something that just happens in development, these anthropologists, sociologists, and geographers document how children struggle to make sense of the constantly shifting terrain of race, racial categories, and racial meanings "over time, through multiple interactions with those who are the same and those who are different" as well as "in relation to the social divisions, real inequities, images, representations, and discourses one encounters in a local, national, and even global context" (Lewis 2003, 6–7). This body of ethnographic research has convincingly demonstrated that the processes by which children learn race are incredibly dynamic, variable, and suffused with resistance. Collectively, research has shown that these processes are a lot more complex than experiments suggest or critical race scholarship assumes, and that we have much to learn about these processes. That is, this body of research has shown that race is decidedly *not* easy to learn.[4]

My research was designed to delve into the irregularities and discontinuities of learning race, and to center on the nuances, contradictions, and struggles that suffuse it. While I insist that learning race is always difficult, I chose to ground my inquiry among a group of kids in a geographical site where it would be more so, where complexity is the key feature. Amid the fiercely segregated landscape of a global city, New York, I chose to conduct my study in the neighborhood of Augursville.[5] Augursville represents what scholars refer to as a "superdiverse" locale, a place with no numerical majorities, where residents have life histories and relationships spanning the globe and represent all socially defined races with many defying easy racial categorization, and where race is not simply superimposed over religion or class. Because schools are the most important meeting place for kids in such diverse locales, I chose to conduct my study primarily in a school, Public School AV (PS AV) that mirrored the neighborhood's demographic complexity. How would kids in such a space encounter and interact with one another on a day-to-day basis? What would learning race look like? Would the variable meanings and felt experiences of race in such a context be more or less conflict-ridden? Would kids know each other primarily on the basis of type? How would kids construct belonging: through a universal or "human" identity, or would new collectivities be created—melting pots, multicultures, polycultures, or mosaics where race lurked deeper under the surface?

Although I was primed to capture the subtler racial dynamics lying beneath the surface, I was not prepared to encounter something that had not been fully theorized. After spending two months with an "accelerated" fifth-grade class in May and June where the kids' understanding of race was akin to multiculturalism with its muted but no-less-present hierarchies and divisions, I resumed fieldwork with a heterogeneously grouped fifth-grade class in September. I was so struck by these kids' unique stances toward race that I shifted my plan and continued participant observation with them for the duration of the school year.[6] These nine-, ten-, and eleven-year-old kids had an open, savvy, and sophisticated orientation to race that represents antiracist forms of being and relating. Their improvisational interactions were fierce critiques of our racial baggage.[7] Yet their understandings were different from the academic critiques with which I was so familiar. It was not just the way these critiques emerged from their situated perspectives. More so it was the way the kids playfully and creatively resolved the contradictions of race in their everyday interactions and relationships. I call this ethos the kids' *cosmopolitanism* to index current conversations on the most pressing issue of our time—how to live convivially among our varied differences. I argue that the kids provide a compelling contribution to this issue, and that their critical perspectives have the potential to nourish the scholarship and politics of race as well as the practice of education. For the kids not only made clear why we should continue to fight relentlessly against race, but also widened the scope of the conversation to include what we should be fighting *for.*

THE STAKES OF THE ARGUMENT; OR, WHY THIS BOOK MATTERS

This book argues that the kids' cosmopolitanism represents a rupture of and an "escape" from our racial baggage that emerged as the kids learned race. These kids, like all others in the United States, were subjected to our dreadful racial baggage amid their everyday lives. Alongside and at the very same time, these kids also doubted, rejected, dismissed, and contested these commonsense fictions and created something else in its stead. As I will demonstrate, there were particular conditions that enabled the kids' cosmopolitanism to emerge and flourish, as well as those that constrained it. Despite the favorable conditions in my particular field site, the central argument of this book is that learning race is *always* pregnant with radical transformative possibilities. Subjection and refusal are the two sides of the same coin of learning race.

Thus far, childhood studies scholars of race have focused primarily on the former while opening the window onto the latter. Like many of them, I approached the problem of children learning race from the standpoint of critical race scholarship. My previous experiences teaching in an NYC public school showed me that kids have a sophisticated understanding of race, and I was dissatisfied with the way children's perspectives are dismissed or ignored in the larger field of race scholarship. Accounts of how race is made in childhood are simply absent in larger theorizations of racial formation. I wanted children's perspectives to be included in these conversations, so I set out to demonstrate that children participate in race making just as adults do. I wanted scholarship to take children seriously, perhaps too seriously. For my participants forced me to contend with the fact that kids did not engage with race in the same way as adults. The kids' practices were more dynamic, open-ended, and playful, and they often challenged the meanings of race and put forth alternatives. But how could I represent these practices as political and purposive interventions while retaining their unique character? While representational matters are a serious concern in all ethnographic endeavors, there is an extra burden here. To represent race in childhood is to tread treacherous waters. One misstep and the powerful current of children's supposed nature pulls the narrative and overdetermines it. Suddenly, kids and their deeply felt struggles with race become characters in our dominant narrative of how race is either easy or inevitable to learn, or their defamiliarizations are dismissed as child's play. For this reason I carefully lay out the ethico-political, conceptual, and methodological concerns of my research in the rest of this introduction; I establish how learning race is a crucial aspect of racial formation and a particularly strategic site for racial *trans*formation and then outline my methodology for capturing the imperceptible politics of racial transformation. But first I rehearse the high stakes of conceptual clarity, for narratives of children's racial lives function as a powerful site where the idea of race as nature or type or kind is sustained.

MAKING RACE REAL IN CHILD STUDIES

Nearly seventy years ago Oliver C. Cox declared the idea that prejudice is a natural response to people who look different to be "one of the most persistent social illusions of modern times" (1948, xxx). Cox targets the deep, invidious notion that different *types* of people exist, types that are absolute, are fixed, and exist in nature. Despite ritualistic invocations that race is a social construction, Cox's declaration has become truer today. Notions that reproduce race as natural, biological, or genetic continually bombard us. It is continually reproduced and legitimated by a whole apparatus of social-scientific and scientific thinking, and promulgated throughout the public sphere and made common sense by racially targeted pharmaceuticals, academic-commercial "diversity" and "ancestry" industries, popular culture shows such as *Who Do You Think You Are?*, and our endless supply of crime dramas where racial forensics helps nab the culprit.[8] In all these sites, racial differences are re-created as natural types that are absolute, essentialized, primordial, and fixed.

Social science accounts of race in childhood function as another site in which race is inscribed as real human type. Because children are largely associated with nature and the natural, evidence of their racialized beliefs or practices suggests that they apprehend race by merely looking, unmediated by social forces. This supports the persistent illusion that racial categories can be intuited directly and transparently from "nature." This is the canonical mode of investigation and analysis in social and cognitive psychology and has been rehearsed throughout the decades with much the same conclusion: innate human capacities of categorization and group affiliation are conducive to the creation of racist attitudes and beliefs. This interpretive vein in studies of children and race is pervasive—hundreds of such studies are published annually.[9] While such accounts of children's racial lives acknowledge "environmental stimuli," "institutional factors," or "contextual features," they privilege what they see as universal and ahistorical cognitive mechanisms that pit one stable and naturally occurring group against another. The most noxious aspect of this work then lies in its political ramifications—by isolating children's attitudes about race in laboratories, this work lends credence to Cox's persistent illusion: that prejudice is a natural response to people who look different. This is the tragedy of accounts of race in childhood: researchers collude, "wittingly or otherwise, in legitimating 'race' as a valid criterion for differentiating the population" (Hatcher and Troyna 1993, 111). By refusing to recognize how profoundly race has regimented our apprehension of the world, such research inadvertently reifies race and racism, and elides the profound struggle to learn race, the struggle that is at the core of racial *subjection*, with all the force and power that the term suggests.

Like it or not, ethnographic studies of race in childhood communicate in a terrain where experimental methods have reigned for nearly a century and have constructed the dominant narrative by which learning race is understood. We must also consider the fact that children have, until quite recently, been understood through either of two extremes in the structure/agency pendulum, both of which naturalize children.[10] On one end is the adult in the making, where the child is passively enculturated or socialized by adults and institutions. The passive child relies on a simplified and false division between individual and society, where reality is "out there," separate and distinct from subjectivity "in there." On the other end is the agentic child "in its own culture," instinctively constructing distinctions and meanings seemingly free from adult influence. The active child also artificially separates children from society and suggests an innocence that easily slips into instinct. Both of these constructions assume an automatic and unproblematic view of learning race. If learning race in not depicted with its inherent complexity and messiness, if the refusals, the playful, and the surreal are omitted, or if the emphasis is on what children know without a focus on *how* they know it, the danger lurks that our accounts are interpreted through the dominant narrative. That is, when we present race as too easy to learn, we contribute to making race real.

RACIAL FORMATION—WITHOUT THE CHILDREN

Critical race scholarship has formed the primary assault against the fallacy that race is a valid natural type. Through countless points of evidence, this body of work has upheld that race is not a self-evident grouping but an arbitrary social category constructed in relatively recent history and continually reproduced and transformed in social life. The misfortune is that this scholarship has had so little to say about children and childhood. Before I discuss how this scholarship dismisses childhood and argue for the importance of correcting this omission, I sketch the general contours of this work's emphasis on complexity and change.

For despite the myopia regarding childhood, it represents a foundational conceptual resource for this research.

Michael Omi and Howard Winant's (1994) "racial formation" perspective is one of the most useful frameworks with which to analyze how race is continually created and transformed through complex processes of social struggle. Emphasizing open-endedness, this perspective directs focus to the circumstances that produce race as relevant, and bodies, spaces, and practices as racially meaningful in the terrain of everyday life.[11] This framework intersects with one of the larger themes of anthropological investigation: analysis of the extraordinary effort exerted in the social production of seemingly natural differences. Anthropologists' unique contributions have been probing how people in specific times and places construct, reconstruct, and deconstruct racial categories and meanings by paying attention to the nitty-gritty details of everyday life. They have demonstrated that people don't just do race. In fact, race may be so pernicious because it is entangled in the basic cultural dynamics of identity and belonging in everyday life (Hartigan 2010a; 2005).[12] These sociocultural processes centrally involve meaning making, the "active interpretive and performative work we do when we encounter or engage the significance of race" (Hartigan 2010a, 14). In the past decade, geographers have contributed much to our understanding of race making by calling attention to how race materializes, in the fleeting yet affect-laden "perception, judgment and action in the here and now of an encounter" (Swanton 2010, 2336; see also Price 2013; Saldhana 2010).

Ethnographic approaches open the door to understanding the complexities of how race is lived at the sensory, affective, subjective, and relational levels. As historian E. P. Thompson wrote about class, race is not an abstract structure or category, but "something which in fact happens (and can be shown to have happened) in human relationships" and is "embodied in real people and in a real context" (1966, 8).[13] As such, ethnography is more than method; it is a political stance that insists that ordinary people constitute the social world in the continuous flows of everyday life. It is within the productive and innovative stir of everyday life that possibilities for alternative social arrangements emerge (De Genova 2005, 1).[14] This perspective gives anthropology its notable "moral optimism" (Trouillot 2003) because from this standpoint, race looks much more fragile, dynamic, and changeable.[15] Behind the façade of rigid and static structures, ethnographers document how they are a product of human actions, thereby revealing stasis *and* change in everyday life. Various sites in social life do not have an equal proportion of stasis and change, and the degree is an open-ended question. However, there are certain arenas with more potential to rupture the seemingly smooth reproduction of social life. Childhood is one such site, one that has unfortunately been ignored.

Although their racial formation framework is one of the most useful for setting the parameters for empirical exploration into how race is produced, Omi and Winant do not mention children or childhood. Their only implicit reference is when they explain "racial subjection," a process that is learned without "obvious teaching or conscious inculcation": "Race becomes 'common sense'—a way of comprehending, explaining, and acting in the world" (1994, 60). Likewise, John Hartigan Jr.'s only mention of children in what he purports is a book about "how we learn and perform race" is the following: "We learn these types of seeing and acting very young, and they generally stay with us, unconsciously, throughout our lives" (2010a, 2). Despite sophisticated frameworks attuned to struggle and change in everyday life, for these scholars race just magically happens in childhood.

Of course, there is something magical about race, a point of departure for critical race heavyweights Barbara J. Fields and Karen E. Fields. Their recent intervention is titled "racecraft" (2014) in order to parallel our submersion in the pervasive collective beliefs, practices, and imaginings of race to witchcraft in other places and times. Culture provides "an immense accumulation of supporting evidence" for these beliefs; and in medieval Europe "there was little to impose the idea of absurdity or of improbability on the stories about 'old women riding on broomsticks'" (24). Their work relentlessly documents how the magic of race is supported and entwined in the structures of American life. But they predictably falter when it comes to childhood. Their only mention of children is that "Americans acquire in childhood all it takes to doubt stories of witchcraft, but *little in our childhood leads us to doubt racecraft*" (24, emphasis added). By ignoring the important work of child scholars documenting the complexity and struggles inherent in racial learning, these scholars can so easily euphemize racial learning and contribute to the pervasive narrative that race is easy to learn. These scholars not only risk reifying race, but miss an important opportunity to solidify the crucial insight that racial formation entails transformation.

LEARNING RACE AS RACIAL TRANSFORMATION

This book argues that childhood is a strategic site to intervene in scholarship and politics of race because children are more likely to defamiliarize race, reveal its most problematic and taken-for-granted aspects, and enact alternatives. Children's potential for critical oppositional and alternative perspectives is due to their marginalized status or liminality in relation to adult-centric life (Burman 2015, 3) and the sheer fact that they have spent fewer years alive. Their experiences are rich but have not acquired the repetitive and taken-for-granted status of adults. As Christina Toren argues about learning throughout the life cycle in her unified theory of mind, "The processes of mind are subject to change and continuity, but as we grow older they become progressively less subject to *radical* change precisely because they are already highly developed" (2012, 29, emphasis original). Children's critical perspectives are not due to their enlightened nature, or because they are ostensibly bounded and protected in an innocent "children's culture." Rather, their unique positioning vis-à-vis the social world is such that they are fully competent social beings able to stand outside common sense, if only for fleeting moments.

Philosopher Walter Benjamin's theorization of the inherently transformative potential of childhood is compelling. He considered children's play a site for enacting the mimetic faculty, the ability and practice of discerning and producing resemblances that characterize human symbolic interactions (1978 [1966]). He saw the revolutionary potential for refusing accepted meanings and creating new fields of meaning residing in play.[16] This highlights the radical potential in the oft-forgotten anthropological truism that culture is never simply replicated in transmission. Cindi Katz (2004) engaged with Benjamin's notion of the imaginative, creative, and destructive faculty of mimesis in her ethnography of children's participation in agricultural development in rural Sudan. In her analysis of the inseparability of children's work and play, she finds not only those "flashes of insight" that "spark a realization that the original is also made up" but also the recognition that "things, relations, and selves could be otherwise" (2004, 98–102; 2008). Within children's play and work, she discerns the production of the central relations of social life, their dynamic nature, and their transformation.

Inspired and enabled by the way this work reveals the radical potential in childhood while insisting that children's sentiments are embedded in sociohistorical dynamics of change, I merge critical insights from various fields to provide a view of learning race as transformative, active, and embodied multisensory meaning making that emerges in everyday practices in the world. It is a posthuman account of learning that foregrounds kids' subjective apprehension of the world and their relations with other humans, spaces, and things.[17] I show how racial learning occurs within the improvised practices, processes, encounters, momentary sensory apprehensions, and rituals of everyday life. It involves flashes of insight, subtle shifts in awareness, fleeting emotions, as well as significant leaps in perception and realization, incremental expansions of understanding in extended debates and long-lasting relations. All of these variable ways of learning race are unpredictable and, ultimately, transformative.

The transformative nature of learning race makes it a form of imperceptible politics. There were multiple interactions when the kids clearly overturned racial common sense; when kids transformed the meanings and values of specific differences and difference itself. There are others when the changes are subtler or below the surface, and there I draw out the shifts in a kid's perspective. Less obvious still, I include interactions in which racial meanings are seemingly reproduced. As I demonstrate, kids never simply mimicked adult constructions of race or understood things in exactly the same way. If we take seriously the charge that interpreting race in everyday life involves active work, that reality is never just "out there" in the world separate and apart from human intervention and engagement in the world as well as the dynamic open-endedness of social life, then we can begin to understand how learning race is a form of imperceptible politics. Every moment in which race materialized or became live involved the kids reconstructing racial knowledge from their particular standpoint, making race meaningful through their embodied experiences. These moments were also opportunities to defuse race or make it into something else. These struggles were not always won, but they were struggles nonetheless. Conceptualizing them as such reveals new insights about how race operates, how it is meaningful, and why it is alienating. For the kids, racial baggage was an obstacle to expressing and experiencing the self in ways they desired; an obstacle in constructing social relations beyond difference; an obstacle to belonging in the classroom, neighborhood, city, nation; an obstacle to being and becoming human. In moments that ranged from dramatic to humorous, somewhere in between or both at the same time, racial baggage is what they tried to escape.

ESCAPE AND IMPERCEPTIBLE POLITICS

While it is possible to think about the kids' cosmopolitanism as a form of resistance, I find the concept of "escape" more analytically useful. Dimitris Papadopoulos, Niamh Stephenson, and Vassilis Tsianos employ the concept to capture the subtle exuberance of those unfamiliar, ambiguous, and imperceptible shifts in subjectivity and sociability. It is a concept that enables us to "imagine, see and interrogate those ordinary moments when people's actions put processes in motion, processes which are effective in confronting the social order with a force of change that cannot be avoided, silenced, neglected, erased" (2008, xix). They purposefully distinguish escape from resistance (or revolt and refusal) because it cuts to the heart of social conflict, the stakes of which are joy. "Joy marks the routes of social transformation. Joy is the ultimate proof," they unabashedly claim. This framework guides the analyst toward moments when people create alternative modes of being and relating within and outside of alienating conditions. These are forms of politics where the "laughter and joy of those who partake in the world through remaking their embodied existences defy seriousness, disperse fear, liberate the world and reveal a truth that escapes the injustices of the present" (Papadopoulos 2010, 144–145). The kids' modes of being and relating suggest a desire to be treated with respect and dignity, to connect with other humans that is just as, for lack of a better term, primal. Escape is a way to gesture toward the unpremeditated impulses that exceed racial subjectification. Escape is a way to reinforce the open-endedness and hopeful possibilities that are always present when learning race.

Analysts who take on the playful or the ambiguous reveal the cracks, ruptures, momentary "freedoms," and interesting possibilities that are present within our dreadful racial baggage. Robyn Wiegman (1995, 35) argues that "shifting the frame of reference in such a way that the present can emerge as something less familiar, less natural in its categories" is a worthy political project. In much the same way, the kids' struggles with and challenges to the meanings and meaningfulness that inhere in racialized bodies, racial categories, Blackness, and whiteness re-present the frustratingly familiar in a new way. What is more, their struggles show how alternative ways to be and relate against and outside race exist. These social relations and subjectivities are the imperceptible politics that are often missed in scholarly accounts. This book represents those flashes of other ways to be, see, and experience race within everyday life, flashes of insight that are euphemized and ignored among not just children but also adults. It is my hope that readers will recognize some of these ruptures and possibilities that exist in everyday life, and deepen them in their praxes, whether as educators, scholars, citizens, or humans.

LOCATING THE POLITICS OF METHODOLOGY

In her critique of the "metaphysics of race," Denise Ferrera da Silva (2011, 139) forcefully argues that "no critique of racial subjugation can afford not to investigate that which renders this common knowing possible." From its conceptualization to its representation in this book, this research is guided by this ethico-political project. These concerns informed the methodology—the who, what, where, and how I produced data—and are inextricable from the politics of my location. The politics of the "I" do not just dictate what is worthy of study and how it will be studied, but suffuse the human encounter at the heart of the ethnographic endeavor. Drawing on feminists' insights on the role of subjectivity in research, Mary Thomas (2011, 19–20) discusses how this is never simply determined by listing one's identities. Of course it mattered that I am an able-bodied, heterosexual, white, middle-class, cisgendered woman with US citizenship. But, as Thomas argues, how this matters cannot be predicted in advance. For subjectivity is not transparent and fixed, nor determined by the various identity categories one inhabits. As I strive to show regarding the kids, subjectivity is irreducibly relational and continually becoming. My "I" is not excused. My interactions and relations with the kids also impacted my racial learning and subjectivity. I offer remarks on the "I" who is writing this book to orient the reader's attention to the various ways it mattered in the processes represented herein.

I chose to conduct my work in PS AV not only because its demographics mirrored the neighborhood, but also because I instantly felt comfortable there.[18] Administrators, faculty, and staff were relatively relaxed about having a researcher in their midst because PS AV participated in numerous projects that brought in various observers: visitors, student teachers, district personnel, administrators, and coordinators. I was to be one of many adults learning and observing, distinguished by the fact that I would be forming relationships with students and would be called by my first name (an important point for me and a source of annoyance to adults who insisted on calling me "Miss" Maria in front of kids). After subsequent meetings with the principal and assistant principal during which I expressed interest in studying with a fifth-grade class, the administrators introduced me to Ms. Anastasia, the fifth-grade teacher of the "accelerated" class. She was receptive and thought her "extremely bright" group would make for a great study. I met with the kids to discuss my research and distribute parent consent and student assent forms. They were enthusiastic and posed tons of questions, the most pressing of which was when I would begin. We set a start date for the beginning of May.

Although the first day of fieldwork was action-packed, I had a feeling of unease throughout the day. I recognized that I was deliberately placed with Ms. Anastasia because of how "exceptional" school personnel found her students. Moreover, I realized that this was the only fifth-grade class without any African American kids. The racialized dynamics were also different than anything I had experienced or expected—these kids were enthusiastic multicultural subjects. On my very first morning, the kids were displaying their multimedia presentations on the topic of their choice. Over two-thirds chose to present "my country" or "my culture." Although I was prepared to deal with multiculturalism, I was not prepared for the way Ms. Anastasia continually constructed me as a fellow Greek American in front of the kids—speaking Greek to me, referring to me as Greek, and making statements that assumed I identified and practiced primarily as such.

A clarification of my discomfort helps illuminate how my subject position informs my research and evolving relationships with the kids. My primary objection to the Greek American subject position involves its entanglement with the racial positioning of whiteness. As Vilma Bashi Treitler (2013) convincingly argues, ethnic projects, born of race in the United States, have historically shored up the racial system of human hierarchy. The historicity of Greekness vis-à-vis whiteness has perhaps made it easier for me to refuse the whiteness on which contemporary Greekness was built. In public schools in NYC in the 1980s, Greeks were, depending on whom you ask, either newly established whites or not (yet) quite white. Following groups like the Irish, the Jews, and the Italians before them, Greeks have left the ambiguity behind and whitened in the intervening decades. Growing up, I understood my position in the racial universe not as white or "Greek" (multiculturalism had not yet hit the schools), but Other. I did not understand this Otherness to be unique or singular—I saw how my best friend experienced Haitianness in relation to Blackness in a somewhat parallel manner. This estranged position allowed me a unique angle of studying race and whiteness in particular, in what eventually became a lifelong pursuit. The intersection of my early biography and history forms the background of a long story of my ambivalent relationship to whiteness that need not be rehearsed here. Today, I reject whiteness because I find race traitor the only tenable position for one defined white. As Black, indigenous, and fellow race-rebel scholars and activists have demonstrated time and again, whiteness is not emptiness but false, oppressive, and demonic.[19] Rejecting whiteness is not simply admitting one's privilege and moving on. It is a continual struggle to reject all that whiteness stands for—hierarchy, oppression, and domination in all its forms, and struggling for all that is its antithesis—justice, equality, humanity, and something we can't quite name.

The problem for the initial period of my fieldwork in Ms. Anastasia's class was that my identity was assumed and determined. Even though multiculturalism prevailed in that classroom, I did not want to be understood to be a party to its implicit omissions and valorization of whiteness, even if it made me fit in. I eventually built close relationships with a few kids who had an ambivalent relationship to multiculturalism. But two months was too short a period to overcome the obstacle of my manufactured identity to build trusting relationships with kids who were alienated by multiculturalism or school. Furthermore, Ms. Anastasia and I did not develop a relationship wherein I felt comfortable to be more than a professional anthropologist in the classroom. In other words, I was unable to encounter kids as fellow humans until I was invited to Ms. Lee's class.

I met Ms. Lee, who is Korean and the only nonwhite fifth-grade teacher, during my initial period of fieldwork with Ms. Anastasia. Because schools are highly racialized spaces where race is always either present or lurking close by, it doesn't take long to figure out with whom you are allied. Ms. Lee and I often had to bear witness to implicitly racist remarks and humor of her colleagues. Discovering that we were the only ones not laughing or making attempts to counter such talk, we quickly bonded. At the end of the school year when I was wondering how my fieldwork would proceed and trying to navigate administrators' expectations that I would continue my research with next year's "accelerated" fifth grade (this time with another teacher), Ms. Lee invited me to participate in her class. It was with Ms. Lee's kids that my fieldwork shifted profoundly. I was able to form relations with kids as fellow humans, which opened me up to their exuberant interactions and embodied stances toward race and shifted my focus from how kids reproduce race to how they transform it.

As an inherently flexible and responsive methodology, the ethnographic endeavor insists that our knowledge can be built only through relations based on mutual respect and care. My ability to enact the principle of relationality—to surrender my agenda, follow the kids' lead, and learn *from* and *with* them—was in no small part due to the way I had more flexibility in my positioning, racial and otherwise, in Ms. Lee's class.[20] Whereas in Ms. Anastasia's class the question had only one answer, in Ms. Lee's class the kids implicitly set out to ask, "What *kind* of white are you?" In this classroom race did not begin and end with bodies but had to be performed. And whiteness did not necessarily cohere to white skin. Although Ms. Lee constructed me as Greek occasionally, it was in the context of bridging with her Koreanness. Ms. Lee and I also bridged through other commonalities: our pride in being born and bred in Queens, as well as some shared pop cultural affiliations. These bridges, our easygoing relationship, even our clowning around, were important performative signals. For instance, early in the school year Ms. Lee had teams of kids construct and perform a "punctuation rap" that she and I would judge *American Idol*–style. The last team was notably lacking enthusiasm, with two of the five kids sitting through their routine. I interrupted them to offer a critique: "This ain't folk music, it's rap!" Ms. Lee fell to the floor in laughter, and needed a minute to collect herself as the kids observed us with studied amusement.

Such performances and the different context in which they occurred were such that my Greekness was distanced from the available model of Greekness in Augursville, as a white ethnic group oriented toward itself and exhibiting strong sense of pride and belonging. In many ways, the kids taught me how to be and express Greekness in a way that was open-ended and detached from whiteness. Together with the kids, it was constructed as one of my many overlapping belongings, not necessarily the most significant, and one that related to other belongings in a horizontal rather than hierarchical relation. My positioning—the way I signaled it, the way the kids played with it—was produced in the real time of interaction and a key aspect of building and enacting my relationships with the kids. It didn't take long for the kids to socialize me into their milieu. After a few weeks I was reflexively using my Greekness in reciprocal processes of bridging and crossing differences that cemented our relationships and flattened out the power differentials that inhere in our racial positionings (see chapter 2). The fact that some Black, Latino, and Asian kids decided that despite being formally white I wasn't "*really*" white" or "white white" opened up the channels of relationality. In the beginning of my fieldwork, I asked kids if they wanted an interview only when I sensed they were comfortable with me and wanted to chat with me. The way Yanely, a second-generation Mexican girl, first asked me for an interview illustrates how important my racial performances were in establishing close bonds with the kids. It was mid-October and I was casually hanging out in the classroom when Eliza, along with Jacinta, came up to me to lodge a complaint about something minor. In a playful mood, I responded in an exaggerated "Valley girl" voice: "Oh my God! This is unjust! We should overthrow the school! Have a revolution!" When the girls laughed and left, Yanely sidled up to me and stuck near me the rest of the morning. At one point she said to me, "That was really funny when you were acting like that before." I laughed and didn't think much of it until she later asked me if she could have an interview. By humorously marking whiteness, Yanely saw me in a different light, perhaps someone she could trust. And we eventually became so close, with her confiding things that I would not include in this book, that Ms. Lee joked that I was her "guru."

Through performances, interactions, and relations, the kids even constructed my phenotype as open-ended, and they manipulated it to include me in various circles of belonging. Some Latinas/os argued that I looked Spanish, Mexican, or Brazilian, and some Middle Eastern and Asian kids decided I looked like I could be from their "country." Such practices were enacted similarly to the kids' performances. For the kids, these were part of the rituals and symbols of friendship and crucial to establishing that I was more than a professional anthropologist, a person with many facets, relationships, passions, and a sense of humor. For me, they were crucial to enacting the principle of relationality that allowed me to surrender to the kids' agenda.

SURRENDER: A METHODOLOGY OF INTELLECTUAL LOVE

Relationality is always wrought with tension and made more problematic when there is a power gulf between researchers and researched. Just as significant as race is the fact that I was an adult conducting research with kids. In their rethinking of the ethical conundrums of ethnographic research with children, Francesca Meloni, Karine Vanthuyne, and Cecile Rousseau (2015) suggest that ethnographers should not fix power in rigid categories of adult and child, but rather reflect on the intricacies of how power is negotiated in the research. In that spirit, I offer remarks on how I managed my intellectual aims amid the larger ethico-political concerns of this research. Surrendering to the kids' agenda was my most important strategy in the daily practice of fieldwork and in representing the research in this book. Surrender entails giving the most precious resource in the process of fieldwork, time, and its representation in the product, space.[21] The reward is indexed in accounts of the ethnographer's tool kit by the term "rapport," or what I would like to call a properly *human* encounter. It is easiest to illustrate what this entailed in my practice in an embarrassing encounter when I violated this principle. On this day, I was able to stay in the field for only two hours. I came in rather determined to get "good data." Rather than casually participating in the cafeteria interactions, I grasped onto a "lead" in a conversation about a kid who was try-ing to be "down." Knowing that authenticity was implicated in notions of race, I started firing off closed-ended questions: "Who is down? Who thinks they're down?" Keisha turned to me with a disapproving look and asked, "What's wrong with you today, Maria?" I looked up from my notebook a bit taken aback. Steven concurred, "Yeah, Maria, why you asking all these corny questions?" These ques-tions were undeniably corny, and the manner in which I asked them suggested that I was interested only in my research, not human interactions and relations.

Without fail, when I tried to impose my research agenda, the kids censured me by avoiding my questions and talking about what they wanted to talk about. I realized that this represented what was important for them; it was the partici-pants' agenda. As Pierre Bourdieu (1999, 614) eloquently put it, allowing par-ticipants to take over research and "find a 'sort of relief' and 'a joy in expression'" represents "intellectual love." Listening carefully to talk about Mets and Yankees, mean and fun teachers, Pumas and Nikes, Daddy Yankee and Don Omar was my way of expressing this love. I spend more space documenting these concerns than other ethnographies of kids' racial lives because race was often entangled in these concerns. More importantly, the humanity of the encounter insists that I represent the kids more than simply racial beings. If anthropology is to be more than the study of humans but a humanizing endeavor with humans, then we must honor and represent our participants' full humanity.

Honoring the kids' humanity meant that I interacted with them in ways that were not "unobtrusive" or "objective" researcher. In many of the interactions described, I am veritably a part of the social scene, a participant. My relation-ships were, like all relationships, fluid, negotiated, and constantly evolving. Inso-far as I did not consider the kids solely as racial subjects, they did not see me solely as a researcher with a notebook. Although I had a unique relationship with each kid, the analogy best befitting my relationships would be the cool aunt who doesn't have kids—I was thirty-one when I began fieldwork and did not yet have a daughter. With many kids I developed strong bonds that were characterized by warmth and affection. By late winter/early spring, I was jokingly referring to Joseph as "my son" because he always seemed to be within arm's reach. My affec-tion toward him indirectly affected his status in the classroom. Ms. Lee noted that his attendance and demeanor had dramatically improved, and I discerned how girls to whom he was previously invisible now thought he was one of "the cutest." My cool aunt role with most kids meant that I was a trusted confidant and one they could act silly around. When conversations turned toward things that were told to me in confidence or when I understood them to be directed toward me as human, not researcher, I promptly turned off the recorder or shut my ever-present notebook with finality. With some kids, the cool aunt was more of the distant eccentric relation that does not quite fit other known categories. Regardless of the degree of closeness, all kids accepted, appreciated, and manipulated my presence for their own ends, most often simply to have someone who was interested and attentive, willing to listen, joke, and have fun. It was not unusual for kids to foist the formal social-scientific role upon me—"Ask us (more) questions!" And I did so only to have my interviewee take over what began as a more formal interview. All interviews with kids that were scheduled formally—initiated by me or the kid for a specific time—became casual encounters with us hanging out and doing whatever they wanted: walking around the school, looking at magazines, playing a game, or drawing. The other strategy I frequently employed to give kids more power during interviews was to conduct them with other kids. These interviews turned into raucous affairs and were an important source of data precisely because in these contexts the kids outnumbered me and largely directed the interaction (see Christensen 2004).

I wielded my "natural" adult authority only when kids' safety or my fieldwork was being jeopardized. Otherwise, I did not care if they broke school rules; there were many regulations I did not adhere to myself. I chewed gum and even gave them gum (making them swear that if they got caught they didn't get it from me), I sat in chairs "improperly," I did not discourage the mayhem that erupted when inept teachers took charge, and once an "f bomb" slipped out. It was during the pandemonium of an unprepared teacher where the kids didn't have much to do and the newly discovered fact of my (then) two white hairs were of paramount interest. Kids hovered over me, touching, pointing, and laughing, which made the white hairs stand up. It was hot and noisy in the classroom, and when the pencil Joseph poked at my head came too close to my face, it was too much. "Fuck off of me," I said, wildly spreading my arms to clear some personal space. The kids roared with laughter and approval. "I *knew* she cursed!" Joseph said. As they laughed, I crossly remarked, "Not so funny when my eye is on a pencil." Joseph hugged me and Jacinta, Sabrina, and a few others followed suit (I suspect the girls joined in to sneak a hug of Joseph). I shooed them away.

Fieldwork was a physical and emotionally laden experience: annoyance, frustration, exhaustion, humiliation, boredom, anxiety, and awkwardness were a few of the negatives. My feelings are included as part of the book because they too are the responses of a human participant: my jealousy at the smart class's successes, my extreme discomfort when a kid got yelled at, even my dread of going to school when I got a pimple and knew I would be made fun of. It took about two minutes after my arrival for Steven to quip, "Yo Maria, what's that on your chin? You a teenager or something?" "You just wait," I ominously repeated with each new crack throughout the day. When the inevitable erupted on his nose a few months later, Steven remembered his debt and avoided me. I didn't have the heart to exact my revenge, but I enjoyed that its lurking possibility signaled a relationality that was much more than professional observer.

The kids recognized and respected my earnest participation, emotions, and affections, although that's not why I expressed them. I revealed I was a hip-hop fanatic in my youth with a (now-fading) encyclopedic knowledge of its "golden age" only after months of being with Ms. Lee's kids, busting out the verses to Public Enemy's "Black Steel in the Hour of Chaos" to jaws predictably dropping. I initially held back because it would too easily win kids over and perhaps align me more with those who liked hip-hop or, worse yet, suggest that I was trying to be cool with them. I finally did so after I had developed relations because it is an important part of who I am, explaining just as much or maybe more about me than knowing, say, I'm Greek. And to be plain, it was fun. I liked debating rappers' skills and best verses. I liked it just as much as seeing how MASH, the fortune-telling game of my youth, played out, watching a fortune unravel with the same amused anticipation as I did at their age. I liked playing Connect Four and chess, small talking with the recorder off. I liked asking girls to rank the celebrities du jour based on their criteria of "hot." And I allowed myself the time to enjoy these activities, establishing and verifying to the kids that I was, first and foremost, a fellow human pursuing relationships with my fellow humans. Indeed, I pursued this research after being a teacher of similarly aged kids in the late 1990s when I realized I was much more interested in having fun learning with and from kids than in teaching them. In the spirit of relationality that characterized my research, I hope that you will experience a modicum of joy in your encounter with the kids. For whatever blind spots the discipline of anthropology has, and there are many, ethnography, its distinguishing method, enables a politics of knowledge rooted in relationality, joy, and love. These qualities of the encounter opened up the window into the kids' cosmopolitanisms.

ACTUALLY EXISTING COSMOPOLITANISMS

At the dawn of the new millennium, Paul Gilroy (2005) and Robyn Kelley (2002) convincingly argued that contemporary race scholars had made it abundantly clear what we were against, but not so clear what we were *for*: there are very few articulations of alternative *forms of being* in an antirace present or future. Where Kelley finds alternative visions in the work of radical and revolutionary figures and surrealist artists and poets, Gilroy argues that poetic, transcendental, and imaginatory possibilities offered by art are also present, if submerged, in the mundane practices and experiences of regular folk who live and engage with difference in their everyday lives. Indeed, the changing global circumstances have now made "superdiversity" an empirical fact in many settings throughout the globe (Meissner and Vertovec 2015). Superdiverse locales contain vibrant possibilities for if not antiracist, then at least convivial sociabilities.

Superdiversity is a property of specific locales that indicates more than a numerical property of diversity, as in more minorities or greater percentage of people from more points of origin, although it does include that.[22] Super-diversity connotes a dynamic mix of multiple axes of diversity, including race, class, language, legal status, migration history, religion, sexuality, and lifestyle that intersect in various unpredictable ways. In the past decade, the mundane forms of relating to difference within superdiverse locales have inspired scholars who have found relationships with difference that depart from fear, suspicion, and conflict that has characterized some diverse locales, and that difference is thought to provoke in mainstream accounts. Instead, they have documented everyday "diplomacy," "civic virtues," "cultural literacy," "normalization of difference," "openness to otherness," "convivialities of interrelatedness," and "sociabilities and social relations of inclusiveness" (Glick Schiller, Darieva, and Gruner-Dominic 2011; Noble 2013; Nowicka and Vertovec 2013; Sennett 2012). These positive relations to difference are not necessarily the dominant ones in specific settings. Some scholars excavate brief encounters of civility within neighborhoods characterized by separation and suspicion (Karner and Parker 2011; Swanton 2010), while others have found public mixing and private separation (Wessendorf 2013). The terms used to describe such forms of being and relating have included everyday multiculturalism (Wise and Velayutham 2009; 2013), interculturality (Dervin and Risager 2015), and increasingly, cosmopolitanism.

With a variety of nuances and accents, the concept of cosmopolitanism has flourished as scholars articulate moral, emotional, aesthetic, and political perspectives defined by the ability and desire to engage with difference.[23] It provides compelling answers to questions implicitly posed by the life conditions of urbanites in global cities, as well as working-class laborers, refugees, and individuals in out-of-the-way villages: How do we engage with and relate to difference? What is the proper notion of belonging amid this superdiversity? When the concept initially resurged in the early 2000s, it was justifiably criticized for its classed and raced parochialism, its "detached" and "rootless" formulations marking elite forms of cultural tourism, appropriation, and fetishization of Otherness.[24] Current scholarship excavates forms of cosmopolitanism where broad attachments coexist with rooted or more local forms of community, religion, culture, race, or nation, referred to in terms like "vernacular," "discrepant," "rooted," "vulgar," or even "visceral" cosmopolitanism. These purposefully contradictory terms hark back to the absurd humor of the original coiner of the term, the Cynic philosopher Diogenes (412–323 BCE). When asked by his contemporaries where he was from, Diogenes troubled the prevailing norms of fierce attachment to city-state and declared that he was a cosmopolitan, a citizen of the world. This conception no more existed then than it does now. It was a satirical rejection of the narrow parochialism dividing his peers as well as a pronouncement of a desire for bonds beyond it. Diogenes's provocation was absurd, humorous, surreal, and imaginative. It was irreverent toward inherited conceptions and playfully gestured toward something that did not exist but whose pronouncement prefigured it.[25] This captures the spirit of the kids' cosmopolitanism.

OPERATIONALIZING THE KIDS' COSMOPOLITANISM

Writing about the variety of definitions of actually existing cosmopolitanisms, Greg Noble (2013) notes how difficult the concept is to operationalize. He asks scholars to attempt to do so not to fix a definition, but to allow for clarity and dialogue. In this spirit, I outline the key features of the kids' cosmopolitanism, and follow by illustrating how it was expressed on the ground. The kids' cosmopolitanism was a local assemblage of practices, dispositions, and modes of being and relating with others. This ethos cut to the core of our racial baggage in that the kids regularly refused race's "essentialism"—its basis in the body, blood, and birth *and* its hierarchical ordering. The kids did not just negate entrenched racial ways of thinking and doing. They also enacted alternative meanings and modes of being and relating with race. The kids' practices intervened into how things were and how they should be. They were inherently political although imperceptible as such because the forms they took are so unconventional: playful, joyful, improvised, embodied, oriented toward the now, and often surreal. If one holds a traditional or predefined notion of what constitutes politics, that is, civic participation or involvement in social movements, it is easy to dismiss the kids' contributions as politically meaningless. Instead, this project relies on an expansive view of the political arena that maps how struggles in the power-laden fields of everyday activities and relationships can change sensibilities and the immediate social realities of existence (Papadopoulos 2010; Tuck and Yang 2013). That is, the kids' practices were political because they transformed their lived reality of race.

Consider the following playful banter on the playground that was guided by and contributed to the kids' cosmopolitan ethos. While certainly amusing, it seems rather trivial if one is not attuned to the rhythm and texture of the kids' interactions or holds a rigid notion of politics. I had arrived at PS AV after a brief vacation during which I acquired a deep tan. The kids were fussing over my tan, questioning me about my vacation and updating me on stuff I missed. After the crowd had dissipated, ten-year-old Mark came up and exclaimed, "Daaaamn Maria! You got dark!" Checking me out, he pulled up his sleeve and challenged,

"You almost as black as me!" Steven and I instantly pulled up our sleeves and lined up our arms for an impromptu skin tone inspection. Keisha shoved her arm on top of the mangle of limbs and exclaimed triumphantly, "I'm blacker than all of y'all!" "You blacker than O.D.B.!" Steven yelled as he started backing up and running.[26] Keisha bit the bait and started chasing him as they howled with laughter. Steven's head start made the chase brief. They stopped and caught their breath, Steven smiling victoriously at Keisha. She nodded to let him know she would get him soon enough.

Let's examine the interaction more closely to highlight how the kids challenged the racial baggage they have inherited *and* transformed its lived meanings. First, Keisha, Steven, and Mark pierced the contradictory logic concerning the racialized body. On the one hand, the visible body is the ground of our racial common sense—the way we use skin to categorize people into races. On the other hand, we are supposed to be "color-blind" and "colormute" toward any bodily trait on which race is based, lest we be considered racist for noticing race. Instead, Mark, Steven, and Keisha took the body as a source of fascination and humor within the dreadful taxonomy of race. They defied our racial baggage's determinedness and color blindness's erasure to recover bodies and put them on inspection in a playful way that revealed the impoverished logic of racial taxonomy itself. The kids also highlighted the mutability of bodies and the fact that racialized traits are overlapping rather than belonging to discrete types. Our skin colors, the key trait used to categorize us as belonging to three different races (conventionally Steven is Latino, I am white, and Keisha and Mark are Black), were actually remarkably similar. Their playfulness implicitly relied on, brought forth, and emphasized the absurdity of race.

The humorous, tactile, and kinetic qualities of this interaction should not detract from the fact that the kids intervened in the politics of race. Mark and Keisha seized the opportunity to outdo Steven and me and valorize their darker brown skin, using their phenotype to invert the hierarchy of Black and white. Furthermore, they intervened in what must have appeared to them as incredibly contradictory—the aesthetic embrace over the temporary dark skin of one defined as white and the concomitant devaluing of the dark skin of one defined as Black. Although Steven's "You blacker than O.D.B." seemingly reinscribes Blackness as negative after Keisha's evaluative flip, this was not how Mark and Keisha understood his remark. They understood it to be playful, one among equals that did not involve racist undertones. Such interpretations involved being highly attuned to various subtleties in meaning. If a remark violated the core principles of the kids' cosmopolitanism, there was trouble.

Consider one such interaction that looks similar at the surface. Mark and Steven were in the classroom working on an assignment together on a laptop while Steven was leading the way rapping. I remarked that I wasn't familiar with the song, and Mark reassured me that this was okay, "I don't even listen to rap music." Steven quipped, "That's 'cause you a white boy!" They both cracked up with laughter. Sebastian, a white kid who was sitting nearby, jumped into the conversation, "How could he be a white boy! Look at the color," while pointing at Mark. The boys abruptly stopped laughing. Steven stiffened and looked at Mark. Mark kept his focus on the computer screen in front of him and flatly said, "Shut up, Sebastian." Sebastian insisted—"But look at!/" Interrupting him, Mark said more forcefully this time, "I *said* shut up, Sebastian!" Sebastian heeded Mark's warning and walked away befuddled.

Sebastian's comments violated the local cosmopolitan ethic, abruptly shifting the humorous encounter to one overwrought with tension. The differences between Steven's and Sebastian's remarks are subtle, yet the boys instantly knew Sebastian's were problematic. Sebastian reinforced the business-as-usual way we do race; they were hegemonic. He insisted that the visible body was the most important, indeed the only factor at play in assigning racial identity. Although Steven's quip, "That's 'cause you a white boy," relied on the body's racialized markings and conventional racial taxonomy, he did so to ultimately subvert the body as the ultimate determinant of Mark's being. In the local cosmopolitan ethos, the ascription of bodies could be subverted to one's practices and tastes, that is, to one's own making. Whereas Mark and Steven, as well as Keisha, called forth the contradictions of race and implicitly put forward positive valuations of Blackness, Sebastian was simply reinforcing established meanings.

INTERPRETING COSMOPOLITANISM ON THE GROUND

Decontextualized, Steven's "You blacker than O.D.B.!" seems more troubling than Sebastian's "How could he be a white boy?" The former appears to suggest Blackness is ugly, while the latter seems to simply reiterate an obvious and neutral fact. The kids interpreted remarks by being attuned to a multitude of contextual features including the immediate surrounding talk and setting of the interaction, the speaker's motivation, social relations, multiple belongings, and interactional history. Even the speaker's general stance toward race colored the meaning of a remark. Mark and Steven were instantly troubled because Sebastian's statement was burdened by the weight of interactional history and his stance toward race in general and Blackness in particular. For instance, one time when Sebastian was sitting with me, Mark, Steven, Connor, and Assad, he abruptly looked at Mark and asked, "How come Black people's hair don't look like ours?" It was a tense moment that could have erupted into a fight. Connor and Assad were stunned and looked to me to do something. Mark asked him in disbelief, "Did you just say what I think you said?" Sebastian explained, "I meant colored people. It's all like . . ." and mimed unruly hair. Steven jumped in and warned, "You being mad racist right now. You like, 'How come. . . .'"

The rupture of the jovial mood and the boys' censuring of Sebastian highlight the kids' sophisticated interpretations of intensions and motivations. The boys knew Sebastian wasn't maliciously or intentionally racist, but that he didn't get it. He did not get that whiteness is not the norm and reference point by which to compare others. He did not get that none of us, ambiguously or newly arrived white (both me and Connor), Latino (Steven), Middle Eastern (Assad), wanted to be recruited into a hegemonic whiteness through the traditional channel of denigrating Blackness (Morrison 1993). And finally, he did not get that Blackness was much more than the inverse and negative pole of whiteness. It was not because Sebastian is white. There were white kids who were equal parties to the cosmopolitan ethos, like Connor. Sebastian's repeated blunders were due to the fact that he had recently arrived in the school and neighborhood from one of the most homogenously white neighborhoods of NYC. Throughout the fifth grade, as Sebastian violated the ethos, the kids censured him in various ways. Although he was hardly a virtuoso by the end of the year, you will encounter Sebastian throughout this book stumbling along with various successes as he tried to belong. Sebastian's case draws out key analytical aspects of the kids' cosmopolitanism. Being an expert cosmopolitan participant required more than complex knowledge (which cannot be reduced to simple rules). It also included certain attitudes, values, and an embodied stance that guided practice.

COSMOPOLITANISM AS CULTURE

The kids' cosmopolitanism was the local culture, a term I employ to analytically highlight certain features of the kids' cosmopolitanism. Not only was it constructed, transmitted, purposive, and meaningful; it was internal and external. It was internalized in embodied knowledge, habits, and dispositions that were gleaned through experience, experiment, and error; and externalized in practices, social relations, and coercive social facts. This does not mean that kids never expressed any hegemonic talk or attitudes about race, by which I mean reproducing prevailing racial common sense. Beyond Sebastian, other kids wrestled with cosmopolitanism. It was not automatic. But it was the dominant way of being and relating to difference in the public domain of interaction in Ms. Lee's classroom. In Ms. Anastasia's class, the other classroom in which I participated, cosmopolitanism was *not* the dominant ethos. I explore the reasons for the marked difference in chapter 3, but here I briefly highlight the differences in the classroom cultures, for they underline the political dynamics at play in the kids' ethos.

There is no denying the social savvy, cultural capital, and worldly knowledge of the kids in Ms. Anastasia's class. To illustrate, I was extraordinarily amused when, during the planning for the annual graduation barbecue, Ms. Anastasia was trying to fill out the paperwork on the dietary restrictions in her classroom. She was having trouble and asked the kids. A crowd of kids amassed to impatiently inform her who was which religion, that Muslims don't eat pork, and that Hindus don't eat beef and debated among themselves if all Buddhists are vegetarian! But this worldly knowledge was not cosmopolitan in the way I employ the term. Their orientation to difference lacked its characteristic spirit and radical edge. These kids also had multiracial networks; they bridged and crossed differences with their friends and romantic partners, sometimes even deep crossing into unconventional belongings (explored in chapters 2 and 5). However, these practices were largely unidirectional, either toward the higher status kid or toward the higher status difference as defined by our racial baggage. For example, amid his romance with Anna, a girl of Greek ancestry, Blake began claiming an Italian identity although he was Ecuadorian. In Ms. Lee's class, these processes were reciprocal and rarely if ever oriented toward whiteness. Indeed, in the way Ms. Anastasia's kids were quick to use any tool at their disposal to one-up the other, including race, I can say that many of them aspired to or inhabited the heart of whiteness. Although a few kids embodied a more radical form of being and relating to race, and others expressed it some of the time, it was submerged. The dominant relation to difference was akin to conventional multiculturalism with its implicit hierarchies.

This points us toward two key features of any cultural formation. First, the local ethos in Ms. Lee's classroom was *fragile*. It was not free-floating but emerged within specific conditions that both enabled and constrained it. Second and more crucially, it was *contested*. This highlights the dynamics under the surface of any cultural norm, dynamics that help us grasp how social change occurs. Even the most dominant and taken-for-granted ideologies do not hold a monopoly. Our familiar racial baggage is not the only game in town. The kids' cosmopolitanism was a "behavioral ideology:" it was unsystematized, unfixed, grounded in experience, and constructed somewhat in relation to the established ideology of race.[27] This emphasizes the inextricable connection of the kids' cosmopolitanism to the circumstances from which it emerged. My insistence on the locally embedded nature of the kids' ethos has already been made clear. If we do not take pains to show precisely when, where, and how racial learning occurs, then our smooth accounts suggest that race is easy to learn. This book demonstrates that learning race is always a struggle, a struggle of which we do not know the outcome.

argument

main Point

HOW DID COSMOPOLITANISM EMERGE?
THE ARGUMENT VIA THE CHAPTERS

This particular group of kids' cosmopolitan ethos emerged as they struggled with the way that race weighed upon them at specific places and specific points in historical and biographical time. These struggles were suffused throughout the kids' everyday lives, but there were five particular "hot spots" of racial formation. I devote a chapter to each: (1) navigating urban space, (2) building friendships and consuming pop cultural objects, (3) laboring in school, (4) being subject to the school's disciplinary apparatus, and (5) enacting sexualities. I have somewhat artificially constructed these domains for purposes of exposition; in reality they were porous. For example, kids built friendships while they were laboring in school and interpreted "good" and "bad" kids in reference to specific urban spaces. Yet, this organizational structure captures the domains that crucially preoccupied my participants. As one of the goals of this book is to document what it feels to be a racial subject at a particular place and time, I strove to represent what it was like to be a ten-year-old kid in Augursville, engaged with concerns other than race: feeling anxious and excited about "growing up," trying to evade a teacher's surveillance, being exhausted by endless math test preparation, feeling exhilarated by the open space of the playground, pining for a chance to wear a wrestling belt, feeling gleeful at being shown a curse word in the dictionary. Race was sometimes entangled in these practices, but these practices cannot be reduced to race.

I have tried to balance this broader view with the purpose of mapping the kids' cosmopolitanism among its conditions of emergence. Consider each chapter a piece of a puzzle that illustrates how each site posed specific constraints and possibilities. Each chapter is united by the substance of the larger argument: the urgency of inserting children in our understandings of racial transformation, and showing how learning race is entangled in and constitutive of struggles of age, class, gender, sexuality, and space. Each chapter is also unified in showing how kids made meanings based on their racial, gendered, and class locations, and their embedded social networks, spatial histories, and aesthetic sensibilities. Within each chapter, I chose specific material to throw light on different angles in the multifaceted aspects of learning race/being a racial subject/racial transformation.

Rather than providing a description of the setting in the conventional sense of background to the processes of interest, chapter 1, "Sensing Urban Space," considers how navigating the superdiverse neighborhood of Augursville was an important aspect of racial learning. I explore how learning race occurred in two interrelated ways: through the multisensory experiences of navigating urban space, and through spatial struggles of belonging. I establish how the

Point of ch. 1

infrastructure of Augursville encouraged the kids' cosmopolitanism via regular and habitual interactions with diversity, and how the marginalization of Blackness from the otherwise rich tapestry of diversity posed contradictions that constrained its emergence.

Chapter 2, "Loving Friends and Things," explores how kids formed multiracial friendships and how the ethic of cosmopolitanism was put to practice in poetic and political ways within them. I demonstrate how race emerged only to be transformed in the kids' struggles to craft selves and social relations beyond the dictates of essentialized racial types and degrading hierarchies. The kids' attachments to their friends and things were sites for gender and class formations, and creative and counterhegemonic racial meaning making.

Chapter 3, "The Collective Labors of Conviviality," explores how institutional policies, teacher practices, and kids' labors had profound effects on the students' social relations and their racial learning. Through comparison of Ms. Lee's and Ms. Anastasia's classrooms, I highlight two circumstances that were key in the development of the kids' cosmopolitanism in the former: activities where kids regularly labored in collaborative tasks and the submergence of the embodied hierarchy of intelligence.

The focus on institutional practices moves to the site of discipline in chapter 4, "Racist or Fair?," where I argue that learning racism is a key aspect of learning race. I analyze how kids made meaning of allegations that a teacher was racist and map how this drama, which predictably unfolded within the site of discipline, was incorporated into kids' racial understandings. I then focus on Ms. Lee's disciplinary practices, arguing that the way she disrupted the disciplinary assemblage of race/style /"good or bad" contributed to the kids' cosmopolitan ethos, and inspires us to think anew about discipline and racial justice.

Chapter 5, "Enacting Sex Ed," reveals how the deep historical entanglement of race, sex, and class emerged in the kids' lives most forcefully in sexuality. In parents', teachers', and the public's regulation of their sexuality, kids were subjected to the dreadful discourse that people "naturally" belong with those of the same "type." I illustrate how critical transformations lurked as a possibility as the kids anxiously navigated these controls. In an ironic twist, the panic of child sexuality functioned to make the bare bones of our racial baggage hypervisible, and compelled some kids to mediate it through creative meaning making. Sexuality was thus a site where kids actively crafted subjectivities and social relations beyond the logic of race.

The kids' critical engagements with our racial baggage suggest many possibilities for concerted action by teachers, administrators, educational and urban policy makers, as well as others desiring antiracist and convivial futures. Within each chapter, the reader will find apparent tangible practices and policies such as being attuned to how race and other forms of hierarchy play out amid kids' informal interactions, recognizing and encouraging kids' multiple positionalities and belongings in the classroom, submerging "smartness," and making cooperative learning a habitual aspect of classrooms. Others will involve broader policies and resources, such as making commitments to build diverse neighborhoods and child-friendly urban spaces. Instituting any of these practices and policies entails rethinking the purpose of schooling, refusing the multiple embodied distinctions and hierarchies that structure our world, and reimagining our ways of being and relating in this world. Interactions with texts are open-ended, but I trust that readers will engage with this one in ways that foreground kids' critical knowledge of everyday life. This is after all the radical potential of childhood studies—the insistence not only that kids' perspectives are worthy of being heard, but also that these perspectives can reveal and problematize our own conceits, our most taken-for-granted categories and values. In the conclusion, I reflect on the stakes of rejecting race and, more specifically, of moving "out of the heart of whiteness" as not solely an intellectual task but a deeply emotional one that children, not in the abstract, but real-life, animated, and relentlessly demanding kids, can help us achieve.

1 ◆ SENSING URBAN SPACE

"It's great, because *everything* is right here," Fawwaz explained when I asked him what he thought about Augursville.[1] He underlined his point by comparing his neighborhood to the one his sister lived in, "where there's nothing around." Looking at a map Fawwaz drew of his immediate neighborhood, one is struck by the proximity of the important places that make up Fawwaz's world.[2] The points labeled within a five-block radius of his home include his school, PS AV, two supermarkets, a subway entrance, a playground and public square, a candy store, a pizza place, a barbershop, a cousin's home, and three friends' houses. A bit farther out but still within a mile radius are his father's work, his brother's house, two highways, his favorite taco spot, two fast-food chains, and the multiacre park. Fawwaz gave excellent directions to any of these or other places of interest. He thought I might find quality espresso at this "Italian bakery," and directed me to pass "the blue-and-white cart with the souvlaki," "the mosque that looks like a store," crossing the street, "yeah, the really busy one" until I would find myself right next to the store "pumping Spanish music." Fawwaz's understanding of Augursville combined the formal knowledge of street names and cardinal directions with the sights, smells, and sounds of his personal experiences (McFarlane 2011).

Because Fawwaz, like all my participants, primarily moved through Augursville by walking, he had a sensuous and intimate knowledge about and relationship with Augursville. From the Athenian philosophers to current social critics, architects and urban planners, and writers, artists, and experimental theorists in between, walking has been theorized as key to the urban experience. Prefiguring currently popular ideas about the embodiment of space, the nineteenth-century poet Charles Baudelaire wrote of the urban stroller intoxicated by the "universal communion" with the crowd and absorbing "all the professions, all the joys, all the sufferings that chance presents" (2009, 22). Current scholarship emphasizes how urban dwellers form attachments to place and cultivate sociability with those around them, as well as the link between walking and neighborhood desirability, convenience, health, and environmental sustainability.[3] A mode of transportation on their scale, walking has special significance for kids. As John Horton and colleagues (2014, 101) note in their rethinking of the "new walking studies" through childhood, children's walking is a constitutive feature of their geographies, characterized by rich and intense "sociality, narrativity, playfulness and taken-for-grantedness." Even when accompanied by an adult or restricted in their range, kids are able to control their pace and attention and suggest routes, detours, and stops in ways that they cannot in cars, buses, and trains. When walking, they have more agency, actively moving through the city rather than being moved through it. Walking allows kids to form an intimate relationship *with* the city; to inscribe their spatial practices, meaning making, and interpretations on the city at the same time that its sights, smells, sounds, and ambient feel shape them as subjects.

This chapter explores how learning race occurred through the multisensory experiences of dwelling, navigating, and making meaning of urban space. In ways, the point is rather banal: you can't understand the kids' cosmopolitanism without taking into account the local setting in which it emerged—amid the rich diversity and dynamism of Augursville. I doubt I need to convince anyone that Augursvillian kids, by virtue of walking about and seeing, smelling, and feeling different bodies, seeing various ethnic supermarkets and places of worship, hearing different languages and feeling the beat and rhythm of various hybridized forms of music, smelling and tasting cuisines associated with different bodies and giving them their different smells, would perceive difference quite distinctly from suburban kids in a homogeneously white neighborhood, driving home from school as big-box supermarkets and chain stores whiz by their view. The analytic task of this chapter is to explore precisely *how* the dynamics within Augursville enabled and posed challenges to the emergence of the kids' cosmopolitanism. For not only are urban multicultures spaces of positive intercultural encounter, they can also be spaces of fear, suspicion, hostility, and indifference.

GEOGRAPHY LESSONS: SENSING RELATIONALITY

Geographer Colin McFarlane describes "learning the city" as the ways adults and children "feel their way through" the built environment of the city, its materials, embedded knowledge, and resources. Through their spatial practices, urbanites produce and transform the city, while the city shapes them as social subjects. In this formulation, the city, or any place for that matter, is not a passive object. Rather, space has agency in its ever-shifting activities, its perpetually contested ideologies, the way it "enters into our unconscious and holds sway over the imagination" (Larkin 2013, 333). Physical space *does* things. As Jan Blommaert notes, physical space is also cultural, social, and *political* space: "Space offers, enables, triggers, invites, prescribes, proscribes, polices or enforces certain patterns of social behavior; a space that is never no-man's land, but always *somebody's* space; a space of *power* controlled by, as well as controlling people" (2013, 3, emphasis original). As such, encounters with space are dynamic and inherently contested. Space is a battleground. Dwelling, moving, playing in, and making meaning of space are never solely practical, but also political.

Geographers are increasingly calling attention to children's spatial meaning making as "moments of political formation," where "children [are] recognizing and asserting themselves as particular subjects, in relation to others, and to subject positions that may be imposed on them" (Elwood and Mitchell 2014, 4). The task of tracing how the specific space of Augursville shaped the kids' racial learning is made complex because kids dwelled in, moved through, and made meaning of Augursville's multiple semiotic systems differently. Their interpretations and evaluations were shaped by their experiences, memories, spatial biographies, aesthetic sensibilities, and intersecting positionalities. This chapter demonstrates how kids learned race as they decided who has rights and who belongs in particular neighborhood spaces, and which spaces are good, bad, ugly, safe, or dangerous. Through struggles to make meaning of their neighborhood, kids transformed the lived experience of race and contributed to the convivial structure of feeling that was evident but submerged in Augursville.

MODELS OF RELATIONALITY

Augursville is a vibrant and bustling "superdiverse" urban neighborhood, and the overlapping relations between different bodies, cultures, and languages constitute its placeness. These relations could be read off multiple semiotic systems at the visual, olfactory, sonic, sensual, and linguistic levels: the built environment; the movements, distributions, and encounters of people; the placement and ordering of visual signs; the sounds of languages, speech, and music styles; the unarticulated yet well-known and contested norms governing behavior in different spaces; and the explicit and implicit everyday discourses of and about the neighborhood and its diversity. The "particular arrangements of bodies, bricks, things, and settings" allow us to trace what Dan Swanton (2010) calls the "ontology of encounter," how the "billions of happy and unhappy moments of encounters" are structured (Thrift 1999, 302, cited in Swanton 2010, 2341). Infrastructure, the built networks that facilitate the circulation of people, goods, and ideas, is thus practical and poetic, "semiotic and aesthetic vehicles . . . that sometimes can be wholly autonomous from their technical functions" (Larkin 2013,

329). That is, infrastructure can bring people together or keep them apart materially and symbolically.

The relations between differences in Augursville ranged from hierarchical ordering of difference to ways of being separate yet together and forms of comingling and amalgamation.[4] Each of these four models was complex and inflected with local meaning. The *hierarchical* model tolerates and ranks differences according to how they compare to hegemonic white "Americanness." Some differences are silenced, are ignored, or barely register in this model. Despite the striking superdiversity of Augursville, the hierarchical ordering of differences was evident and could be apprehended in the universal dominance of English on Augursville's public buildings, civic associations, street signs, and corporate advertisements. Hierarchy was explicit in the spatial marginalization of Augursville's housing project. Like much public housing in the United States, Augursville's projects were located at a geographic endpoint of the neighborhood. Although the projects were only about a mile from the school, the subway, and vibrant commercial districts, walking to them was a slow progression into inactivity, industrial buildings shuttered up in the daytime, blocks with boarded-up and dilapidated buildings. The bustling placeness of Augursville is absent; only a few poorly stocked bodegas and a supermarket surround the area. Residents of Augursville who did not live in the projects simply had no reason to be there and did not venture there. More problematic was the racialized suspicion with which Augursvillians perceived the young Black residents in public and commercial spaces. Because the majority of Augursville's African Americans lived in public housing, Black male bodies were perceived through what Sara Ahmed (2000) has productively described as "stranger danger," a racialization compounded by spatial and classed fears. As "matter out of place," Black male bodies were understood as not belonging—loitering in public space and endangering those with spatial rights. While this hierarchical model predominates in public spaces in the United States, Augursville differs because it simultaneously coexists with other models.

The second model of relationality evident in Augursville is the *horizontal* ordering of differences, a separate and equal model best encapsulated with a variant of the oft-heard motto of polite separation, "we all do our own thing." Its voicing in local speech ranged in tone from acceptance and enthusiasm for the "live and let live" attitude of residents to guarded suspicion and defensiveness regarding any perceived encroachment that would upset the balance of diversity. Horizontalism easily slipped into hierarchy when adult residents unfavorably compared groups to their own with statements such as *"we* take (took) care of the neighborhood; *they* don't." This is not to say that any resident, white or otherwise, held one view of Augursville's diversity. After complaining how newcomers from Latin America were not learning English as her parents' generation had, Eliza's mom, a longtime resident of Augursville, extolled the neighborhood because of its diversity in the very next breath. The horizontal model is visually prominent in Augursville, a byproduct of groups' everyday life experiences and Augursville's historical status as a receiving point for new immigrants. Diverse religious infrastructure punctuates the neighborhood. On a commercial strip a few blocks from the school, every other business seems to be created by and for a particular group: a storefront offering telecommunication services to Latin America with its large vitrine covered in Spanish signs; a building serving as mosque, madrassa, and Bangla school; a barbershop with a large Dominican flag and map of the island on its vitrine that featured photographs of low and high fades and buzz cuts; and a Greek supermarket with a poster of a smiling woman exclaiming, "We support Greek products and our space" in Greek. But no group lived a separate or parallel existence. Residents regularly visited one another's grocery stores, restaurants, and travel agencies (one neighborhood in which this business still thrives). There were many opportunities to mix it up in Augursville.

The third model of relationality in Augursville is a *patchwork* model where differences overlap and abut in shared spaces. This model prevailed in the arrangements of bodies, languages, and things in public and commercial spaces. As one large supermarket proudly exclaimed, "We carry a full line of Greek, Indian, Italian, Brazilian, Mediterranean, and European, organic & natural products." Inside the market, products were mixed together without any geographical schema. The kiosk-like corner stores that were a key feature of the neighborhood also exemplify the patchworking of differences. Their outdoor newspaper displays had newspapers in at least ten different languages. Every day saw a different paper centered or on top of others, with the *New York Times* and *Daily News* often obscured by Spanish, Korean, Russian, Albanian, and Polish dailies.

Augursville's patchwork of architectural styles marked the spatial mixing of class. Buildings of varying types, styles, and ages occupied the same block. One of my participants lived in a beautiful yet modestly maintained Federal-style wood-frame two-story building over a century old, on the same block as two other fifth-graders, who lived in a sprawling eight-floor apartment complex built in the mid-twentieth century. These buildings face three-story row houses, brownstones broken up into multifamily homes, and squat buildings of indeterminate age covered in aluminum siding. Virtually all of these structures have been modified with little thought of architectural integrity. One brick structure had four different patches of siding, some of aluminum, others of faux stone, each showing its age. Newly arriving professionals found this patchwork of architectural styles disorderly, its "ugliness" a constant source of humor and critique. The cobbled-together model was featured prominently in commercial spaces, perfectly represented by Abir's Bakery a few blocks from the school. Although Abir had erected a handsome dark green awning with his store name and "halal" in both English and Bangla, the vitrine was also painted with a stereotypical Italian baker holding an Italian flag and the previous owner's Italian name. Inside, pairuti sat alongside Italian loaves, cannoli, baguettes, challah, and health-conscious multigrain loaves. Was it a Bengali bakery, a Bengali bakery with Italian goods, an Italian bakery with Bengali goods, a Bangla-Italo-French bakery? No one in Augursville bothered to ask, accepting it for what it was.

The last model of relationality is the various modes of *amalgamating* differences. Togetherness transforms individual parts to create something new, with varying degrees of integrity of the parts. These include youth cultural forms that blend by virtue of interaction and sustained relationships. It is not as visible in the built or semipermanent structures of Augursville, although it does appear sporadically in new fusion restaurants opened by a younger generation of entrepreneurs. It is more visible in the ephemeral syncretized practices of residents—a teenage girl wearing tight jeans tucked into knee-high leather boots and a hijab giggling arm in arm with a girl with "chola-fied" eyebrows and henna on her hands. This syncretic model troubles neat packages of difference. When walking about or staying still on a busy corner, you encounter people whose bodies do not match the language or clothing style you would expect, who eat or worship in places you would not envisage. The ambient sounds of Augursville also form an amalgam, the dizzying array of languages, beats, and lyrics coming out of cars, storefronts, headphones all converge. The subway arrives and the whole neighborhood trembles, the sound of metal on metal temporarily drowning out and uniting all sounds.

These four models of the relations of difference (hierarchical, horizontal, patchworked, and amalgamated) overlap to produce superdiversity's key feature—complexity, "a multitude of crisscrossing and overlapping features of diversity, packed within a relatively small area" (Blommaert 2013, 112). The neighborhood's dynamism ensures that these models are not static. Horizontal arrangement of differences can become a patchwork, like the Romanian church that turned into a de facto ecumenical one. Changes are not permanent or unidirectional. Separation can emerge from the patches, as when the ecumenical church turned into a Korean Presbyterian church within a year's time. Simultaneous class dynamics transform the signature row houses, each with their patches of garden that blend seamlessly with one another. On one block, an absentee landlord illegally renting one of the row homes neglected his plot. Desperate neighbors separated their carefully tended rectangles, one with a short chain-link fence, another with bushes. In contrast, in another row of homes purchased by developers, the emblematic patchworks of gardens altered in a way that seems to please the eyes of the newer professional middle class trickling in to Augursville, with uniform plants by professional landscapers. Superdiversity's complexity entails not only perpetual motion, but that "layers upon layers of historically conditioned activity" occur at different speeds and with different form simultaneously (Blommaert 2013, 17). Kids had to make *sense* of this complexity as they went about their business moving through space in their daily lives. In doing so, they contributed to complexity and its ongoing dynamism.

SENSING AUGURSVILLE FROM DIFFERENT VANTAGE POINTS

Because all of the kids had ties to other parts of NYC, regularly visiting, having lived in families or visiting kin in various parts of the city, the kids often talked *about* Augursville, perceiving it in relation to these other places. The kids' spatial biographies, along with their multiple positions, shaped how they made sense and evaluated Augursville's dynamics. In general, all of the kids had positive connections to their neighborhood, and like Fawwaz's introductory statement, signaled Augursville's density when speaking of it favorably. In fact, kids' talk about Augursville often flowed into a discussion of diversity and difference and vice versa, establishing how important space was for racial learning. For example, when I expressed surprise when Besnik first told me that he was part Albanian, he continued by discussing the neighborhood. "There's lots of other Albanians in Augursville. And a lot of Spanish cultures. I'm Spanish too," he added as an aside, before continuing, "Egyptian, I know, my friend is from Egypt. What else? I forgot, there's *a lot* of people here. Bangladesh, India, Korea, Tibet, like Sangmu!" Carly, who had been casually listening, piped in, "Oh yeah, like in my building we have twenty people. We have Greek, Arabic, Yugo, um, something Slavia." "Yeah?" I asked. She replied, "I'm fine with it. I don't mind if they're Chinese, Japanese, French, as long as they speak English!"

Consider the contrast in the two kids' perspectives on their relations to difference. Besnik's positive perception of Augursville is partly due to the fact that his daily practices and embodied experiences mixed cultures, races, languages, and religions. His father is a Dominican-born Catholic, and his mother is an Albanian-born Muslim. Part of his enthusiasm for Augursville's mixity must have also been due to his spatial history, having lived with his maternal grandparents for a time in a neighborhood that was predominantly white and "boring." We could imagine that there his mixity was viewed if not negatively, then at least as a curiosity. The hierarchical model limits the degree of mixing that it tolerates. On the other hand, Carly, white and self-proclaimed "just American," perceived Augursville through this hierarchical lens—"as long as they speak English." It was nearly identical in formation to a white adult resident who remarked about Augursville's multilingual store signs, "I don't mind the signs in all these languages, as long as they're in English too!" But Besnik didn't subscribe to the hierarchical model. With his considerable spatial autonomy, he and Raiden, a fifth-grader from another class who was "all mixed too" (Japanese and French), would skateboard all around Augursville when school let out.

When I asked ten-year-old Salma what she thought of her neighborhood, the limits she raised were of a very different order. "I love it! Augursville, it's like a little town, a cozy town." When I asked her to elaborate she replied, "Lots of stores and lots of friends, it's kinda like . . . its cozy! There's hundreds of stores, you can buy anything. Plus, the park is way cool!" She continued to rattle off the places she frequented, excitedly describing Augursville in a sensual manner. I jokingly remarked that she must have a pretty good nose, after her mentioning the aroma of schwarma from her favorite restaurant, or the incense she would try to grab and sniff at the kiosk if her mother wasn't in a hurry. She pointed out the costs to her sensitivity—she hated the smell of smoke and "the drunk people." For Salma, the older Europeans were problematic. Her family just wanted to have a picnic in the park, but the smokers aggravated her asthma. Salma often brought up Augursville and the interesting lessons about diversity she would learn just by being out and about. When telling me about her Bangla school, she excitedly remarked that although only Bengali people attended the school, "people from all over" came to pray. She then recalled, "There's this African American man who's Muslim on my block!" "Does he go to your mosque?" I asked. "I don't know, they go in separately, but little kids can go wherever." "So how did you know he is Muslim?" I persisted. Salma explained, "Because he kept saying 'As-salamu alaykum' all the time and I asked my dad 'Is he Muslim?' because some people are other religions and they say it, and my dad said yes. Some people just do some things because they like it. In the store there were some Christian people and they had their head covered with a scarf and they weren't Muslim but they liked that part." Perceptive and curious about differences, Salma enjoyed having her assumptions about difference contradicted. Augursville's density and diverse demographics meant that navigating space was an opportunity for Salma, like many other kids, to tease apart the tight configuration of race/culture/language/religion in hegemonic understandings of difference.

The incoming professional middle class did not register in the kids' perceptions of their neighborhood. Attracted by Augursville's commercial strips, ethnic restaurants, considerable nightlife, and proximity to and ease of transportation to Manhattan's business districts, young singles were dribbling in, as were a few families with kids in PS AV, although they were all in the lower grades at the time of fieldwork (kindergarten to second grade).[5] Although the area has experienced some uneven gentrification in the past decade, it had not yet matched developers' expectations. Newer and more expensive units were conspicuously vacant, stalled development in the form of empty lots and inactive construction sites, as well as absentee landlords without any interest in the neighborhood beyond their capital return resulted in predictable illegal rentals, overcrowding, and abandonments as they waited for a more favorable market. Some kids from upwardly mobile families (white, Latino, and Asian) perceived this as a downward spiral in their neighborhood and misattributed the shifts to "Mexican" people, or that there were "too many Mexicans." Other kids invoked a moral panic about criminality in their neighborhood. Augursville is a relatively safe neighborhood, with a crime index significantly lower than the city and national averages (there was an increase in robberies in the five years preceding fieldwork, which dipped back down again when the economic downturn was in recovery). Some kids perceived the neighborhood was *becoming* full of gangs and gang violence, a dynamic that they racialized as Mexican or Black, the latter seen as emanating from the projects.

The public housing project was officially *a part* of Augursville and shared the neighborhood's name and postal zip code. However, both kids who lived in the projects and other kids recognized that it was *apart* from Augursville as well. Where they differed is how they evaluated the projects, and how resident kids worked to legitimate their perspectives. I was hanging out with Keisha and Jacinta during a lull in activity when Steven came up to us, put his arms around the girls' shoulders, and remarked, "These kids right here? They're from the *hood*!" Keisha beamed with pride, nodded, and gave Steven a pound. Jacinta giggled. Playing naïve, I asked, "What's that?" "The hood!" Keisha repeated loudly, tilting her head at me as if I should know this most basic term. I kept up the role, "Is *this* the hood?" All of them burst out exasperated, "Noooooooo!" "This, this is like a *suburban* neighborhood," Jacinta explained pedantically, pausing before she added, "They're all white people here." Steven continued the lesson, "In the hood, there's only Black and Spanish people." "Yeah right, over here the houses are all nice and neat," Jacinta explained, making little squares with her hands. "Yeah, over there there's no, well, hardly even any white people," Steven continued. I winked at them and quipped, "Except cops?" They all laughed, knowingly agreeing, "Yeah, the cops." Steven added, "Cops, detectives, undercover."

Steven, Keisha, and Jacinta considered their housing development through the double view that characterizes many marginalized subjectivities. On the one hand, they expressed pride of belonging to what they constructed as a vibrant and authentic *urban* space. This perspective was partly informed by their knowledge of how others viewed the projects. That is, they understood how other residents could easily and did avoid the projects and their associated fears. It was an issue that implicitly came up whenever teachers gave assignments that had to be completed after school. It was simply out of the question for a friend to come to the projects, about a mile away from school, to work cooperatively. It was difficult for kids to cement friendships with home visits, for they would have to walk the mile by themselves or take a bus. Considering that for half of the academic year this would have to be negotiated in the dark, these visits were extremely inconvenient to parents, most of whom had no access to a car. Steven, Keisha, and Jacinta understood but did not accept this spatial marginalization. Rather, they used it to paint a picture of Augursville that was distinct from that of other kids', straightforwardly racializing the neighborhood as a hierarchical and explicitly white space. Although Jacinta's view was more ambiguous than Keisha and Steven's celebratory rhetoric, her characterization of Augursville as "suburban" was dismissive. Accompanied by an eye roll, her hand gesture of uniform squares suggested a staid and static order in contrast to the lively dynamism of "the hood."

KIDS IN PUBLIC SPACE

While all kids interacted with the public spaces of Augursville, they experienced the conflicting narratives concerning young people in public differently. On the one hand, we like to imagine that public spaces—parks, playgrounds, sidewalks, and squares—are designed for children and are ideal for their development.[6] On the other hand, young people in public space are thought to be endangered and a danger to others, "out of place simply due to age" (Gray and Manning 2014, 652). As ten- and eleven-year-olds, my participants were on the precipice of transitioning from older childhood to teenage youth, a period that is marked by, among other things, a growing spatial autonomy. Even the most protective parents who walked their kids to and from school realized that their kids would soon be "out and about" without them and began allowing them to navigate certain routes without adult supervision. Parents' spatial regulation of their kids fell along predictable gendered and classed patterns, rehearsed daily at three o'clock, when the kids dispersed from the school building.

On one afternoon on a chilly day in early April when the heat had been relentlessly pumping in the building, the kids were more exuberant than usual upon release from school. I scanned the environs to see where my kids had scattered in the disorder of the hundreds of running, yelling, and hooting kids radiating in every direction of the school. Lillian and Selena marched to pick up their younger siblings, holding tightly to their hands as they made a beeline to a local after-school club. There they would be able to do their homework, be amused with various activities, and, most important, not be "all around in the streets" as their parents feared. Jacinta and Keisha walked to the public bus stop for the short trip to the projects. I could see Jacinta longing to dawdle about with her friends Sabrina and Eliza. But she didn't like going on the bus alone, especially a little later when it was crowded with "crazy" teens. She followed Keisha who preferred to be in her "hood," hanging out with her older siblings and their friends. Besides, Keisha's best friends, Darryl, Mark, and Steven, were preoccupied with flirting with some girls. Sabrina and Eliza ran about, chased each other, pulled one another's hair, and made fun of their little brothers as their mothers chatted while mixing and switching between Albanian and English as they waited for the girls to release some steam. Abdul was already down the block, his mom's black abaya visible from afar, one of the few boys whose mom came to pick him up. Luis, Juan, Hakeem, Sebastian, and Lucas began the preliminaries of wrestling matches that would continue for the next hour across the street at Verrazano Square. Omar was chasing his friends around until he was panting and nodded his head in goodbye. Steven was being grabbed and chased by three girls as Mark and Darryl tried to participate. This interaction continued at the corner store across the street where Steven usually bought candy to share with his friends. Yanely and Ashley made their way about the schoolyard as a team, going in and out of flirtatious encounters with various boys, including James, who was being chased by his own crew of admiring girls from other fifth-grade classes. As kids dispersed, Yanely and Ashley lingered.

The spatial politics that structured the gendered and classed variations in the kids' spatial autonomy are somewhat predictable. Girls were more likely saddled with responsibility of picking up their siblings, boys were allowed more time and space to interact, middle-class parents had the ability to personally supervise their children, and many working-class parents instilled fear in lieu of their presence. Some adults' exaggerated fears of the urban persisted as a background threat and were articulated in ways that explicitly or implicitly indexed Blackness. These anxieties arose when bodies of Black youth were seen to be out of place, as was the case on this April afternoon. It was about a quarter after three when I finished talking to Ms. Flores, the former head of PS AV's Parent-Teacher Association. Her son Blake had been one of my participants in Ms. Anastasia's class the previous year, and she updated me on his difficulties adjusting to junior high. Walking to my car, I came into view of the group of kids in front of the candy store, now Steven, Mark, Darryl, Yanely, Ashley, and Amy. The kids were in full-on flirt mode, their faces flushed and their bodies charged with expectancy and the potential of the unpredictable. When they spotted me they all started hooting and yelling my name. For performative effect and to signal our closer relationship, Yanely ran toward me begging for a ride home, a regular request that was always denied. I was uncomfortable witnessing the palpable excitement of their raging hormones. A car rolled by pumping "This Is Why I'm Hot" by rapper Mims. The boys yelled and waved their arms in recognition. As they turned their heads to follow the car's beat, I took the opportunity to shout my goodbyes. A few minutes after I left, a teacher drove by and saw the kids doing much the same. She found it so inappropriate that she got out of her car and demanded that they go home. She went home and informed the principal and the girls' teachers by telephone, and their behavior was the disapproving gossip among the teachers the next morning. The girls were called to the principal's office and told to go straight home after school from then on. Other staff concerns quickly eclipsed the drama. Some kids tried to find out why the girls were called to the principal's office. Steven and Mark pretended not to know anything and were uncharacteristically quiet. There was no dramatic resolution. Only an aura lingered about them for the day, a mixture of guilt, confusion, resentment, violation, frustration, and powerlessness.

However atypical was the teacher's policing the kids' use of public space, it highlights politics that are operative yet mostly concealed. The spatial struggle was emblematic of adults' attempt to control children and children's attempts to wrest autonomy to conduct their social affairs. This struggle was also embedded with sexual, racialized, gendered, and class meanings. The age and gendered dynamics are obvious in the teacher's censuring of the girls. Less obvious are the sexualized and racialized aspects of the teacher's indignation—it was the "out of place" boys who threatened the girls. The boys were all from the projects, and Mark and Darryl were Black. The interracial, sexually saturated encounter in unregulated public space tested the limits of acceptability. The teachers' protective talk about the girls was not about shielding them from sexual predation. In fact, the girls were considered to be more sexually mature than the boys. The teachers were instead keen to protect the girls' reputation from a vaguely defined public, personified in a former parent of the school that was active in local politics. "Imagine what DeMarco would have done?" one of the teachers mused, as the rest laughed in relief that he was no longer a constant presence in the school, judging, complaining, and questioning.

A few days later, I was chatting with Yanely. She had told me about the incident the day after it happened. It was apparent that she was unsatisfied with the nonevaluative tone I had taken and, moreover, how all parties involved (including me) knew that race was an integral aspect of the dramatic stance the adults had taken but did not name it. As we ate pizza, Yanely filled me in on the gossip of the girls in the ELL class, hoping to force me into a position and get me to name the role of race explicitly. Yanely vacillated in her desire of wanting me to judge and condone the girls' behavior as her stories escalated in danger. Some of the girls were dating boys from the nearby junior high, she reported. "Mmm," I noted. Some of the girls went looking for the boys around their school. "Mmm hmm." "And Darryl likes Flora," she said, looking intently for my response to gauge if I, like all the adults she knew, drew a line at dating Black boys. "Does Flora like him back?" I asked neutrally. She shrugged and responded with a story that I would hear again: Flora's mom had recently seen her daughter at the edge of Verrazano Square after school. She grabbed Flora by the hair and dragged her across the street. Yanely told this story in horror, "Can you imagine pulling your daughter's hair like that?" she wondered. I asked if her mom would be mad. "Maybe," she mused, but maybe not if she was "just playing." Yanely understood too well that "not playing" was danger-ous business.

Yanely's story telling of Verrazano Square was just as much an act of spatial learning as her own actions on the sidewalk, for the city is also learned in translo-cal processes that transcend that particular place (McFarlane 2011). Yanely was making hegemonic norms and codes of conduct explicit and inspecting their lay-ers of meaning. The immediate context of her narrative framed Flora's actions as violating the boundaries of age, sex, race, and space. These tentative musings about adult power and regulation of children's space were linked to her grow-ing spatial autonomy and her own experiments pushing the boundaries of spatial belonging and racial mixing. I was to find out a few weeks later that Yanely was entertaining a flirtation with Darryl herself. Yanely's spatial meaning making—in her real-time interpretation of the event, in her musing, telling, and retelling of the story—represented claims of spatial citizenship, processes entangled with her emerging sexuality and racial meaning making.

Verrazano Square was an important touchstone in the kids' spatial practices and imaginaries. It figured prominently in the kids' more-or-less concealed struggles to define to whom this public space belongs. The way kids related to Verrazano, the meanings they made of it, and their practices within it were partly shaped by the design, construction, and physical materials with which Verrazano Square was built. It was designed as a gathering place, with a central open space and benches and small tables linings its perimeter. The layout perfectly distrib-utes the pairs and small groups of old European men for whom the square was created, giving them a sense of being in public and out of the private, feminized space of their home while still able to have private conversations. The design itself is not accidental but a product of local history and politics. Originally a playground with climbing equipment, sandboxes, and handball courts, the square was rebuilt as a tribute to one of the "original" European groups in the dis-tinct paths of ethnic succession encoded in the city's neighborhoods. Its Italian name engraved on plaques announces its European ownership to the newer and now younger immigrants from Latin American, Asia, the Middle East, and the Caribbean. A statue of the explorer himself looms over the square, the bronze and granite stubbornly and unbendingly insisting European ownership. Early in the morning the square seems veritably public, belonging to no one and every-one. Augursvillians of all ages, genders and races hustle and bustle and shortcut through it. From the hours of nine to two, Serbian, Polish, Croatian, Albanian, Greek, Romanian, and Italian are the languages of the square, the continuous stream of thick smoke emanating from old men's cigarettes ensuring their day-time monopoly of the square. In the afternoon, moms staked their claims as they waited to pick up kids from school or to give their toddlers freedom from stroll-ers. They gave dirty looks and loud coughs and conspicuously waved the smoke from their personal space to the calm obliviousness of the men. Some women, including me, preferred to take the longer route around the square rather than be the spectacle of the old men's lazy gazes.

The kids' experiences, memories, and social relations shaped their meanings of Verrazano. Jacinta, who had to walk alongside it on her way home, once made a remark that suggested the old men were creepy. Her best friend Eliza, whose grandfather was a smoking regular at Verrazano Square, immediately contested her interpretation, and tried to educate Jacinta on the functions of such spaces for old men, to catch up "about their countries." She is of Albanian descent, her mom born in the United States to Albanian immigrants and her dad born in Albania. At this point, Eliza often and eagerly performed herself as Albanian, and it was an important part of her life. She visited in the summer, anxiously waited for her grandparents to come back and live with her when they were visiting, and frequently communicated with relatives in Albania, typical experiences for kids of the second or 2.5 generation. The way Eliza spoke about the square with nostalgic reverence reflected her emotional attachments to her grandfather and "her country," and spilled over to the spaces he dwelt.

Boys had different perspectives and experiences with the square. Although designed and partly privately funded by the older European generation for themselves, Verrazano Square is operated by the New York City Parks Department and subject to its safety codes. The soft protective surfacing that surrounds and extends outward from the small playground unintentionally invited groups of rambunctious boys to conduct their wrestling matches. On any day without rain or snow, the square was filled with bodies of boys in unthinkable contortions by a quarter after three in the afternoon. They yelled and cheered as they waited their turn or jumped in the mangle of bodies. If there were rules, I did not want to know them. I still marvel that no serious injuries resulted, although I did not have the stomach to stick around and watch the matches. The boys waited until most moms dispersed because there would always be one who, even if she did not recognize them, would yell or try to pry them apart. In addition to the absence of adult supervision, Verrazano Square was a cherished spot for wrestling because the boys were protected from the ridicule of other boys for their obsession with wrestling. Those boys did not frequent the square because they were preoccupied with girls, who couldn't be in the square. For a good hour, boys gloried in their wrestling. They struck a silent truce with the remaining old men. As long as they kept to the center, the old men were as interested in their movements as if they were squirrels, if not less.

The arrival of teenagers in the late afternoon gave new meaning to the space and displaced the very young and old. Style and the new reigned: piercings, tufts of pink hair, baseball caps, beanie hats, hoodies up, tighter-than-tight jeans, ripped jeans, hanging-off-the-hips jeans, and the latest, most colorful sneakers.

Unruly bodies sat on the backs of the benches, arms around one another, hugging, kissing, laughing, cursing, playfully hitting. No drinking or smoking weed, yet the mixedness of the teens and their unruly sexuality—their unauthorized couplings and their very bodies gave the space an illicit feel. To my participants, this made Verrazano a site for exploration and education.

The public space of Verrazano fluidly entered the kids' spatial imaginaries, as it did during a moment of anticipation in the cafeteria as the kids waited to be allowed into the schoolyard for recess. I was listening to Amy recount how she and Yanely had seen Mia's ex-boyfriend at a fast-food place about a mile from the school yesterday. Mia challenged, "I thought Yanely wasn't *allowed* to go outside her house." After going back and forth on this point, Mia one-upped her with a tale highlighting her considerable spatial freedom (she was a year older than most of the fifth-grade kids). When *she* walked through Verrazano yesterday afternoon, she had seen two girls making out. Steven yelled, "If my daughter was a lesbian, I'd kick her out of the house!" As the girls laughed, Martina reasoned, "No you wouldn't because that would still be your daughter." "Well," he acceded, "I would tell her, you better shape up or you gonna have to get out of my house." Amy and Mia then reminisced about a day when they were walking along the commercial strip and "lesbians" approached them to support "gay rights." They laughed about how the young women approached anyone and everyone and mimicked some of the confused and horrified responses they received. Such experiences in and talk about Augursville were emblematic of the educative function of kids' struggles to make meaning and wrest more autonomy in Augursville's public spaces. Their interpretations and experiences affected how they viewed particular spaces like Verrazano and Augursville's dynamics in general and how they cobbled together notions of difference.

BRINGING THE HOOD INTO THE SCHOOL

The school is itself a social space, a web of "intersecting relational geographies" (Massey 2005). It is embedded within the spatial dynamics of Augursville but has spatiotemporal contradictions of its own that kids interpret, struggle with, and contribute to. It should come as no surprise that multiculturalism, the hierarchical model of difference expressed in many US schools, also prevailed within PS AV. The hierarchical model greets all visitors with PS AV's public message board outside the school. Five announcements under headings of PTA news, school news, and parent coordinator news appeared in English, and one announcement each for Spanish, Bangla, and Arabic. At first glance, the visibility of the non-Latin scripts grabs the attention and seemingly welcomes the families speaking different languages. While acknowledging the fact that many parents did not speak English, the information posted in other languages was not as thorough, and the professionalism of the translations was uneven. Spanish was centrally placed and typewritten, while the others were handwritten.

The hierarchies and silences of multiculturalism are also evident upon entering the lobby of the school. One is visually struck by a multipaneled "multicultural" mural painted by a local artist, a piece that continues into the auditorium, the second-most public space of the school. The artwork depicts people of various skin tones and manners of ethnic dress and adornment, including a woman wearing a sari, belly exposed in a sensual dancing pose. The omission of any woman in traditional Islamic clothing becomes apparent upon exiting the school at three o'clock with the group of parents waiting for their children, front and center are the mothers in hijabs, burkas, and nikabs.

Multiculturalism was the dominant visual motif throughout the school and individual classrooms. Colorful graphs and pie charts with "the countries we are from" or "our many languages" made the school bright and cheerful. Despite the dearth of Italian students, "Italian Day" was celebrated with gusto, with a special assembly and food served in the cafeteria, and a local news station to document it. Every visitor I encountered inevitably marveled at the colorful representations of diversity and at the colorful bodies of the kids themselves. None of them picked up on the multiculturalism's implicit hierarchies and omissions. Despite the sizable proportion of Muslim students, Christmas decorations were everywhere in the school, hallways, and classrooms in December, and the entire fifth grade went to Radio City to see the *Christmas Spectacular* show. I was not aware of any staff member questioning the wisdom of having students participate in a letter-writing campaign to US troops in Iraq and Afghanistan. Nor did visitors pick up on the school's marginalizing, ignoring, or devaluing of the local African American experience in a multicultural model wholly based on the immigrant experience. Black kids' experiences were excluded not only from the visual celebration of languages and countries but from everyday classroom practices that incorporated this multicultural model. Black History Month was celebrated in conventionally impoverished fashion—focusing on the achievements of historical figures like George Washington Carver (inventor of peanut butter) and contemporary famous African Americans like Oprah and ensuring discussions of racism stayed firmly rooted in the past with celebrations of the "end of racism." The only schoolwide breach occurred during the talent show, where Black and Latino kids sang and danced to hip-hop and R & B numbers to the delight of the kids. Teachers and administrators preapproved and sanitized each performance to make sure there were no inappropriate language or body movements. But they knew too well how impossible it was to discipline bodies in exuberant motion. The adults watched these performances in nervous apprehension and vigilance, ready to pull the plug.

While Blackness was marginalized in the space of the school, each teacher had her own method of regulating performances and embodiments of urban youth style with which kids expressed Blackness (see chapter 4 for an analysis of how Ms. Lee disrupted the disciplinary assemblage of skin and style). Related to this, teachers knew which kids were from the projects, labeled them as such, and considered the projects and their residents in ways identical to how they were positioned in the neighborhood—problematic, marginal, and best kept that way. This was so even among teachers who could be said to be sympathetic to these kids. For instance, I had noticed that a lot of the kids from the projects were in band, one of the few extracurricular activities with which they were involved and enjoyed. When I asked the music teacher how the band gets chosen, he explained that he culls them from music class, inviting kids who exhibited a particular talent. He correctly figured the reason why I asked and started talking about his steep learning curve with the "project kids" and the various strategies he experimented with to make sure they behaved. He did not allow the project students, unlike other kids in band, to take instruments home, fearing they would lose, steal, or otherwise damage them. He told a story of a third-grader from the projects who was caught smearing feces in the boys' bathroom and shuddered at what went on "over there." Despite the free way that teachers talked among themselves about the "project kids," I never heard them mention the projects in front of the kids. Perhaps they thought it was an object of shame or that they did not think they could muster a neutral tone when doing so.

The kids from public housing intervened in this marginalization through various stylistic performances that constructed the projects as a source of urban authenticity and savoir faire. Keisha kept trying to get me to visit. "Oh, you'd love it!" she said and explained the gathering of kids and chasing games and all the fun. These performances educated other kids on the alternative spatial meanings of the projects, Augursville, and the urban. The following event was spectacular. Ody, one of the janitors, was passing through the cafeteria. He was extremely conspicuous to the kids because he was the only youngish janitor, had tattoos up both arms, and always dressed nicely in the style admired by the boys—hip-hop-associated name brands and baseball caps. Whenever he appeared, the kids followed his every move until he was out of sight, slowing down or bringing whatever action to a stop. On this day, Steven, sitting on the end of the bench, stood up and boldly approached him as he came his way. I was sitting at the other end of the long bench watching how heads were turned to follow their interaction. At one point Steven called out to Mark, who was across the lunchroom, "Yo Mark! Where I live at?" Mark yelled, "Tha projects!" Steven turned to the janitor and held his arms out with a "see, I told you so" stance. Ody gave Steven a pound on his back. Steven started recounting all the kids who live in the projects, and the janitor asked about Steven's parents.

They went through all the people they knew in common. Ody seemed amused by Steven's charisma, gave him another pound, and went about his business. Mark had made his way over to bask in the glory as Steven repeated bits of the conversation. The kids looked on starstruck.

Such performances of alternative spatial meanings were an important part of the classroom culture because Ms. Lee provided space for it in her lessons. She was unique among teachers I observed in making efforts to inform herself about the kids' pop cultural consumptions, and using them as a pedagogical tool. This allowed kids to display their competencies and perform identities and allegiances. One particular noteworthy performance occurred in the context of an intensive, monthlong high-stakes math test preparation using a book that focused on test-taking strategies. To engage the kids, Ms. Lee picked a different "accent" every few days in which she required the kids to read aloud passages from the book—among them "British," "Southern," "Boston," and here, New York.

Ms. Lee called them over to the meeting area for the teaching point of the day, "reviewing Kaplan strategies." Ms. Lee told the class that today they would be using New York accents. "We moved from the South to California, and now back to New York. Maybe next we'll go to other countries. Maybe Jamaica, yah, mon." She asked them to repeat after her "New Yawk!" The kids repeated loudly. Then she said, "Add a little head bop—New Yawk, New Yawk!" The kids repeated, pumping their fists in the air. She introduced the strategy for order of operations in complex math problems. Sebastian was very excited and pumped his fist in the air, "What up, dude! No, no. What up, bro!" Steven called him out dismissively, "Yo, you sound like my grandma." I turned to hide my laughter only to be met by Steven's mischievous grin when I turned back. He was satisfied that someone appropriately responded to his comment. Most of the kids were too excited over the call and response to have noticed. Sebastian did, and was sheepishly getting his face back together.

Ms. Lee asked for volunteers to read the next example. Hands shot up. She chose Steven and he came up to the front of the class and began reading in his regular voice. When he came to a pause, Ms. Lee said loudly, "I want to hear some New Yawkers." Steven replied, "New York, New York son. A'ight son." He read the next paragraph: "*Yo*, my dear aunt sally is just one of the memory aids you will learn in the program *son*. Keep a list of the memory aids you find useful *a'ight* and review them before test day, *you dig*? A'ight son!" The class was enthralled. Ms. Lee cracked up in delight and answered his call, "A'ight!" Keisha, giggling and nodding her head in approval throughout his performance, reached over to slap Steven's hand in allegiance as he walked back to his place. Some of the boys looked anxious as they wondered how they could compete. Sebastian saw an opportunity to redeem himself in the excitement, "Your aunt Sally's dead!" Ms. Lee, still laughing, gave a faux shocked "Sebastian!" to censure him gently but keep the playful mood alive.

After Ms. Lee had the kids discuss the next example with partners, she asked for a volunteer to read the next passage. There were considerably fewer hands than the first request, and the arms were more tentative than enthusiastic. The volunteers were a mixture of the confident and bold like Keisha and James, and those with little social savvy like Sebastian, Juan, and Assad. Ms. Lee chose Juan. He began reading with no audible modification in accent. Sebastian loudly called out, "Where's your NY accent bro!?" Juan looked down dejectedly. Ms. Lee asked, "Are you up to this?" He shook his head. At that moment, someone made a loud fart sound and the class broke into hysterics. Some kids started chanting "Oh! Oh! Oh!" Ms. Lee told them that the commotion had cost them ten marbles, part of a communal behavioral system that gained or lost them privileges. There would be no free time today.

I wish to highlight the high stakes involved in this performance, even for Steven. Rather than diffusing his charismatic power in that curious dialectic that characterizes the mainstreaming of subcultural styles, the institutional legitimacy conferred upon his performance served to heighten his status. Indeed, he did not take these performances lightly, and his little warm-up (New York, New York, a'ight son) and his walk "offstage" had the out-of-body seriousness associated with theatrical performances. His successful performance was ratified by the kids' awe, Ms. Lee's delight, and Keisha's hand slap. These displays were ubiquitous in the informal interactions of the school, sealing and ratifying Steven and other kids' association with an urban Black youth culture. These performances ratified this particular style as *the* urban mode of being. While there are many New York accents, Ms. Lee initiated the activity with the stereotypical Brooklynese with an exaggerated "r" deletion, associated with the white working class. However, Steven quickly changed the accent to one he thought more appropriate. His performance presented an *embodied* aesthetic. It was not just an accent and use of certain slang. Steven shifted his posture, gesture, facial expression, indeed his whole body to signal a mode of being that was at once "real," urban, and associated with Blackness. Steven and Keisha were redefining New York and urbanness at the same time as they figured Blackness a key to multiracial hip-hop culture.[7] Implicitly rejecting constructs in which the "hood" and its residents are an entanglement of degeneracy, pathology, and violence, Steven and his friends worked to flip the valuation. They constructed the projects as a vibrant and live source of urban authenticity. The kids claimed dignity and social and spatial belonging in the urban context. Steven and Keisha established the projects as a dynamic part of the school, neighborhood, and city.

The kids' practices, although partly an expression of their lived circumstances, were purposeful interventions into their racialized landscape. These kids were among the few who perceived the hidden contradiction in Augursville's and the school's celebration of diversity. The kids' expressive practices worked to affirm their belonging, and educate other kids to alternative orientations to Blackness and associated categories of the urban. There were limitations to the conceptions that the kids put forth. Yet, these practices were a rich site for reinvention that came from the productive performances of Black kids and their allies, educating others about the pleasures of Black cultural forms. The kids' efforts highlight the major fault line in Augursville's conviviality—the exclusion of Blackness, one that characterizes many vibrant urban multicultures. This fault line was crystallized in the racialized and spatialized fears of their impending entry into junior high school.

MACHINE GUNS AND WEDGIES: FEARS OF A BAD SCHOOL

For many elementary students, junior high school looms on the horizon with a mixture of excitement and anxiety, becoming more palpable as summer approaches. For the fifth-graders of PS AV, this anticipation was a site of hegemonic racial meaning making as some kids wondered what junior high they would be attending, and others tried to come to terms with the fact that they would be going to "the bad school," Junior High School Maya Angelou (JHS MA). Zoning regulations had about half of PS AV students going JHS MA, and the other half to Junior High School Walt Whitman (JHS WW). The schools' reputations were inverse images of one another, as was their actual ratio of Black to white students (one to three and three to one, respectively, with nearly identical percentages of Asian and Latino students). JHS WW was universally praised as a good school with rich programs, great teachers, a sound administration, and good students. JHS MA's reputation was the stuff of urban legends, with little semblance to reality: a bad school where kids brought weapons (knives, razors, even a "machine gun") to school, sold drugs and condoms in the bathroom, "jumped" new kids or white kids, and gave freshman "wedgies," and teachers paid no mind. So although about one-third of its students were Black, JHS MA's "bad kids" were colored by a seemingly endless supply of racialized imagery that constructed the school as a dangerous space.[8]

Fear is a common emotion as kids prepare to leave the comfort of their elementary schools and on to the unfamiliar territory of junior high, where they will be the newest and youngest students. Other childhood scholars have discussed some of these fears as entailing the opening of spatial horizons and decreased adult supervision (Nespor 1997). These rather normal anxieties were compounded by the broader and local equation of Blackness with violence, criminality, and predation. This specter was thought to pull boys with gangster-like tendencies into its orbit as predators, with innocent boys as their prey. During a conversation with two of my kids in the accelerated class, Salma told me how her mom had obtained a phony address for her to attend JHS WW. When I asked why, she explained about JHS MA: "The classes are good, but the students are horrible!" Daniel seconded her opinion, "It's not the school, it's the students!" While other kids expressed anxieties about going to JHS MA, Joseph was excited and unperturbed by other kids' fears. Part of Joseph's excitement was because he had cousins and a sibling who attended the school. Other kids explained Joseph's nonchalance as proof positive of his future descent into criminality, and predicted that he would be carrying a knife and joining a gang in no time.

In the late spring of the school year, JHS Maya Angelou organized an orientation for kids from PS AV. I accompanied the kids on the visit, many of them dressed in their favorite outfits for the occasion. Teachers and administrators warmly welcomed them, explained the various programs on offer, and then sent them to the auditorium to watch performances by students from the choral and dance programs. This was a performance that the kids would normally enjoy—fast-paced, lively, with current music, and starring young people. Almost all the dancers were Black, their bodies on spectacular display, and the rhythms, movements, and sounds were all borrowed from African American and African forms. I sat next to Keisha, the only African American girl in the class, who was elated to be in a veritable Black academic space. Throughout the visit, she was sitting at the edge of her seat, exclaiming her approval, wondering if she was going to see her cousin currently attending the school, and smiling about how she was going to be following her older sister's footsteps. I had never seen her so excited about anything school-related. Although Ms. Lee had done a wonderful job of turning Keisha's orientation around through love, attention, and a good dose of favoritism, she still had a reluctant attitude toward schooling (see chapter 3). But the sight of so many successful Black students, not in the conventional sense of book smart and obedient, was empowering to Keisha. She planned the programs and classes for which she was going to sign up, and her excitement persisted for the rest of the day. Keisha was optimistic about her future.

At one point in the performance, as I was laughing at Keisha's pained desire to be chosen as a volunteer to go on stage, I noticed some kids frozen or sinking in their seats in their hopes of remaining unnoticed. These kids had been uncharacteristically sullen throughout, not reacting in their characteristic "oohs" at the more impressive feats, nor laughing at the funny segments. These were some of the same kids who, however admiring they were of Black youth cultural forms, were extremely uncomfortable being in a Black space. For some of them, it was their first time doing so. Later when I asked Sabrina what she thought of the visit, she reverted to her earlier expression of fear and shock and responded wide-eyed, "That school is bad!" When I asked why, she just shook her head and walked away. Needless to say, she came in the next day in a chipper mood, announcing to anyone and everyone that her mom was going to get her into Whitman Junior High. Indeed, her mom was successful, and like her kin Eliza's mom, they made sure to protect their daughters from their fears. As another parent explained to me, sending "innocent girls" to Maya Angelou was unthinkable, indexing a whiteness that was related more to sexuality, class orientation, and aspiration than to skin color.

Much more surprising for me was Steven's reaction to JHS MA. His sharp barbs that served as running commentary to every event were absent. He had been noticeably silent, pensive, and nervous during the visit. When the cloud dissipated a bit later in the afternoon, I approached Steven and asked him if he was excited about junior high. He replied, "I don't like that school too much." "Why?" I asked. "I just don't like it there that much." After a pause he continued, "They say they beat up kids like me, 'cause I look white and stuff, cause of my hair and my eyes." "Who?" I demanded suspiciously. Steven just shrugged, unable and unwilling to articulate his inner conflict. He could see that junior high meant facing difficult choices and changes. At this point, Steven had a rather charmed life. He was both of the projects but not confined to them. He spent weekends with his father who spoiled him with expensive clothing, jewelry, and technology. Steven was at the top of his social hierarchy and personified the cool of hip-hop culture for kids in PS AV.[9] Steven identified as Puerto Rican, sometimes as "African." This was the first time I heard him even implicitly identify himself as white, even though his blondish hair and green eyes contradicted his performed racial identity. Like Keisha, when he contemplated junior high, he was seeing his future. What he foresaw, probably correctly, is that his ambiguous racial identity and his expensive gear, things that made him and would continue to make him attractive to girls of every race, would also make him the object of negative attention. His loyalties and authenticity would be tested, and he would have to prove himself. He may also have had premonitions on the unsustainability of his friendship with Darryl, who would likely start hanging around his older brothers and their friends, characters who were always in trouble. Steven aspired to go to college and become "an entrepreneur," and I imagine that some of the "man-to-man" talks his dad regularly gave him suddenly became all that much closer.

I wanted Steven to articulate the way these dynamics were entangled with race, so I jokingly bounced it back to him, "What, they beat up white kids there?" Steven answered, "The basketball team is all Black and there's just four white kids." "What about Latinos?" I asked. "It's not just Black and white, is it?" As a few other kids had gathered around to listen, he nudged his chin toward Joseph (who is Mexican) and said "Yeah, but they all Mexicans." Joseph reassured him,

"You think you're gonna get beat up 'cause you look white? Just get a tan, man."
Joseph's cool nonchalance here was related to his spatial savvy. He exercised considerable spatial autonomy because both his parents worked long hours in their café and Joseph was often under the charge of his older siblings who were very lax about regulating his actions or movements. In the beginning of the year, Joseph was often absent, staying home to play video games or roam around the neighborhood. Once the kids even spotted him riding his bike around the school during lunch! Another time Mark spotted Joseph riding his bike by the projects, and announced the fact the next day in the classroom. At first, Keisha thought Mark was lying. When Joseph confirmed, she nodded at him with amused approval. By the end of the year, kids began recognizing that Joseph was one cool kid.

Joseph was quiet, small, and observant; his clothes were not flashy but serviceable. This enabled him to navigate Augursville and other parts of the city relatively unnoticed. Along with Fawwaz, he was my go-to contact for information about Augursville. Joseph's expanded spatial practices and savvy were linked to his embodiment of cosmopolitanism. In his short quips and musings, Joseph regularly expressed its improvisational flexibility and counterhegemonic politics. For example, when Joseph referred to one of his white friends as "vanilla," Jacinta challenged him and asked if he would call a Black kid "chocolate." He simply replied "no." Jacinta retorted that it was because "they would hit you." Joseph rolled his eyes and waved her off. He was unable or unwilling to explain how "vanilla" humorously made whiteness visible and nonnormative while "chocolate" may not have the effect of leveling the racial hierarchy. Nevertheless, he knew this cosmopolitanism intuitively. Joseph often expressed disapproval of anything that bolstered hierarchies with his characteristic "Yo that's fucked up." This was what he told Yanely and Lillian when they were making fun of one of their peers for living in a rented room (despite Joseph's parents' relative economic comfort). One of my favorites was when he dismissed the giggles of two of his male friends. "They're laughing about maxi pads," he informed me when I went to check out what the fuss was. When the boys cracked up even more at uttering the offending term aloud in front of a woman, Joseph rolled his eyes and said, "What's the big deal? I get them for my sisters." Although Joseph does not often appear in these pages because he did not explicitly articulate cosmopolitanism as well as some of his peers, he represents another way that it was expressed. Although inconspicuous, his reserved but knowing social savvy critically perceived the contradictions and hegemonic hierarchies of space, race, class, even gender. His critical stance was forged through his intimate relationship with his surroundings, much like Fawwaz, who opened this chapter.

SPATIAL CONTRADICTIONS AND
LIMITATIONS OF KIDS' COSMOPOLITANISM

It is no accident that kids with greatest spatial autonomy were boys. As this chapter illustrated, navigating space was imbued with struggles of race, gender, class, and age. The kids' embodied and intersecting positionalities meant that they were subjected to and interpreted spatial contradictions in varied ways. A near universal contradiction for kids in the United States is their limited spatial entitlement. Augursvillian kids were fortunate that there were plenty of parks and public spaces in which they could congregate, at least in daylight hours, although somewhat restricted for girls. The kids all walked through Augursville's vibrant and bustling public and commercial spaces, however circumscribed their individual radius or adult supervision. As such, Augursville kids perceived the superdiversity of their neighborhood through multisensory channels and understood difference as an ordinary feature of social life. By moving through, living in, talking about, and interpreting space, they developed social savvy and inflected Augursville with their practices and racial meaning making. These spatial struggles were a critical part of their cosmopolitanism, as both cause and consequence. That is, Augursville did not exist as an inert setting in which the kids' cosmopolitanism was contained, but experiencing its spatial contradictions helped *develop* the kids' critical stances.

As this chapter demonstrated, the central contradiction of Augursville's celebrated diversity is its marginal positioning of Blackness. Some kids pierced and partly resolved it through their spatial struggles and meaning making and educated their peers on alternative spatial and racial meanings. Although these contradictions were mirrored in the space of the school, Ms. Lee allowed these exuberant displays in the classroom. The space of the classroom was also the primary setting for the forging of friendships. The next chapter explores the unique constraints and possibilities posed by the unique bond of friendship and the learning and transforming of race that occurred therein.

2 ◆ LOVING FRIENDS AND THINGS

The cafeteria was where "it all goes down!" The frenzied outburst of interactions produced a roar that, if the windows were open, could be heard half a city block away. On a rainy day in early October, I walked into the cafeteria after stepping out to get my own food and the kids greeted me as usual, waving, yelling, and coaxing me to sit next to them. Jacinta, Eliza, and Sabrina begged for me to watch their "Glad Bag experiment." They proudly showed me how they piled up their uneaten food on napkins and shook it to see which napkin would hold up the best. The task was more about anticipating the inevitable rip of the school-issued napkins, at which point the girls would crack up with laughter. Keisha watched the girls, chuckling at their enjoyment and shaking her head at their silliness. She was also keeping an eye on Steven teaching James how to do various hand symbols. Steven would first display a sign, and James earnestly observed and imitated as Steven perfected his handiwork. Mark was complaining about the food, "Look how ghetto this is!" He opened up the foil-wrapped sandwich and pointed out that cheese was on only one side. He turned to me, "Don't they know that kids go like this and throw it?" He crushed it into a ball and threw it against the table. "These lunch ladies are not too smart, they need to go back to school!" Ms. Kiki the lunch lady eyed Mark to let him know not to take it further. She then noticed Assad was not eating any lunch. It was the month of Ramadan. She fixed her gaze on him and yelled across the bodies, "Why aren't you eating?!" Mark and Joseph explained at once, "He's fasting!" "What?" Ms. Kiki yelled over the noise. "Fasting!" Steven repeated. Ms. Kiki shrugged, "Oh, okay." Assad said to no one in particular, "My mom said I could eat if I want to." "Do you know what fasting is?" I asked Steven. "Yeah, in his religion on some days they can't eat." I nodded impressed, "How did you know that?" "I learned it, in school. That's what you do in school *Maria*—you *learn* things," he intoned sarcastically. Point well taken.

I turned my attention to Leslie and Selena playing patty-cake. Because they were sitting across the table from one another, they kept messing up and were laughing in mock frustration. Abdul exclaimed, "I want to play too!" Abdul and Selena started playing while she sang, and he quickly caught on to the hand motions. They started going faster and faster until Lillian complained, "Hey, you're doing it better with him than with me!" Inspired by this, Nedim and Lucas busted out in an arm-wrestling match, soon followed by Omar and Joseph. Within three minutes, the arm-wrestling game became a kicking contest under the table, at which point Omar and Abdul joined in. Soon enough, Assad got involved too. It was now three boys across the table from another three, intently kicking, hooting, screaming "Owwwch," and laughing in response to giving and receiving particularly painful kicks. They were having a ball of it, until Ms. Kiki felt the table shaking and yelled at them to stop. The game shifted once again; the challenge was now to remain absolutely still and expressionless while sneaking in good, hard kicks. The new iteration pleased them just the same.

I moved toward the other end of the table just as Sebastian tapped Allison and said, "I know who you like—Gregory!" Gregory who had been playing with a tiny skateboard on the table snapped into attention, "Right! *You* like her!" Sebastian screamed over to Abdul, "I know who likes you! Eliza!" Lucas interjected amid his kicking to defend his friend, "I know who likes you!" Sebastian cut him off: "I know who likes you—Hakeem!" He cackled and turned his attention elsewhere. Lillian informed me that Hakeem and Sebastian "were just insulting each other. They were calling each other 'faggot.'" She was hoping I would get the boys in trouble.

We watched Ashley and Yanely try to grab Oscar's ice cream, Oscar relishing the attention from the girls. Yanely had a whole act—first she pretended she was mad and looked away with her arms crossed and then went right back and tried to pull it again. Sebastian yelled at Allison, "I am not *gay!* Man, you crazy!" and stood up to do the crazy symbol with his hand twirling by his head. Allison was trying to get anyone to play Truth or Dare. She got Hakeem to choose truth, but then he declined to answer the question she whispered. She asked Gregory, who chose dare. She dared him to eat the leftover slop of food on her tray. He pretended he was going to but then refused. Hakeem turned the tables and asked Allison to choose and she selected dare. He said, "I dare you to lick the table." She did. Hakeem and Gregory screamed "Iww!" Hakeem said, "That's Clorox on the table!" She licked her shirt and giggled at her intrepid act. The lunch ladies halted all action, shouting directions for the ritual of hustling kids to throw out their food and go into the auditorium for the rest of the lunch period. The kids would not be going out to the playground on account of the rain. On such days, the women had the unfortunate task of escorting hundreds of kids through a hallway that passed the principal's office and the main entrance. They readied

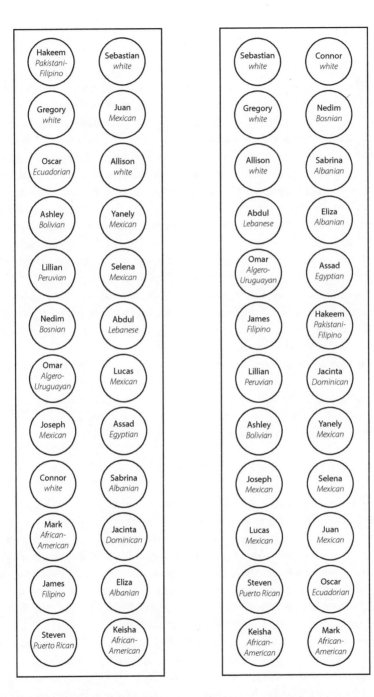

FIGURE 2.1. Cafeteria seating among Ms. Lee's class in the mid-fall of the school year.

FIGURE 2.2. Representation of a fictive seating arrangement predicted by racial homophily.

the kids for the march, their threats of revoking playground privileges eventually producing quiet.

Despite the chaotic frenzy of kids yelling, laughing, conspiring, observing, playing, complaining, sharing and begging for food, and telling fortunes, there was an order to the cafeteria interactions. The cafeteria was the place where kids were finally allowed to enact the basic desire they struggled for all morning—the freedom to choose with whom they wanted to associate. Indeed, lunchroom seating was the most visible marker of friendship. The way the kids sat on the long cafeteria bench became a pattern early in the school year that, while exhibiting some flux, persisted until the end ten months later. In addition to its relevance to the kids, seating patterns in the cafeteria are of interest to scholars, as they function as loaded symbols of racial segregation, veritable thermometers of race relations in schools. Beverly Tatum's (2003) book may partly owe its best-selling status to its provocative title that asks what previously went unquestioned—*"Why Are All the Black Kids Sitting Together in the Cafeteria?"* Anyone concerned with this question would be pleased that the kids violated this pattern.[1] That is, the Black kids were *not* sitting together, nor were the white, Middle Eastern, Asian, and Latino kids either. Figure 2.1 represents the seating arrangement on the day described.

Why have scholars spent so much time wringing their hands over racialized clusters within children's friendship? What is the potential of the unique bond of friendship in racial formation and transformation? And why *weren't* all the Black/white/Latino kids sitting together in that all-too-familiar pattern (as represented by figure 2.2)?

BIRDS OF A FEATHER?

One who will make your soul blossom (Marcel Proust), gives value to life itself (C. S. Lewis), makes the heart run over (Ray Bradbury), represents a world in us (Anaïs Nin). Every great author has meditated on the power of friendship, a mysterious bond that eludes explanation. Scholars have also made much of friendship, when it intermittently becomes the focus of their attention. Aristotle was the first to focus on the far-ranging significance of friendship for civil society and politics. It served as the founding metaphor of his political thought, where friendship was seen as a "rehearsal for citizenship" (Gandhi 2003, 17). In his tripartite definition of friendships based on utility, pleasure, or virtue, Aristotle placed the latter on his hierarchy because it bonds communities together. Anthropologists have also recognized the socially integrating function of friendships. However, friendship has received scant attention in anthropology because of the discipline's traditional focus on kinship. When compared to the neat structures of kinship, friendship appears to be its antithesis. It is an achieved rather than an ascribed relation, is technically free from its ritualized obligations, and exhibits more fluidity and informality. This is precisely what makes friendship so interesting to its practitioners and to the few scholars who have focused on it—"it stands in contrast to other ways of relating" (Killick and Desai 2013, 2). This uniqueness gives friendship its potential power: it creates bonds and intimacies where they would not exist, widens the circles of belonging, and creates something distinct in its enacting, however much that enacting varies across the scales of social life.

Children's friendships have rarely been considered in these deeper moral and political terms. Aristotle dismissed children's friendships as unable to cultivate the loftier democratic goal of virtue, for the young "quickly become friends and quickly stop"; they "love and stop loving quickly" (1999, 122). The future-oriented perspective denies the meaningfulness of children's social forms because of their unique temporality. This dismissive tone concerning children's achieved relationalities is not the only problem with the Aristotelian legacy. Leela Gandhi critiques the homophilic assumptions within Aristotelian conceptions of friendship where "a friend is another self . . . a friend is what is most similar." Citing Jacques Derrida, she points out the "schematic of affiliation: stock, genus, species, sex, blood, birth, nature, nation" that largely goes unnoticed within this genealogy of friendship (Derrida 1997, vii, cited in Gandhi 2003, 17). Assumptions of homophily have guided thinking on friendship in the intervening millennia so much so that they have become utter common sense. Who doesn't know that "birds of a feather flock together"?

It is unfortunate that the dominant strand of research on children's friendships for the past half century not only assumes that similarity guides friendships, but operationalizes similarity to mean the same race and prioritizes racialized homophily as the most important principle governing friendship. Citing this "large body of literature on homophily," James Moody writes that "friendship segregation in heterogeneous settings" is unsurprising because "individual level preference for similar friends suggests that, all else equal, when people have the *opportunity to choose* relations within their own race they will" (2001, 680; emphasis added). I have made clear how the assumption that people naturally prefer to associate within their "own" race (and by this logic, that different races are naturally repulsive) is a dangerous correlate that derives from reifying race as essentialized type or kind (see the introduction). Such work pays the requisite lip service to contextual features such as demography and various institutional factors, and constructs complex mathematical formulas that predict how likely children are to associate by race. By neglecting children's perspectives on their friendships and the local ideologies and means by which friendships are made, such scholarship euphemizes children, denying them any agency, and ultimately reduces friendships to molecules colliding in space, attracted or repulsed by race. To fully problematize racial homophily we need to interrogate homophily itself and ask, on what basis do practitioners construct similarity, and to what extent do friends have to be similar, if at all? For the conception of the individual informing the principle of homophily is one with a unitary identity, a stable and coherent self. If instead we turn to contemporary theorizations where the self is conceived to be complex, continually in flux, and embedded in multiple experiences and belongings, then what it means to be similar becomes an open-ended question to be explored empirically. We can expect the answers to vary tremendously by field site, between individuals within any such site, and by individuals at different times and settings.

FRIENDSHIP AND BECOMINGS

In her "materialist theory of becoming," feminist philosopher Rosi Braidiotti argues that the question "at the top of the agenda of the new millennium" is not "to know who we are but rather what at last we want to become, how to represent mutations, changes and transformations rather than Being in its classical mode" (2002, 1). It would seem children, the "changelings" par excellence (Lancy 2014), are the perfect candidates with which to explore such questions. Regrettably, the child's perceived "becoming" has been imbued with a naturalized teleology of development or socialization (James and Prout 2015 [1998]). Change is represented within a unilinear paradigm of "growing up" rather than with the unexpected trajectories and multiplicities of "anti-linear becomings" (Renold and Ringrose 2011), what Kathryn Stockton (2009) has productively referred to as "growing sideways." Perceiving this problem, many child scholars have swung the pendulum away from what is *done to* children to emphasize what children do by themselves in their "own culture." As recent critiques have contended, this exaggerates children's agency and renders their varying forms of power and ability to act meaningless (Bluebond-Langner and Korbin 2007; King 2007; Kromidas 2014; Lancy 2012; Rosen 2007). Because friendship is defined by choice and because children's friendships are often enacted differently from those of adults, it is easy to fall into this trap and consider these relations to be free or unencumbered from all constraints. Instead, the task is to consider children's friendships from the standpoint of *relative* freedom, their desires and agency constrained by their embedded social locations and the constraints imposed by local and wider settings. Taking kids as relational beings that are *somewhat* of their own making opens up the exploration to how kids saw and desired to see themselves, how they wanted others to see them and, equally important, how they navigated the obstacles that stood in their way. The struggles to enact the joys of friendship provide an opportunity to see the kids as relational beings of their own making under conditions not of their own choosing.

Whenever kids represented themselves, they did so in terms of their relationalities; their friends, families, and things. Things—eye shadow, Xboxes, wrestling mags, team jerseys, songs, pop stars, and stickers were crucial aspects of friendship relations. As Gillian Evans writes in her ethnography of similarly aged kids in a working-class school in London: "Objects are obviously crucial to the way that social relations among children (and, indeed, adults) are both formed and transformed. . . . Objects . . . become the bridges over and through which children encounter and make sense of each other in particular ways. This means that if we are to understand children's social relations we have to find out, in any situation, which specific objects and practices mediate peer group formation" (2013, 187–188). Objects have taken on new status and analytic focus in the human sciences, from inert objects to dynamic interactants that can surprise us in the way they will be "done." Ash Amin explains how current work considers how attachments to objects, previously dismissed as corrupting social ties and alienating humans from one another, are "part and parcel of human identity [and] part of the human condition, proof of the constitutive hybridity of humans and subjectivity" (2012, 27–28). Objects "shape the nature of our ties with humans," Amin argues, and have potential to create new alliances and allegiances, spaces of identification, belonging, and ethics of care (29–30). From the fierce to humorous rivalries over the Mets and Yankees that divided boy groups to the way a humble pencil triggered the tender memories surrounding the origins of Lucas and Abdul's friendship, objects were laden with affects. Relationships with objects were crucial in the making of friendships, as well as in the formation of gendered and racial subjectivities. The practices challenge linear mappings onto race and gender and could and did lead to new belongings, as other child scholars have established (Ali 2002). These insights are firmly ensconced in studies with teenagers, but rarely has objects' transformative potential been explored within younger kids' relationships.

The task of this chapter is to delve into how relations contributed to racial transformation and the emergence of the kids' cosmopolitan ethos. How were bonds formed with others and things a key aspect of their cosmopolitan selves? How and when did race materialize, and what obstacles did it pose within these relations of affection and admiration? How did kids navigate race when it did emerge? And what are the limits of friendship relations in fomenting antiracist forms of being? These questions are subsumed under a broader exploration of kids as relational beings. In the next section I explore the principles guiding kids' friendships, paying attention to their temporal dimensions in the multiple trajectories of "growing up" and "growing sideways."

FROM ROOTEDNESS TO BRANCHING OUT WITH STYLE

Unlike romantic relations, where race was a chief organizing principle and concern, friendships did not have to "make sense" in terms of race. Friendships had their own logic, revolving around the kids' cultivated styles that were in turn related to their object relations. The kids recognized this logic, and would remark on a friendship's oddity if it violated this principle. Style was superimposed over and alongside three default mechanisms from which friendships were built: those based on shared residence, kin relations, as well as race. I use the term "default" to indicate that friendships are established on such basis when bonds based on kids' achieved relationalities could not be or had not yet been established for whatever reason. That is, in contrast to the dominant theme in social-psychological scholarship (see Moody's assertion cited earlier) that children choose to associate with those of similar race above all else, my work argues the opposite: kids had friends within their own racial group when their opportunities for association were circumscribed. When kids had less freedom to foment bonds of their choosing, the default mechanisms were operative. The default mechanisms were themselves interrelated—parents formed friendly or child-care relations with one another based on race, ethnicity, religious status, or residence, and these bonds would embed kids together in various ways. These bonds were important insomuch as they grounded kids in a social network and served as roots. But they depended on whether kids decided to further develop these bonds or to branch out from these roots based on their own cultivated styles and stances. Default mechanisms were thus fragile. Some scholars might consider these bonds stronger because they might persist for longer durations of time as compared to bonds based on style. However, I consider the strength of bonds of friendship in the here and now of their enactment and "measure" them in more qualitative terms, the joy, enthusiasm, admiration, and affection that were the marks of friendship. There were some friendships that had no logic at all—not based on style or any default mechanisms. While the bases of these friendships remain somewhat of a mystery, they were characterized by those decisive factors. In the following, I explore how friendships developed during the year in terms of rootedness and branching out.

I begin with Lucas and Abdul because they were the quintessential best friends. They referred to one another exclusively as such, enacted this relationship daily by sitting next to one another every day at lunch, choosing one another as partners whenever possible, engaging in small talk, and hanging around together whenever they could. They most explicitly exhibited the tenderness and care associated with friendship. Their friendship was limited to the spaces of the school because Abdul's mother did not allow him to hang around after school or visit anyone's home. Lucas was part of the unofficial wrestling club that convened in the park after school (see chapter 1). Their bond represents one of the more peculiar ones, not because it crossed lines of difference—Abdul was a second-generation Lebanese and Lucas a second-generation Mexican. It was more so because they did not have any activities or fandoms in common. They simply enjoyed one another's company. They loved being interviewed together, and unlike other interviews with boys where the themes revolved around objects, within the interview space Lucas and Abdul expressed their intimacy toward one another and reflected on their friendship, the meaning of friendship, and social relations within the school. The boys were protective of one another, Lucas preempting challenges to his friend (as in the opening vignette in the cafeteria when he thought Sebastian was teasing Abdul), and Abdul comforting his friend whenever Lucas seemed to need it.

The only group that operated with the principle of racial homophily was that of Yanely, Ashley, Lillian, and Selena, respectively Mexican, Bolivian, Peruvian, and Mexican. In an interview with Lillian and Selena in the early fall, the girls referred to themselves as a group. I asked, "So why do you think you guys come together?" Lillian quickly offered, "Because we all talk Spanish." Selena agreed "yeah." When I asked if Spanish was important to them, Selena replied, "No, not really, but, its something unique from the rest of the kids." Evidently, the bond was not strong enough. By late winter the group had splintered into a formation that made more sense. Indeed, when I got to know the girls, I thought the group strange until I understood how default mechanisms operated. Yanely had arrived at PS AV at the beginning of the school year not knowing anyone. Although she was initially quiet and reserved, I could tell that she was containing her more aggressive, outgoing, and sexual persona. Her character was in stark contrast to Lillian's and Selena's, the former focused on academics and the latter just about as sweet and naïve as possible at any age. Ashley was also a newcomer; it was her first year in a monolingual classroom. Previously she was in the ELL (English language learner) class, where the kids' networks rarely extended beyond their classroom. Although she was also quiet and outwardly obedient in the classroom, I soon found out that Ashley was an active social player, flying under my radar because she was still integrated in her social network in the ELL class and hung around with them on the playground.

When Yanely and Ashley began the fifth grade in Ms. Lee's class, neither had friends and arrived in a situation where four of the remaining seven girls— Keisha, Jacinta, Sabrina, and Eliza—were already established as a friend group at the beginning of the school year. Allison was on the margins, and did much to make herself unlikable. Finally, Lillian and Selena remained, themselves split up from their larger group of friends in other classes. Yanely and Ashley were drawn into Lillian and Selena's group by the default mechanism of racial homophily. It easily disintegrated when they had opportunities to develop and express their own subjectivities and achieve their own relationalities beyond their rootedness in a shared Latinidad. This occurred when Yanely and Ashley developed their bond. Their budding styles took off: they began waxing their eyebrows, highlighting their hair, and wearing makeup and nail polish, their shirts and jeans got tighter, when the weather warmed their necklines got lower, their colorful lacy bras became visible, and their activities began to significantly diverge from those of Lillian and Selena. The budding of this transformation could be detected from their cafeteria interactions in the introduction. Ashley and Yanely became centered on their own style developments, their talk focusing on this and evaluating other girls' styles. They also began to focus on boys and spent time teasing, chasing, and talking about them (see spatial drama in chapter 1) and started getting involved in machinations typically considered "girl." One of these involved fomenting a serious conflict with girls in the ELL class. Yanely and Ashley negotiated and built alliances to eventually involve most of Ms. Lee's class in what came to be known as a "war" between the two classes. Their pleasure in the conflict and fear wrought by such dramas was intense. They would return to the classroom after lunch flush and trembling with excitement. Although they successfully denied their role instigating the conflict to the principal, Ms. Lee pieced together the truth and gave them a stern rebuke. As the end of the year approached, Ashley unexpectedly decided she didn't want to be friends with Yanely anymore, a message she sent via Connor. They patched things up on the last few days of school, but it was clear that the relationship had cooled, and this was the end. Ashley rejoined her friends in the ELL class as the boundaries of that class became fuzzier, and Yanely weighed her options under a cool exterior.[2]

The most enduring friendship group consisted of Keisha, Jacinta, Eliza, Sabrina, Steven, Mark, James, and Connor. Respectively, there were four girls, four boys, African American, Dominican, Albanian, Albanian, Puerto Rican, African American, Filipino, and Croatian (see figure 2.3). The group crossed boundaries of race and gender, the latter a near universal division among elementary children's friendships. The eightsome sat together at the end of the cafeteria bench with little variation every day from the start until the end of the school year. This group was connected through cultivated bonds, bonds based on default mechanisms, network-based bonds (friend of a friend), as well as default bonds developed into cultivated ones. The default bonds within the group consist of Sabrina and Eliza, whose parents shared a larger network of distant kin through marriage and ethnicity (both girls were Albanian); and Keisha, Mark, Jacinta, and Steven all lived in the same building, Jacinta's parents sometimes relying on Steven's mom for child care.

Keisha and Steven's bond represents a type with origins in shared residency but developed through their agentic practices. Their bond formed the center of the network because it was the most durable and connected the boys and

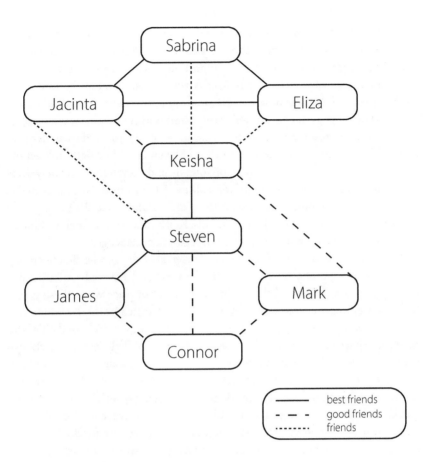

FIGURE 2.3. Eightsome network in the late winter.

girls. Indeed, their seating arrangement in the cafeteria was permanent. They sat across from one another at the end of the table, their occupation making it the de facto "head" of the table. If anyone dared to occupy these seats even briefly, Keisha and Steven just stood there glaring to eject the offending kid. Their bond with Mark was similar, built from their shared residency, and deepened by interactional history and a shared sense of humor and pop cultural knowledge. Because Mark did not enthusiastically cultivate or perform hip-hop style, their bonds with him were not as strong in terms of mutual pleasure and admiration. Keisha and Steven counted him and Darryl, another kid from the projects, as their "best friends." Less strong was Keisha and Jacinta's bond. Although they enjoyed one another's company, their bond would likely not exist if they did not share the experience of navigating the sociospatial dynamics of being from the projects.

Steven and Keisha's relationship was one of affection, admiration, and respect for one another's authenticity, embodied knowledge, and skills surrounding hip-hop. They were linguistic innovators, importing speech forms from their hood into the parlance of the classroom. Keisha and Steven stood at the top of the hierarchy of cool that was based on urban savoir faire. They were proud of their roots and belongings but performed their positions in contrasting ways. Keisha's stance was more reserved; she didn't seem to need or wish to display her proficiency or convince others of it as much as Steven did. They both policed the boundaries of authenticity, Keisha more quietly and Steven more actively. Kids who performed belongings to hip-hop culture deferred to Keisha's knowledge and judgment, including Steven. With three older siblings, Keisha was exposed to more sophisticated tastes than most kids. Keisha and Steven openly admired one another, and each was the other's only legitimate challenger.

Keisha was one of the few girls who transgressed the gender divide among strong friendships. She interacted with the boys and enjoyed rambunctious chasing games with them, although awkwardly out of place when these games turned into flirting encounters with other girls, at which point she would disengage. Keisha performed girl in a unique manner, and she dismissed girls who performed it in more typically "girly" or "white girl" ways, a term that Yanely also used to refer to girls whose stances were more stereotypically girl, and for both a term that was disengaged from skin color. So contrary was Keisha's expression of femininity that she even employed the male-specific speech form "no homo," quickly remarked following anything that could be construed as a phallic reference. Because it required attention to finding an opportunity for double entendre, "no homo" marked a speaker as clever, and was a way to shore up masculine identity in relation to the "specter of the fag" (Pascoe 2011). As strange as it was for a girl to employ the term, no one dared challenge Keisha that she was missing the requisite anatomy to make this humor work. Keisha's appropriation of this talk could be easily interpreted through the tired trope of "penis envy." This would erase all the nuance and creativity of Keisha's practices. Feminist scholars have argued that such practices, rather than mimicry of masculinity, are more productively viewed as indicative of "radical disruptions and displacements" of masculine-based power (Renold and Ringrose 2012). "No homo" was a nonchalant display of the way Keisha could appropriate masculine-based power at her will. She was considered not a "tomboy" but a "tough girl," feared, admired, and respected by all.

Among the girls, Jacinta and Eliza's relationship was the freest and the one characterized by the most affection and mutual admiration. Although Eliza, Jacinta, and Sabrina considered themselves best friends in the beginning of the year and had been so throughout fourth grade, Sabrina and Eliza's bond weakened as Eliza and Jacinta cultivated their own friendship. Eliza and Sabrina's family entanglements began to weigh heavily on Eliza, who expressed how she wanted to break free from her bond with Sabrina, so much so that she recounted various fantasies involving locking Sabrina away or exporting her to a faraway land. Eliza also began to renounce their default ties. Where once she and Sabrina were cousins, Eliza began telling people, "We're not *really* cousins." Where once they exuberantly performed their Albanianness together, Eliza began differentiating herself from "like all those Albanians that only hang out with other Albanians." Eliza began to perform belongings in excess of her Albanianness. Jacinta for her part also performed her Dominicanness and participated in displays of her rootedness in the projects, but did not think of herself nor desire to be considered solely in these terms.

This combination of being both rooted and branching out toward belongings of their own drew Jacinta and Eliza together. Their self-making revolved around cultivating gendered styles through clothing and overall stance. Theirs was a conscious cultivation but yet less intelligible than Ashley and Yanely's, which could more readily be read as a youthful urban Latina style. Both girls prided themselves on their own distinct casual yet cool style that, although not identical, was differentiated from "too sporty," "too sloppy," or "too girly" styles of other girls in the fifth grade. Style often came up in their talk. When Ms. Lee solicited chapter topics for a writing assignment titled "All About Me" books, Jacinta had offered "style." Although Ms. Lee didn't accept her suggestion, when I asked the girls later what they were going to write, Jacinta insisted she was going to write about style anyway (she later changed her mind and added her own chapters about "my hard rough past" and "my hope to be future").

JACINTA: Okay, I'm going to write about style, as in *my own* style, 'cause I don't know, I don't like having the same things, I don't know, when I see someone with my same thing, I have to take it off.

MK: Yeah, I get that.

JACINTA: Like, I have my own way of talking.

MK: What do you mean you have your own way of talking?

JACINTA: I don't know, like she has her own way of talking, she goes "spanks" or whatever.

ELIZA: Spanks ((laughs)).

MK: What's spanks?

ELIZA: Like if she pass me a fork or something, I go "spanks" ((laughs)).

JACINTA: ((laughing)) Spank you! Like me, I don't talk normally, like how I talk with my cousins and stuff like that, cause we make funny jokes and stuff like that, but like, I don't like being the same as everyone else, like wearing the same shoes. Pumas! I don't want to buy those, they're cute and all/

ELIZA: I like those.

JACINTA: Yeah, they're cute and all, but everybody's wearing them.

MK: Okay.

JACINTA: I'd rather just like, like those boots ((points to MK's boots)), no one's wearing them.

ELIZA: I hate when people get my jackets!

JACINTA: Like, my favorite color is light green and I thought that nobody else liked those colors besides Eliza, but it's okay/

ELIZA: I like dark green.

JACINTA: 'Cause she's my friend. I like dark green and light green. Yeah, I'm just like, we're doing the same thing 'cause we're alike.

These cultivated preferences were the object of reflection, admiration, and shared affection from which the girls built up their relationship, created their subjectivities, and distinguished themselves from others. They represented the girls' desires and the means for them to become other than what they were understood to be based on family, race, ethnicity, and residence. Their friendship allowed them a space to experiment with becoming different and becoming other.

Steven and James's relation was also built on their careful crafting of aesthetic sensibilities and study of hip-hop culture. This was enacted differently than Steven's bond with Keisha because it was a site for them to cultivate heteronormative masculinity. In their "All About Me" books, both boys chose to write about their styles. This is how Steven described his "bangin style" as he titled the chapter: "My style is very unique. I don't wear bootleg clothes or sneakers. I don't wear Payless sneakers. I like baggy clothes. I like to wear Nikes, Jordans, and Timberlands. I like to wear jewelry not too flashy but to catch someone's attention." For his part, James included a description of his style in the introduction to his book that he titled "This is me."

> My style is baggy pants and oversize shirts. There are many reasons why I love it. One, it feels like I am wearing a blanket over my body and two, I can move better. Somehow I got hooked to this style. I used to wear normal-fitting clothes. But now things have changed. But the style I'm wearing makes me feel like a little baby with big clothes.
>
> Sometimes it gets annoying when my baggy pants fall down. I always buy loose fit pants and I thought that will kinda stay up. But I was wrong. Sometimes I buy my clothes at [local store]. By looking at their clothes, it has very cool designs and the shoes are nice. It is kind of pricey though. I choose clothes wisely and carefully that will make me feel and look good.
>
> My hair is my priority though. And as they say, never mess with my hair. I make it a point to have my hair cut every three weeks or less and that makes my mom crazy.

The boys' styles were similar but not identical, differing in the way James incorporated athletic elements and Steven donned dressier items like button-downs and jewelry. The boys' efforts paid off. They were known as the best-dressed kids in the fifth grade, and were the boys whom the girls in the fifth grade desired most. The boys bonded on their "ladies' man" status, and they gave advice on being a "gentleman" to boys foraying into romance, including how to properly groom, how to be assertive and honest about one's desires, and how to buy and give gifts.

The odd one in this eightsome was Connor. None of his primary friend bonds with Mark, Steven, or James can be explained in the way most bonds could—they were not ascribed through default mechanisms nor achieved through shared object affections. By the kids' conventions, Connor would be nerdy: his main object interests revolved around airplanes and airports, he was a "math whiz," always prepared for school and outwardly complied with teacher instructions. This may partly explain why the kids in his network admired him. He expressed himself differently; his observations and humorous contributions were of a different order. For his part, Connor was smitten with his peers' playful and combative humor and his infectious laugh encouraged them. Despite being a nerdy Croatian kid with glasses and protective professional middle-class parents, his friends considered him "down." In a low-key manner, Connor defended, contributed to, and embodied the local cosmopolitanism. Once when Sebastian had taped a piece of paper on his head, Connor tapped me and crossly reported, "He's making fun of people's religion." When I went over to Sebastian, now singing a song about "Hindus," and asked him how he would feel if someone was making fun of his religion, he simply retorted, "No one's a Hindu in this class—so?" Jacinta demanded, "Take it off, Sebastian." He did so to get us off his back.

Connor's relationship with his friends represents, much like Lucas and Abdul's bond, the mysterious nature of the affections of some friendship. But their mutual warmth and tenderness were just the same. These multiracial solidarities created an ethic of care that transformed race, implicitly through the creation of intimate ties across its dreadful boundaries and explicitly in the way they injected alternative meanings to racial categories and flipped conventional hierarchies. Much in the same way that the kids from the projects constructed their residence as a space of vibrancy and savoir faire, the kids in this network and others denigrated whiteness when it implied a hegemonic racial stance, but decidedly not skin color. To illustrate, in the mangling and jostling of bodies in the lineup to enter the auditorium, Sebastian and James got into a tussle when the former pushed the latter. James responded by calling Sebastian a "wannabe," "Slim Shady," and a "McFlurry," to the laughing approval of Connor and Steven. Sebastian replied, "You look like brown pudding!" James accepted it as a compliment, smiled and coolly replied, "So?" and looked him square in the eye. McFlurry, a white soft-serve ice cream treat from McDonald's, and Slim Shady, one of the personas for Detroit white rapper Eminem, disparaged a particular kind of whiteness by indexing commodified mass-market goods, the veritable antithesis of authenticity represented by the boys' localized expressions and stylistics. The boys recognized how Sebastian selectively tried to claim the masculine toughness associated with hip-hop style, minus any identification with counterhegemonic racial politics.

WRESTLING WITH MASCULINITY

Wrestling was not confined to the matches in the park after school, but was a big deal in the classroom as well, the object relation around which the other boys formed a loosely clustered network. Wrestling became live in the way boys congregated around objects associated with it (magazines, pictures, websites, and merchandised objects), the talk about it, the relationships built through it, and the way that wrestling knowledge served as a way to forge bonds where they didn't exist. The friendship network shifted slightly day by day and included Oscar, Sebastian, Hakeem, Joseph, Nedim (respectively, Ecuadorian, Pakistani-Filipino, Mexican, Bosnian), Gregory (white), Juan (Mexican), and Omar (Algerian-Uruguayan). Abdul (Lebanese) and Lucas (Mexican) also participated, although Lucas more so than Abdul. Assad (Egyptian) hung around the margins.

Wrestling was a site for boys to craft and claim masculinity, although a contested one. This was partly due to its uncool status in the beginning of the year, especially vis-à-vis the local prominence of hip-hop style. It was perceived as less masculine, and coded more white because of its wider fandom and the majority of professional wrestlers themselves. As such, the masculinity of wrestling had to be reinforced by emphasizing its heterosexualized character. In an interview in December with Gregory and Omar, I asked them what they were talking about with Assad in the cafeteria. Even though Assad was reveling in being included in the interaction, I worried that the boys were making fun of him somehow. Gregory replied, "Me, Joseph, Hakeem, and Nedim, we give him quizzes on wrestling." He laughed, "He can't answer any of the questions!"

MK: Oh no. Why you try to, he likes wrestling now?
OMAR: Me?!!!
MK: I know *you* like wrestling, Omar.
OMAR: I'm going to the website right now ((heads to the computer)).
GREGORY: Did you ever see anything in wrestling?
MK: No, I'm not really into it.

OMAR: They even got a bikini contest.

MK: A bikini contest huh? You like that?

OMAR: [Yeah!

GREGORY: [Yeeeaaahhh. ((mimes panting))

MK: Oh goodness, okay. Who is like, your favorite?

OMAR: Trish Stratis of wrestling, the women's champion, used to be; Mickie James. She's mad crazy, she likes Trish Stratis, she even kissed her!

He detailed various matches as he got on the Internet. "Come and see Mickie James!" I finally acceded and moved over to the computer. Omar wasn't thrilled with the first image, "Over here, she looks ugly."

GREGORY: Ooooohh!

MK: Gregory seems to likes her.

GREGORY: No, I only like the part right here. ((points to her breasts))

MK: Oh my god Gregory!

BOTH: ((giggling))

GREGORY: Just kidding.

OMAR: Look, this is the girl that I like.

MK: What do you like about her?

OMAR: She beated the hell out of Tory Wilson!

GREGORY: Go for more girls, now go back to more girls!

OMAR: Let me show you more girls.

I walked away, telling the boys I was going to work on my crossword puzzle. Gregory halfheartedly tried to get me to stay, but quickly returned his attention on the screen. I worked on my puzzle as the boys went to different websites. When Greg expressed delight at Omar's finds, Omar told him, "You want to get babes, stick with me, man."

Omar relished in his expertise vis-à-vis Gregory and Gregory's respect for his knowledge, as well as his opportunity to enact masculinity through gazing at women's bodies. Despite the hegemonic expressions of masculinity and the problematic although more complex expressions of femininity within the sport, I understood and respected Omar's (and other boys') sincere enthusiasm for the drama and performativity of wrestling, if not the sport itself. I sympathized with Omar's need to validate his interests and belong to something larger in the classroom, and his need to claim masculinity through recognizably heterosexual desires and practices. Omar was the most avid and first public wrestling fan of the boys, his obsession with it was considered decidedly uncool. By October, the kids at his table were already tired of his wrestling talk. When James and Keisha were discussing how the Tigers got eliminated in the baseball finals, Omar interjected "You know Rey Mysterio" (a wrestler), only to be cut off by James, "We're not talking about wrestling! Every time we talk about any sport or anything, he always talks about wrestling!" Omar just looked at them. A more painful incident occurred a few weeks later. I noticed Omar sitting on the bench crying in the cafeteria. I went over to ask if everything was okay and Mark explained that Steven was "calling him gay because of his magazine." A WWE (World Wrestling Entertainment) fan mag sat on the table in front of him. He was sullen the rest of the lunch period and tucked the offending object into his desk as soon as he returned to the classroom.

Steven also directed his homophobic taunts about wrestling to Sebastian, another avid wrestling fan, although to quite different effect. I was sitting with Sebastian, Mark, and Connor while the kids waited for the technology teacher to give them directions. Sebastian was staring lovingly at a picture of the Mets he had on his binder and pointing out his favorite players. Mark quipped, "I don't like baseball." Connor agreed, "It's boring." Mark said, "I like street football!" Sebastian agreed, "I like when they tackle each other! It's like wrestling." Steven had come over at this point, and began with his wrestling taunts: "All it is is two sweaty mans touching each other's butts in spandex. What is that?" Sebastian did not get ruffled and defended wrestling thus—"It's entertainment! And they have girls in it! And they're half stripped!" Mark and Connor laughed. Steven walked away and came back a few minutes later and Sebastian was still talking about wrestling. Smitten with his humor, Steven asked, "What's so nice about wrestling? The girls?" Sebastian looked at him and asked, "Why are you even here?" Steven delivered his punch line, "Or 'cause the sweaty boys?" He cracked up and I told him to hush up. Ignoring me he tried to disparage Sebastian again, accusing him of liking wrestler Mickie James. Sebastian loudly denied it, "She's lesbian!" This drew eyes around the classroom and Steven cracked up again, "You mad loud, they all hearing you." This interaction apparently won Sebastian some respect because he and Steven began one of their more civil exchanges. It was about baseball, a topic they had previously fought about in the Yankees versus Mets rivalry. They talked about players and what positions they played. Steven said he didn't like being a catcher, and Sebastian agreed, "I hate doing it. I stink yo!" Mark who had no interest in the baseball talk stopped and looked up at Sebastian's use of slang. Perhaps he was waiting for Steven's regular disparaging of Sebastian's attempts "to be down." It didn't happen, so Mark reentered the talk, shifting it back to playing football in the park.

By the midwinter, wrestling fandom had achieved, if not respect, then at least a status of not being ridiculed. No longer an untouchable emblem of gayness lying on the cafeteria table, Sebastian's wrestling fan mag was the object around which several boys conglomerated in the cafeteria. The next day, pictures of beefy-looking topless wrestlers from the mag were decorating the notebooks of Lucas and Oscar, gifts that carried no obligation for reciprocation. Through his spirited defense of wrestling's rampant heterosexism, Sebastian had managed to elevate wrestling's status and allowed a wider network of boys to participate and revel in the joys of the bonds created through fandom.[3] Boys who had trouble fitting in, like Omar and Gregory, even Assad, formed bonds of friendship that while not characterized by longevity, nevertheless contained the practices, affects, and feelings of belonging that are associated with such bonds. The hierarchies created were, like those surrounding hip-hop, based on knowledge and sincerity. But these hierarchies were more fluid because they were detached from cool. Consider the way Hakeem and Assad discussed the wrestling hierarchy in an interview when Assad declared Nedim "the master of wrestling." Hakeem disagreed, "No! Sebastian is!"

ASSAD: Not really the master, the second. Every question I ask him, even if it's a tricky question, he answers it.
MK: Oh yeah, you're the test giver?
ASSAD: Yeah.
HAKEEM: I give him some questions too.
MK: Oh yeah? You guys like to quiz each other to see who knows more?
HAKEEM: ((nods))
MK: So who knows the most?
HAKEEM: ((pats himself))
MK: You?
ASSAD: Sebastian!
HAKEEM: But Sebastian knows a lot. He watches every single day.

Unlike the masculine competition of cool based on hip-hop style with its attendant rewards of status and admirers, there were no stakes and therefore no resentments attached to wrestling competitions, both the live matches in the square and the knowledge-based ones in the classroom. As such, the interactions were predominantly about pleasure. They were games in the philosophical sense, a site where the larger rules of social life are suspended and players enter another universe where relevant distinctions were fluid, transient, and of their own making. It brought boys into exuberant physical and emotional contact (while also allowing some to craft their gendered and sexual selves) and branch out beyond their embedded locations to ultimately form social relations across race laden with affection and pleasure.

WIDENING THE CIRCLE OF BELONGINGS: BRIDGING AND CROSSING

Friendships held transformative potential beyond the bonds of affection they forged between kids of different race. Friendships were a site where kids explicitly transformed race—its essentialized and static core; its basis in blood, birth, and bodies; and its hierarchical ordering. The kids did this through three unique processes: bridging, crossing, and deep crossing. While these practices also occurred in the context of romantic endeavors and in attempts to forge new friendship relations, the way bridging and crossing occurred within friendships reveals much about the unique bond as well as how race itself operated on the ground. These ubiquitous and spontaneous practices within friendships were joyful, symbols of affection and admiration, explicit and exuberant displays of the becoming other that characterizes friendship.

During the time they were best friends for the good part of the year, Sabrina, Jacinta, and Eliza often bridged their differences. I use bridging to refer to practices that made differences functionally equivalent in speech acts that ranged from prosaic to poetic. Sabrina and Eliza had ties with Albania (their parents were ethnic Albanian) and Jacinta with the Dominican Republic (her parents were born there). Besides reaching across differences, the group had an additional hurdle—Jacinta could feel excluded by the other two girls' Albanianness. These challenges arose and were dealt with in interaction. One way the girls navigated this obstacle was that Sabrina and Eliza, while referring to Albania as such in their talk together, would use the term "my country" when either of them were with Jacinta or when all together. Along with that strategy, the girls made their differences equivalent by juxtaposing repetitive phrases with patterned variation, a poetic device known as parallelism. In what follows, the girls built bridges by paralleling the use of "my country," possessive pronouns, and content. Tracing shifts in pronouns and possessives reveals the momentary and shifting construction of membership and categorization (see Ensink 2003; Wodak and Reisigl 2003). Eliza was explaining the "legend" of the mythical two-headed bird in "my country" while Sabrina busted out her key chain to show me "our flag." Jacinta continued, "Our legends are mostly about ghosts," and explained what the colors of the Dominican flag represent and its significance to "how we got our country to be made." Eliza continued, "There's this thing in my country, a gypsy, but we call it a *majipe*."

MK: What's that?

SABRINA: You know those poor people that walk around but/

ELIZA: They're like gypsies. I'll tell her, I'll tell her. Right next to her house is my cousin's house [. . . . .]

JACINTA: In my country, there's this thing, it's called a *brujo*, and they do magic, to make people disappear, to make people/

MK: You guys are scaring me!

SABRINA: One more thing about the gypsy person. Whenever the car stops, like if it's a red light, they always come to the window and they go ((imitates begging))

JACINTA: You know in my country there's al/

After an interruption in the conversation, Eliza continued softly, "You know what's weird . . . there's a lot of Black people in my country."

JACINTA: Me too, they're all dark, 'cause of the sun.

ELIZA: I never knew though, 'cause there's mostly white people and the black people only come for war.

JACINTA: There's a lot of Haitians in Santo Domingo.

MK: What do you mean they come for war?

ELIZA: Because they want our part of the land, because our part of the land is huge, we have like/

SABRINA: Lots of farms

ELIZA: Lots of farms, we have like huge apple trees, and banana trees, cranberry bush.

JACINTA: We have banana trees, and coconut trees! They're so beautiful. There's this place, oh God! Plata it's called like Platano. . . .

The excerpt begins with a display by Eliza using the typical first-person possessive "my country." Sabrina changed the possessive from the singular to the collective ("It's on *our* flag"). Jacinta joined the conversation using the plural possessive herself, "*Our* legends are mostly about ghosts," and continued with this use in her next turn ("how *we* got *our* country . . ."). Jacinta's use of the collective constructed equivalence in the girls' subsequent talk—the frame was now in the terms of "our difference." When Eliza switched back to the singular ("there's this thing in *my* country"), the use of the singular possessives persisted until Eliza introduced the plural again—"Because they want *our* part of the land. . . ." Jacinta again responded by maintaining a poetic equivalence. This extract represents how the ubiquitous phrase in the kids' terminology, "my country," strategically constructed an openness in which other kids could respond equivalently, allowing bridges to be constructed through poetic means. The girls also likened the particulars of their countries, making the practices and beliefs of their "countries" equivalent. In these few moments, the flags, legends, flora, and even the racial demographics (!) of Albania and Dominican Republic were made equivalent; gypsies and *brujos* united through creative speech acts.

If the analysis did not mimic the girls' careful attention to their own talk, the bridging of the "cultural stuff" would stand as the most conspicuous, eclipsing the subtle shifts in pronouns and possessives. In such talk, the girls were not trying to explain, reconcile, or tolerate their differences as mainstream multicultural interventions intend. Rather, they were establishing a way to talk about their rootedness so as to transform the static borders of racial baggage. Through their various interactional methods to create bridges, the kids effectively constructed groups that were inclusive of varied differences, constructing an ever-shifting plurality of a larger "we."[4] Bridges worked neither to subsume difference under a homogenous "American" identity, nor to beg acceptance of one's difference from a hegemonic center. Rather, they allowed kids to claim differences that were not sutured off in barricaded borders. Boundaries were made flexible and porous, situationally expanding and contracting to include kids' various allegiances and affiliations. Through their affiliative ties, the kids refigured static boundaries by making difference one aspect of their varied selves.

It should be no surprise that best friends Lucas and Abdul often bridged and crossed into one another's differences. I borrow the term "crossing" from Ben Rampton's (1995) exemplary work among multiracial teen youth in England where he uses the term to refer to the teens' practices of employing language forms for which they did not have conventional access. I also use it to refer to practices where kids displayed or performed knowledge about another's difference. These practices had interactional similarities to bridging: they were routine features of interaction among friends, were performative, and transformed static boundaries of difference. Furthermore, they were reciprocal processes that depended on acceptance to be successful. Consider an interview with Lucas, Abdul, and Gregory, with as many symbolic gestures of the affections between Lucas and Abdul as attempts by Gregory to construct them. The interaction represents how enacting friendships and attempting to build them operated.

The interview began with Abdul eagerly asking me, "Are we going to talk about friends again?" I replied, "We could talk about anything you guys want to talk about." Gregory screamed "Dragons!" After our lack of enthusiasm, Abdul soon found a way to bring it to his preferred subject: "I have more friends in school than out of school." This begat a flurry of talk about the boys' friends, the arc of such friendships, and how they revolved around class assignments and "getting split up" from one another. This prompted the first of many recountings of the origins of Lucas and Abdul's friendship. Like other friends, they often reminisced about the histories of their friendship. These accounts tickled me in their tenderness, tinged with nostalgia and the pains of remembered slights.

ABDUL: This is how we got friends [in first grade]. I asked you for a pencil, right, and then you said okay.
LUCAS: But I couldn't understand English.
ABDUL: This guy, Joseph/
LUCAS: Yeah, Joseph used to tell me what the teacher was saying and all that.
MK: Oh, that was in kindergarten or first grade?

LUCAS: First grade. . . . Well, my parents didn't um, know English.

MK: Yeah, I was the same way. We used to speak only Greek in my house, so I didn't know English until I went to school.

ABDUL: Yeah, me too, I didn't either.

GREG: Maria?

MK: What did you speak, Arabic?

ABDUL: Yeah.

GREG: Yeah, me too!

MK: That's right, you speak Arabic too. You taught me some.

GREG: Maria, you know in kindergarten, Joseph used to beat me up just 'cause I had a girlfriend that he liked.

Gregory interrupted the flow of conversation just at the point when Lucas, Abdul, and I had built a bridge between our differences. Although he is a white kid without conventional transnational ties, Greg had begun claiming he was Moroccan and Muslim (his mom was dating a Moroccan man). I refer to such claims of unconventional belongings as "deep crossings." These practices were also prevalent among friends. They signaled that a kid had *become* other, a claim that ranged in temporality from the ephemeral to the longer lived, as was Greg's. Gregory used these claims to bridge and cross with his peers and to participate in the camaraderie it generated. We can see how quickly he grabbed the opportunity to bridge with us when the conversation moved from our first languages to speaking other languages; he enthusiastically interjected, "Yeah, me too!" when Abdul mentioned he speaks Arabic. When the conversational shift Greg initiated was going in circles (he coyly withheld information on his "girlfriend" so we could beg for it), I brought the discussion back to friendship. This allowed Lucas and Abdul to cement their bond further and gave Gregory a chance to forge bonds with them by crossing.

MK: So, the friendship that started from a pencil.

ABDUL: [Yeah ((nodding and smiling))].

LUCAS: [Yeah ((smiling widely))].

GREG: What? I don't get that.

MK: Well, 'cause Abdul asked Lucas to borrow a pencil/.

ABDUL: But Joseph told him that.

MK: Joseph translated.

ABDUL: Joseph talks Spanish.

LUCAS: He knows Spanish and English.

MK: What other kids speak Spanish?

LUCAS: Lillian! Selena! Uh, let's see . . . [named others] Oh yeah! Abdul, a little bit.

MK: You speak Spanish? ((to Abdul))

LUCAS: I teach him, I taught him last year some words. Tell her some words.

ABDUL: Hi.

GREG: *As-salamu alaykum!*

LUCAS: In Spanish!

ABDUL: *Si.*

GREG: Everyone knows *si.*

LUCAS: No, not everyone knows!

ABDUL: *Vi*, I think like the *b* in the alphabet is *vi.*

LUCAS: Which kind of *v*? The *v* like that ((makes a v in the air)), or this one ((makes a *b* in the air))?

ABDUL: That one ((points to where Lucas had traced the second)).

LUCAS: ((smiles and nods proudly))

MK: When did you teach him?

LUCAS: Last, um, in third grade. He used to, he used to know the numbers from one to ten.

ABDUL: *Uno, dos, tres, quatro* ((continues to twelve with Lucas's help)). Tell us how you speak Greek.

MK: Okay, what do you guys want to know how to say?

LUCAS: *Ela* is like um, hurry up.

MK: It's like "come on, hurry up." How do you know that?

LUCAS: Ms. Z, she used to teach us.

ABDUL: How about *capiche*?

MK: That's Italian.

GREG: Yeah, that's Italian!

LUCAS: *Capiche, capiche!* ((puts his hand to his mouth and moves it out in "Italian" style)) My dad knows a little, because he works in an Italian restaurant. Yeah, he teach me sometimes. I forgot how to say lady, um, and gentleman.

GREG: What else? What else are we going to talk about now? Dragons?

ABDUL: What are we gonna say about dragons? Wings? Fire?

After listing conventional Spanish speakers, Lucas listed Abdul as an honorary Spanish speaker. In the same way that Abdul had earlier veered the conversation back to their friendship, Lucas found a way to do so by coercing Abdul to cross into Spanish. The kids obtained much joy from crossing, as is evident in Lucas's pride when Abdul eventually did so. Abdul's initial humble "*si*" gave Greg an opportunity to join by displaying his knowledge of Arabic—"*As-salamu alaykum!*" When his participation was ignored, he downplayed the symbolic significance of Abdul's knowledge, "Everyone knows *si.*" Lucas crossly maintained it was the special result of friendship—"No, not everyone knows!" Abdul supported his friend by offering more obscure knowledge. Lucas, co-opting the teacher's traditional script of the question, answer, evaluation, got Abdul to continue crossing by counting. Abdul then turned to me and asked me to display some Greek, a reciprocation of my earlier bridge of not speaking English as a kid. This gesture enacted my own relationship with the boys, and was reinforced when Lucas crossed into Greek. Bridging and crossing were some of the ways kids acknowledged and symbolized our friendship. As Gregory's anxious attempts underline, these were not just pleasurable pastimes among friends maintaining well-established relations. They were also prerequisites of new bonds, both friendly and romantic, where the processes were riskier and their outcomes unpredictable.

I have devoted so much attention to bridging and crossing (Kromidas 2011a; 2011b; 2012) because these ubiquitous practices were an important and unique way that kids enacted their cosmopolitan ethos. These practices refigured boundaries between differences within hegemonic constructions of difference. Despite their playful form, they were political acts that purposively transformed race. Although the term "bridging" is employed in mainstream multicultural discourse, there it signifies a process of making presumably opaque differences transparent in order to tolerate those differences. The kids' bridges drastically differed in content and tone. Countries, foods, practices, words, even entire languages were shown to be more similar than different. In their bridges, the kids acknowledged the social fact of difference but expressed ambivalence about the boundaries and content of differences. These practices allowed kids to signal multiple belongings, to establish that belongings were variously felt and that attachments varied situationally and changed through time. Although spontaneous and intuitive, these practices were purposive and had profound effects on how the kids experienced race. In their unique manner, the kids worked to uncouple the tightly bound configuration of race/culture/language and dislodged their seeming primordial connection to bodies and birth.

Bridging and crossing also subverted the hierarchical ordering of differences. Croatian was equivalent to Lebanese was equivalent to African American was equivalent to Filipino was equivalent to Mexican was equivalent to Italian. In one particularly raucous interaction, Eliza and Keisha bridged and crossed Albanianness with African Americanness, both of them clutching their stomachs in laughter when Keisha proclaimed that Eliza's Albanian last name could easily be changed to "Biznitch." Because they were sensitive to the hegemonic status of an undifferentiated "American" whiteness, it was conspicuously absent in the kids' bridging and crossing. Gregory perceived that he could not bridge or cross with "Americanness." So he resolved this problem by deep crossing, claiming to be something other than what he is conventionally understood to be. However much Gregory's case exaggerates the dynamics involved in crossings, his practices were not qualitatively different in spirit. Indeed, other kids performed differences that our racial baggage would not allow them. Jessie, a girl in the ELL class (and one-time girlfriend of Oscar and James), posted on her online profile that she was "50% Rican 50% Mexican and also 50% from Montenegro." Although she was only Puerto Rican, her claims were based on the fact that one of her best friends was born in Mexico and the other in Montenegro. Gregory's claims differed because of his lower social status in the classroom and because his claim was of complete belonging. Although his claims were sometimes dismissed, at other times they were accepted, as in the interaction described earlier. Like all bridges and crossings, it allowed Gregory to "become other." While becoming other is a central aspect of friendship and the formation of subjectivity, in this multiracial milieu "becoming other" had special significance in the formation of the kids' racial subjectivity and in racial transformation, dissolving the conjoined cores of our racial baggage—essentialism and hierarchy.

BECOMING COSMOPOLITAN

In her meditation on the potentialities of friendship for utopian politics, Gandhi brings forth a subjugated perspective informing the philosophical tradition on friendship, one "independent from the burdensome nomenclature of naturalness, homogeneity, origin" (2003, 17; 2006). She finds it in the Epicurean tradition where friendship is based on *philoxenia*, love of strangers. These bonds are necessarily risky, potentially unsettling hegemonic constructions of presumed similarity within nation, sex, creed, and race. She argues that the existential dilemmas posed by the openness and radical insufficiency of this model of the friendship bond are what paves the way to a genuine cosmopolitanism (2003, 18–19). Gandhi's focus on "in-betweenness" echoes wider shifts in social theory where subjectivity is increasingly characterized by creative, open-ended, and relational fluxes. Rather than mirrors reflecting who they were in some closed-ended sense, friendships were, whether enduring or fleeting, sites of ongoing processes of learning where kids brought themselves into being, continually in relation to who they could become (Evans 2013, 183–184). The crafting of self is always political, formed in relation to power-laden discourses of gender, sexuality, class, and race. And the bonds of friendships, loaded with affects of admiration, respect, loyalty, and joy, were the source of an ethic of care and cosmopolitan belonging. Friendships were the site where kids expressed and wrestled with deep desires of self-authoring. They refused definitions based solely on rootedness in family, neighborhood, religion, class, and race. They branched out from these roots to express and define the self with flexibility and openness. I must stress that it was not only the relative unpredictability and choice of the friendship bond that allowed the kids' cosmopolitanism to flourish. That is, kids would not have been able to transform the meanings and livedness of race absent the rich and complex diversity of this particular classroom.

Friendships also posed limitations on the inclusivity of the kids' cosmopolitan ethos. For one, friendships were sites where hegemonic expressions of masculinity and femininity were operative and entangled with heteronormativity and homophobia. Even expressions of alternative, or at least unconventional, gendered formations had to be declared explicitly heterosexual to be legitimate.[5] For instance, Keisha's tough stance and her unique position as the only girl with boys as her best friends ironically relied on the homophobic slur "no homo" to stretch the limits of girl yet still be intelligible as one. Similarly, the physical and emotional intimacy of the wrestling boys' bonds points to alternative expressions of masculinity as well, one also legitimized through a rampant heterosexism. As Emma Renold and Jessica Ringrose (2008, 332) point out, mapping such processes enables us to see how disrupting one norm may reinscribe other forms of domination and Otherization. When we consider the fact that much of the pop culture through which kids mediated their relations was suffused with homophobia, the picture appears rather bleak for an inclusivity that includes LGBTQ struggles. But even within the seemingly immovable heteronormativity of the kids' peer groups, there were glimpses of rupture. Foremost among these was the way that Victor, the only openly gay kid in the fifth grade, was treated. Although he hung out with a bunch of girls, the boys did not tease or taunt him, nor was he an object of ridicule (although there were eye rolls when he danced suggestively in the playground). I saw boys go out of their way to treat him with kindness. These disruptions suggest that educators equipped to deal with such issues (sadly too few; see Payne and Smith 2014) can and should approach them with kids in an open-ended manner that mines the contradictions and alternative figurations that may very well be present under the surface.

Another limitation to a more robust inclusivity was posed by the way authenticity operated within friendships: it could be used to exclude kids from friendship or a sense of belonging in the real time of interaction. Consider an interaction in the art studio when kids were making kachina dolls wherein the pleasures and pains of relationality were apparent. The art teacher allowed kids to talk and roam while working, enabling relaxed and unrushed conversations. I sat next to Jacinta, working intently on decorating her doll in a long fancy dress ("Look, a princess!"). Steven and Mark clustered by us with their dolls and started rapping songs and inserting Jacinta's and Eliza's names. Eliza was working some distance away but could hear the boys, laughing when her name was included. Mark then realized that attaching black pipe cleaners onto his doll's head resembled dreadlocks. Excited with his discovery, he called out across the room, "Look, dreads! Keisha! Look!" She smiled and nodded. He became obsessed with finding more pipe cleaners. "I need black! Yo I need some black!" Steven guffawed "Oh, you a racist!" to the chuckles of the others. When the talk moved to celebrities with dreadlocks, Mark remarked that Flavor Flav is so ugly. Jacinta agreed that it doesn't get much uglier than "Flavor Flavor." Steven cracked up, "She said Flavor Flavor!" Juan, listening from another table interjected, "It's Flavor *Flav*." The kids whipped their heads around to look at Juan, then looked at each other and laughed. Steven added, "Oh yeah, look, he's trying to correct *us*." Admittedly, Juan was sad at the rejection of his earnest attempt to be included in the camaraderie of object relations, and I felt bad for him and embarrassed that I had to witness it. However painful such exclusions may be, these rejections must be distinguished from the way that race functions—denying belonging in the larger circle of humanity. Hierarchies are not all of the same order. The hierarchies that must concern us are those that are embodied, enduring, ascribed, and dehumanizing. Dehumanization is always at stake in race's durable, essentialized, and hierarchized types. Juan was denied through an authenticity that was achieved rather than ascribed—defined through experience, sophistication, knowledge, and sincerity. The authenticity guiding object relations was open, was changeable, and did not measure a kid's ultimate worth. Objects allowed kids, however temporarily, to become other, and forge relations based on their own differentiating principles. These principles were more open-ended than the essentialized and static boundaries of race and authenticity defined by blood, birth, and bodies.[6]

The most significant contribution of friendships to the kids' cosmopolitanism, then, was the way they allowed kids to form ties of affection beyond the dreadful ascriptions of blood, birth, and bodies. These ties provided them with the most powerful ammunition against the core assumptions of our racial baggage—that we naturally prefer "our own kind," and the natural order and value that adhere to these kinds. Significant here for politics and scholarship of race is the fact that kids did not adopt a simplified "we're all the same" rhetoric to achieve friendships. Nor did they ignore differences or tolerate them as it were. Rather they engaged with the racial baggage they inherited, playfully and humorously, but decisively transformed its meanings on the ground. These processes worked to strengthen their bonds and made friendship such a fruitful site for cultivating civility. The other side of the coin of the power of friendship was its centripetal force that tended to exclude others, posing obstacles to a more inclusive cosmopolitanism. This could have considerably constrained the emergence of the kids' cosmopolitanisms if they did not have ample opportunities to engage with other kids in their classroom on humanizing terms. Fortunately, cooperative learning, the subject of the next chapter, provided an opportunity for kids to forge bonds other than friendship. I explore how collaborative labor allowed Ms. Lee's kids to submerge the hierarchy of smartness, and how both these factors contributed to the emergence of the kids' cosmopolitanism and their sense that school was a space in which they rightfully belonged.

3 ◆ THE COLLECTIVE LABORS OF CONVIVIALITY

In their "manifesto of relational pedagogy," Charles Bingham and coauthors argue, "the fog over education has kept us from realizing that learning is primarily about human beings who meet. Meeting and learning are inseparable" (2004, 5). These philosophers are concerned with transforming schools and learning by refiguring the student-teacher relationship. Yet they open up a space to reconsider student-student relations. In this chapter I explore how the school's policy of ability grouping and teachers' use of individual or cooperative instructional methods contribute to racial learning.[1] Although these practices have ostensibly nothing to do with race, I demonstrate how they were decisive for students' experiences of race and trace the distinct structures of feeling in the two classrooms I participated in to these practices. I argue that the kids' cosmopolitan ethos must be understood as emerging in part through the social relations forged through collaborative learning. The humanizing effect of laboring together was key to inspiring the cosmopolitan ethos in Ms. Lee's classroom. My analysis is materialist in that it locates "definite forms of life" arising from "definite forms of activity" (Marx 1970 [1865], 42). The analytic task is more abstract in this chapter than the others, but the effects I trace are no less tangible. Throughout the book I show kids struggling to make sense of race as it materialized or was imposed on them, confrontations in which they often defused or defied racial categories and meanings. Although they were not always immediately apparent, racialized meanings lay near the surface. In contrast, collaborative learning practices often did not draw on race at all. The logic about how these practices figure in racial formation is as follows: Race is a particular social relation, a deeply fractured relation in which we come to know one another as *types* of human, a profoundly dehumanizing process. Encounters in which people come to know one another beyond these ascriptions, experiencing or glimpsing their common humanity, run counter to race making and are, in a word, humanizing.

The humanizing potential of cooperative learning strategies has been celebrated in educational scholarship for decades, as a way to inculcate and foster a sense of community, racial integration, and inclusion of special needs or otherwise marginalized students (Cohen and Lotan 2014; Johnson and Johnson 2009; 2014). However, empirical work has shown how cooperative learning can be a problematic site where students enact and exacerbate inequalities of gender, race, and ability. Mary Christianakis's (2010) ethnographic study among a diverse group of fifth-graders in California showed that cooperative work was a site for reinforcing status hierarchies of intelligence, popularity, and race that were operative in the classroom. More troubling yet, it was a site where intelligence was inscribed as an innate property of whiteness. This underscores my argument about how cooperative pedagogies operated in Ms. Lee's classroom, and their broader potential. The joyful and engaged manner in which kids labored together was possible only because Ms. Lee submerged the hierarchies of smartness in her classroom *and* because they were a way for kids to escape the sorting and ranking function of schooling. Collaboration was dependent on and further encouraged the destruction of hierarchical relations in the classroom. This points to the magnetic power of race to incorporate other seemingly innate hierarchies, in this case smartness.

THE STRUCTURE, EMBODIMENTS, AND INTERSECTIONS OF SMARTNESS

"Do you want to see how a *real* classroom works?" Ms. Lee asked me on a sticky day in June. "Come join us next year," she said with her characteristic nonchalance. This was how I came to be a part of Ms. Lee's fifth-grade classroom when my two months with Ms. Anastasia's class, the "accelerated" fifth-grade bunch, were coming to an end with the close of the school year. The excited talk among the teachers that day was the next year's teaching assignments, particularly who would be taking the coveted spot of teaching the "top" class. Exhausted and disgruntled from the yearlong strain of demanding parents challenging her tests, report cards, homework grades, and award recipients, Ms. Anastasia announced she would be taking an out-of-classroom literacy position. The opening caused a commotion among the upper-grade teachers who coveted the position of teaching the "top" class, despite the demanding parents. It allowed Ms. Milton, a fourth-grade teacher, to use her seniority to grab the sought-after spot. The administration and teachers assumed that I would be continuing my research with the new "top" fifth-graders and

Ms. Milton. Perhaps Ms. Lee sensed my unease at the arrangements. Or perhaps she wanted me to experience the "real" in the spirit of scientific inquiry. It's not that Ms. Lee found the "smart" kids to be exceptional and less real. As a matter of fact, Ms. Lee's stance toward smartness is just as unorthodox as that concerning goodness or badness, the subject of chapter 4. She fully understood the social facts of smartness, as did everyone in the school: students, parents, staff, teachers, and administrators. Unlike her colleagues, she did not naturalize these social facts. She did not vie to teach the "top" class and took her name out of the running. Nor was she particularly endeared to "smart" kids any more than she was "good" ones. As I will show, Ms. Lee used multiple strategies to purposefully submerge the hierarchy of smartness in her classroom. Before I explore how Ms. Lee created an alternative ethos in her class, it is necessary to establish the structure of smartness in PS AV.

The Structure of Smartness

Among the human sciences, it is an acknowledged truism that intelligence and related constructions like giftedness are social constructions that distort complex and dynamic properties. While intelligence testing has been the subject of fierce critique for over half a century, scholars have recently focused their attention on the more informal but no less powerful ways that intelligence is constructed in the everyday life of educational institutions and their implicit theories and practices of "smartness" (Hatt 2012). Schools not only produce smartness as a measurable and incrementally variable property of individuals, but also naturalize these distinctions as innate properties, and justify differential educational treatment on this basis (Stark 2014).

Public School AV, like many schools throughout the United States, employs ability grouping, but segregates only its "top" class. The process begins in the third grade using data from standardized exams and teacher evaluations. As PS AV is a moderately sized school by New York City standards, each grade level had four or five classes that included one accelerated class and one class for English language learners (ELLs). The other two or three classes were "heterogeneously mixed." It would be only a slight exaggeration to say that school personnel treated the "smart" kids like royalty. Although the processes of designating it are somewhat hidden, smartness was a live and locally relevant category. The spoils of smartness were not the small privileges given to smart kids, like special trips, pizza parties, or curricular opportunities. Rather, the prize was inhabiting the distinguished category.

The school distinguished and celebrated the smart kids in various public ceremonies that functioned as de facto degradation rituals for all other kids. In both graduation ceremonies that I observed, the kids in the top class swept the awards, not just obvious ones based on grades such as valedictorian, salutatorian, literacy, and math achievement, but subjectively based ones such as the NYS Attorney General's Triple C (Commitment, Character, Courage) Award and NYC Comptroller Achievement Award for leadership potential and commitment to public service. In the first year I attended, the principal announced awards by class. After the flood of awards bestowed upon Ms. Anastasia's class, the awards abruptly trickled down for the next two classes and ended with a single award to a student in the ELL class, for "Most Improved Scholar." Although I am not sure if my comment to teachers about how awkward I felt was the reason why the practice was changed, in the following year's ceremony the administrators bequeathed awards alphabetically so that the discrepancy between classes was not as apparent.

Despite that small measure, the top classes continued to function as the public face of the school, called upon to represent the school or to display their giftedness to the many outsider visitors, whether local or regional school administrators, college professors, or journalists or television stations covering an extracurricular program or school celebration. They were overrepresented in the student council; they served as the hallway monitors and classroom monitors for the younger kids. They assisted or ran bake sales or lollipop sales. Their work was prominently displayed in important school areas (not just outside their classroom), their activities written up in the PTA newsletter, and their achievements announced over the loudspeaker. After one such announcement celebrating the television appearance of Ms. Milton's kids, Connor complained loudly, "Whenever they interview us, they always use kids from Ms. Milton's class." During another announcement of the winners of the student council, Jacinta, who was running for president, was apparently prepared for her loss. She rolled her eyes and exclaimed sarcastically, "Oh wow, from Ms. Milton's class," and continued her task.

School personnel regularly singled out the top class as models of behavior: Ms. *Milton's* class or Ms. *Anastasia's* class lined up quickly or finished the project in a single period, the intonation always signifying something in excess. Ms. Anastasia treated the kids in her accelerated class as most other teachers, staff, and administrators treated them. She believed they were special, more intelligent, and more articulate, and their perspectives more worthy of being heard. She reminded them every day of their college and professional trajectories, and of the hard work and drive they would need to succeed. These reminders were geared to incite competition with some abstract entity—"I expected more from *this* class," or among students within the class—"Damon, this is the type of work that they expect at Walt Whitman" (the "good" local junior high school, see chapter 1). By the fifth grade when I met them, these students had gotten the memo.

Embodying Smartness

The kids in the top class understood the gravitas of their status. They thought of themselves as smart, related to others as it, and knew one another in the class through the infinitesimal gradations within it, and looked down on anyone lower than them. In short, they embodied smartness. It was an embodiment imbued with entitlement. For instance, upon listening to two girls in Ms. Anastasia's class, Izel and Carly, debate who was going to be valedictorian, I interrupted to ask how they knew it was going to be a student from their class. They looked at me as if they were puzzled by my ignorance. Izel explained, "The valedictorian is *always* from the top class." My further question of "why?" probably cued them that my ignorance was an anthropological trick. "Because we're the Einsteins!" Carly yelled and guffawed as Izel cracked up in laughter.

Not only did these kids incessantly refer to themselves as the top class, they understood all classes to be hierarchically ranked despite the fact that it was only the "top" class that was homogenously grouped. So encompassing was this category that they even incorporated the ELL class into it. Salma explained to me about being a relative newbie in the accelerated program by having arrived in fourth grade rather than in third, "because I was bad at problem solving, but I wasn't in *ELL*!" Likewise Sangmu, another girl in the "top" class, explained to me that when she first arrived in the school, they had mistakenly put her in Ms. Lee's class, which was "almost an ELL class!"

The kids not only were hyperaware of their hierarchical status vis-à-vis the other classes, but also recognized the hierarchy of smartness within their classroom. This was partly due to the way Ms. Anastasia publicly rewarded the highest grades in her classroom as well as the kids' own curiosity, nay, need to know how their peers scored. Every return of a graded assignment, and they were all graded, was accompanied by a flurry of activity as the kids gathered this information, peering at their neighbors and miming their performance to peers across the room. However, the kids' ranking of one another's smartness was based not solely on grades but on their assessment of one another's *natural* and *fixed* capacities. For instance, the kids in Ms. Anastasia's class were almost unanimous in their unhesitant placing of Damon as the "smartest." Kids explained to me that he didn't always get the best grades because either he didn't care or was immersed in his own interests. Deirdre in contrast, was smart, "cared," and worked hard, eventually receiving the valedictorian award. This was in contrast to Blake, who tried hard and cared, but "has kinda troubles" succeeding. The kids predicted, correctly, that Blake would not be joining them in the "top" academy of "top junior high" Walt Whitman. For the kids in Ms. Anastasia's class, effort could go only so far, a distant second to the natural property of smartness. Regularly positioned as winning players in a competitive race, they were invested in the construction of the intelligence hierarchy.

The Intersections of Smartness

My detour through smarts and ability grouping is not haphazard. Ability group-ing is a racial project, and giftedness is a way that whites have maintained and protected their privilege in schools in the era of de jure desegregation (Bor-land 1997; 2005; Staiger 2004; Stark 2014). Tracking is currently the predomi-nant institutional practice that segregates students within integrated, or more appropriately termed desegregated, schools (Lewis, Diamond, and Forman 2015; Oakes 2005). Indeed, I would venture that tracking is the dominant way that young people in desegregated schools naturalize racial inequalities and reify differences of race by unquestionably apprehending the stark chromatics in college/honors/AP/accelerated versus regular or "slow" tracks. I agree with Ingold's (2000) pronouncement that intelligence is, along with race, one of the worst of human fabrications.[2] The grafting of intelligence onto whiteness is for students the most tragic of all. We are only beginning to surmise the devastat-ing effects tracking has on the development of students' racial worldview (Lewis, Diamond, and Forman 2015).

Fortunately at PS AV, the preeminent school hierarchy of "smart" and "not so smart" students was not based on plainly visible chromatics. Although none of the kids from public housing were in the top classes, this fact was obscured by the particular race and class demographics of the neighborhood and the school. There was a higher proportion of white to Black students in the accelerated class, but the sizable number of Latinas/os, Asians, and mixed-race or otherwise racially ambiguous kids masked this fact. While most of the Black kids in the school came from the public housing projects, there were a few Black families that sent their kids to PS AV from farther afield, and those kids were often in the "top" class. The ELL class was predominantly Latino and Asian, although the kids referred to it as the "Spanish" class. The superdiverse demographics of PS AV's students thus subdued the racialized dynamics of tracking. This stands in stark distinction to many NYC's schools, such as in "majority minority" schools where white kids populate the "gifted" class, or predominantly white schools where there is a significantly higher percentage of racial minorities in remedial or special education classes. Whether this relatively subdued racial structure of the "top" class persists in the face of the changing class dynamics of Augursville remains to be seen.

However, when smartness is such a live category, we can expect that it will grab hold of and graft itself over other seemingly naturalized inequalities. Indeed, in Ms. Anastasia's classroom, smartness intersected with and informed how kids viewed one another's differences, and vice versa. That is, their perceptions of one another's differences informed how they perceived one another's smartness. For instance, the kids linked Damon's "natural" smartness with his being Chinese (he was also part Vietnamese), and reciprocally linked Chineseness with smartness. This association was apparent to Damon, which both pleased and irked him depending on the circumstance. When Ms. Anastasia was going over a "math challenge" problem that none of the kids were able to solve, the kids expressed surprised that Damon hadn't come to the correct answer either. "Why, because I'm Chinese?" he responded, his frustration mixed with disappointment at being wrong. Although her whiteness was not explicitly provided as an explanatory framework for her smartness, it bears mentioning that Deirdre, at the top of the smart hierarchy along with Damon and ultimately the valedictorian, was widely thought to be "Italian" or "part Italian" even though she was Dominican and Puerto Rican. More telling than Deirdre's whitening was Besnik's Blackening. Conventionally mixed-race white and Latino and with racially ambiguous phenotype, Besnik was racialized as Black in the classroom. This was partly due to the way the kids placed him at the bottom of the smart hierarchy despite any clear evidence that he belonged there more than any of the other kids who weren't at the top. He was often called "dumb" and "crazy." His very figure came to stand in for an unruly dumbness when Nicolas described to me the structure of the academies at Walt Whitman junior high: "Academy 1 is for the smart kids, Academy 2 is regular, and Academy 3 is for the Besniks." When I replied "Huh?" Nicolas explained, "Like crazy people, all the students turn into Besniks." Besnik happened to walk in late at just that moment and Nicolas had no qualms about turning to him and saying, "Hey, Besnik, I got accepted into Whitman!" "Cool," Besnik said still groggy-eyed, "how will you get to school?" "Bus, city bus," Nicolas answered. Such is the magnetic pull of smartness that despite the absence of explicitly racialized structure of smartness, the kids implicitly created one.

CHALLENGING SMARTNESS

It is one thing to reject the legitimacy of intelligence as a fixed, innate, and incrementally varying trait of human beings. It is quite another to subvert the relevance of smartness when one is essentially tasked to produce it. Ms. Lee managed to do this in her classroom despite being encapsulated by its larger structure. Her most important strategy was her public stance toward smartness in the classroom. Unlike other teachers, she did not openly favor and reward kids who got good grades, nor did she hold them up as models to emulate. When administrators asked teachers to submit a "student of the month," a picture of whom was displayed by the main office, Ms. Lee deliberately chose students who upset the hierarchy, even once selecting Selena, who consistently got the lowest grades. Ms. Lee explained to me that she doesn't like to always give it to the "goody-goodies." She also added that some teachers let the students decide, but she didn't like that strategy either "because it turns into a popularity contest." When she did announce the student of the month in class, she made a point of asking the kids why they thought the student deserved it. The kids never made mention of grades, tests, or smartness in their responses. Instead, they provided reasons like "she does her homework every night" and "he listens." Although it was only a monthly task, it was relevant because of its public nature. In it she deliberately intervened in the preeminent institutional hierarchy of smartness, as well as students' hierarchy of popularity.

Similarly, when asked by the school to submit the "top" students within each class to run for student council, Ms. Lee constructed a "citizens ceremony" based on actions in the classroom that allowed more kids to succeed than traditional tests. Ms. Lee also subverted the emergence of smartness in the routinized activities of the classroom. In the weekly ritual where kids marked their peers' spelling tests, Ms. Lee did not allow them to exchange information about the scores, and announced she would penalize any violation. After going through corrections, she would give the score for each number of errors so the student could write the grade. By the end of September this culture was already established in the classroom. She was going down the list of the amount of errors and exclaimed that she didn't think she would have to continue after seven wrong. James said that she needed to keep going. Eight wrong? James nodded to keep going. The class was oohing expectantly. When he finally signaled she had reached it, he wrote it down solemnly. I watched him carefully to see if he would verbally or otherwise signal whose test he was marking. He did not. Ms. Lee, although very curious about who had done so poorly, waited to ruffle through the papers when the class moved on.

Despite the fact that Ms. Lee's kids were aware of the structure and valorization of smartness in the school at large, it was not an operative category in their classroom. Ms. Lee's submerging of smartness also allowed the kids to redefine it. The kids unhinged it from school knowledge and recognized and valued a much more diffuse notion of smartness—kids who were experts in airplanes, baseball, wrestling, rap, drawing, jokes, Pokémon, or the neighborhood. Expertise was not considered innate (even when the knowledge or skill was somewhat racialized, such as rapping), but based on practice and interest. As the conventional notion of smartness was remote in the perceptions of their immediate peers and dislodged from any association with blood, bodies, and birth, smartness did not intersect with race. It is quite possible that these kids would have rejected the hierarchy of smartness because of their positioning within it. But it is unlikely that they could have dissociated smartness from implicit racial meanings without Ms. Lee's purposeful and habitual submerging of smartness in her classroom.

SMARTNESS AND ASSENTING/REFUSING TO COOPERATE

There was another way that smartness contributed to racial formation in PS AV, in an indirect but powerful manner. Accepting or rejecting "smartness" had an impact on racial learning through the labors of learning, specifically how teachers structured learning through cooperative or individual methods. Teachers themselves responded to students' assent or refusal of these methods. I take it as a truism that, despite the seeming irreducible nature of teacher control in a classroom, students must assent to the arrangements of any classroom (Erickson et al. 2007). It is so with the teacher's method of delivery. Because Ms. Anastasia's kids embodied smartness, they refused to engage in collaborative learning. Ms. Anastasia and the kids implicitly struck a deal to stick to traditional instruction methods.[3] Consistently, whenever Ms. Anastasia employed cooperative strategies—doing so only when it was part and parcel of a larger program to which the school subscribed—the kids took this as a signal that it was not "real work." While there were considerable off-task behaviors during traditional instruction, the classroom exploded into off-task mode when kids were asked to collaborate. It is no wonder really that the kids in the "top" class did not take cooperative work seriously. Knowing they could not be evaluated on them, they were not worthy of their efforts.

Although Ms. Lee did not subscribe to the magic of intelligence, she knew what most teachers know—the "smart" kids are those who outwardly comply when ranking and grading are at stake. As the beneficiaries of the school system, the "smart" kids knew that the gifts of smartness were only previews of rewards on the horizon. Ms. Lee knew that the rewards of grades and future success were not motivation enough for "real" kids. Nor did she fool herself by thinking that obtaining school knowledge was intrinsically rewarding by itself. Rather, she recognized that assigning kids cooperative activities made them work without the threat of punishment or the promise of reward. She saw not only their assent but their embrace of cooperative activities and so employed social pedagogies at any opportunity.[4] These collaborative practices and the bonds created from them were decisive in the emergence of the kids' cosmopolitanism. They provided kids with another tool and opportunity to challenge racial dehumanization, albeit indirectly.

THE STRUCTURE OF COLLABORATIVE PRACTICES

Ms. Lee's use of cooperation was a regular and recurring feature of the classroom. These activities were varied in form, some as brief as asking kids to turn to the person closest to them to give their opinion. Other activities were extended thirty-minute interactions in groups of four with larger goals, for example when

Ms. Lee had kids devise their own experiment to evaluate the best paper towel. The latter were often raucous affairs where kids would be intensely working together on the same task, alternatively or simultaneously laughing, fighting, or even expressing utter hatred of one another. Nevertheless, they were invariably engaged in ways that radically differed from their orientation to other academic tasks.

I confess that although I enjoyed observing these activities, I did not consider their significance until quite recently because I was too preoccupied with my own ideas of what an "authentic" education looks like, along the lines of a Freirian or critical pedagogy. Nevertheless, I faithfully observed and recorded them because my relational methodology directed my attention and engagement to mirror that of the kids. I was bored during traditional instruction (my surveys of how kids amused themselves unbeknownst to teachers were getting repetitive), stirred with the small yet numerous breaches in the classroom order, and woke up during "free time." In Ms. Lee's classroom, the shift in energy with the introduction of a cooperative activity was as noticeable as switching on a light in a dark room.

Consider the dynamics on the morning before the New York State social studies examination in January. Ms. Lee had assigned the kids a task to review the events leading up to the Revolutionary War by making a "social studies foldable," an activity suggested by the textbook. Ms. Milton had conducted it the previous day and recommended it, giving Ms. Lee one of her student's work as a model. The project entailed cutting up a piece of paper, folding it into a booklet and writing specifics using the textbook. Although the kids generally preferred "hands-on" tasks like cutting and drawing to straightforwardly academic tasks, I was frustrated with the activity. It was not just that I thought the activity itself was intellectually pointless, I was irritated by the kids' poor progress and results. Perhaps the perfectly executed model from Ms. Milton's class hung over me and incited my competitive edge—Ms. Milton's kids are no better than my kids! I ran around trying to motivate and help kids along with Ms. Lee. But it was a losing battle. I took a step back and recorded what the students were doing: Oscar and Jacinta were busy coloring the covers of the book and competing over the quality of their graffiti-like font. Nedim and Joseph were smelling markers, still at it when I looked a few minutes later. Gregory was aimlessly flipping through his textbook every time I looked at him. Omar was looking around the classroom, having "finished" the task by scribbling a few words per page. Keisha was thoroughly cleaning her desk. Connor was looking at a book in his desk about airplanes. Yanely was going back and forth to her book bag in the closet. Steven was wondering what time it was at regular intervals, and Abdul was wondering when it was going to be lunch. Only Lillian was faithfully if halfheartedly at work. After a half hour like this, Ms. Lee saw it was going nowhere. She told the kids to clean up, to finish it for homework (she didn't include it on the homework list later, and no one reminded her), and that they would be playing Family Feud. You would be wrong if you thought these kids couldn't move fast or follow directions. They quickly tucked away all vestiges of the activity. It was time for Family Feud!

The kids gave their full attention to Ms. Lee's every utterance as she explained the game, charged kids with distributing materials, and set up teams of four or five. Teams were to compete answering questions they constructed for homework the previous night. Omar, James, Lucas, and Keisha formed one of the five teams. I moved toward their group just as they were coming up with a definition of federalism. James began writing the response as the other three kids moved to huddle around him. Omar inadvertently made a noise with his shoe that sounded like a fart. James, Lucas, and Keisha burst out in laughter as Omar claimed, "It was my shoe!" They turned back to their task still laughing. Omar was happy at the attention and repeated his excuse in hopes of generating more laughter. If this had occurred during traditional instruction or unstructured time, the joke would have been extended well beyond the point at which it had exhausted its comedic effect (see chapter 1 for how calamitous a fart was during whole-class activity, one that was even considered fun). But the others collectively shushed Omar, their bodies and attention oriented toward James writing on the white board. The kids were disappointed when another team came up with the answer before them. James, Lucas, and Keisha gave one another a knowing look—it was the small setback of the shoe fart.

Again without any words, the kids collectively readied themselves for the next question—head nods, eye flicks toward the teacher, and stoic facial expressions. Keisha outstretched her hand to James. He passed her the board. Omar erased it in her hands. They were statue-like until Ms. Lee asked the next question. "What are the four duties of citizenship?" They looked to one another to see who might know. Lucas exclaimed, "I know this is in the textbook!" He bent down, got the book from his desk, and feverishly flipped through it. James and Keisha looked at Omar impatiently, so he started ruffling through their review sheets. He found the answer and pointed it to James, who started reading it for Keisha. She was writing it as Omar and Lucas were cheering her on nonverbally and James was chanting, "Hurry up, hurry up!" They were in a groove, all with one purpose. As Keisha was finishing, Lucas bellowed, "Done!" They raised their hands to signal they reached an answer. Ms. Lee acknowledged that they were the first, waited for other groups to finish, then verified their answer. They allowed themselves a brief expression of glee, which quickly transformed into intense satisfaction before they readied themselves for the next task, all without any words.

The burst of collective energy during the activity was typical of cooperative learning tasks. Despite the fact that kids had only slightly more control over their time, labor, and bodily autonomy, they experienced collaborative activities in profoundly distinctive ways, so much so that the kids did not consider them "work" and suspended their perpetual struggle for free time during these activities (see chapter 4). What was it about these activities that evaded the kids' central struggle for autonomy? What made these activities so different from the wearying work of listening to the teacher or working individually? Why did the kids come alive?

Part of what delighted me about these interactions is that the kids got things done, even while arguing, joking, or both. I remember watching them work like a well-oiled machine and wondering if I had not dismissed Émile Durkheim's (1984 [1893]) *The Division of Labor* too hastily in graduate school. There seemed to be something created in these interactions akin to his notion of organic solidarity. I relished how these activities gave me another view of the kids—their potential for concentration in tasks that were not directly relevant to their lives and their enthusiasm for doing things with kids who were not their friends. One principal reason kids were able to engage in these activities this way was because, even if they were embedded in a competitive structure of winning and losing teams, the individual self was not at stake. In virtually all other school activities, individuals are ranked and pitted against one another, if not explicitly then implicitly. Collaborative activities reduced if not eliminated the possibilities of "face threat," a risk that Frederick Erickson and colleagues argue (2007) is key to understanding students' assent or refusal to learn. From the students' point of view, these moments were not geared toward a future learning outcome or the evaluation machine of which teacher's grading is only a small part. Cooperative activities were fully in and of the present tense. Knowing that a "collective brain" could not be ranked in the same way that an individual brain could, the activity became about play, fun, and enjoyment. Lacking any utilitarian value, they were enacted for their own sake. The pleasure opened up a space for, ironically enough, moments of *authentic* learning—perceptual and sensory shifts where outcomes are unknown, are unpredictable, and can usher in "something radically new in which preconceived notions of self and the world are permanently altered" (Carlin 2010, 240; see also Biesta 2012).

ALIENATED LABORS OF LEARNING

Thinking about the social relations of learning within schools through a framework of humanization/dehumanization allows us to appreciate their significance for racial transformation. Marxist perspectives have been the most radical critiques of the functions of institutionalized schooling within capitalist societies: their credentializing purpose, their role in sorting the population into classes and sustaining the illusion that class is completely achieved and legitimizing

class inequality, and finally their role in constructing a docile populace ame-
nable to the dictates of production and unable or unwilling to challenge their
oppressive conditions.[5] Very little work has considered students' school experiences, and particularly their social relations with one another, from the broader
Marxian rubric of alienation. Alienation is arguably the fundamental Marxian
category, the concept through which "Marx displays the devastating effect of
capitalist production on human beings, on their physical and mental states and
on the social processes of which they are part" (Ollman 1971, 131).[6] Through the
rubric of alienation, Marx diagnosed the unsustainability of capitalism through
his analysis of the radical political inequality of the laborer.[7] In the most potentially humanizing act of creating and transforming the world, the laborer instead
finds herself degraded, controlled, manipulated, or mechanized and the objects
of her labor not her own. What happens to our critique of education if we also
consider learning with the fascination it is due as "a crucial aspect of human
being" (Toren 2012, 27), an inherently collaborative and social act that embeds
learners in webs of social relations with teachers and other learners?

Despite the many parallels between the organization of labor in capitalist
workplace and that of institutionalized learning in schools, scholars have not
applied the alienation rubric to think about the types of relationships forged
through the practices of schooling. Jean Lave and Ray McDermott (2002) are
among the few to engage this analysis by substituting "learning" for "labor" in
Marx's "Estranged Labor" essay of 1844 (1964). The critique of institutionalized learning is thrown into sharp relief when contrasted to authentic learning
in communities of practice, that is, the way *Homo sapiens* have used learning to
survive and thrive for millennia, and the relatively unproblematic way humans
learn complex knowledge outside of schools (i.e., no one "fails"). The inherently social character of learning not only is excised from schools, but also seen
as antithetical to the purpose of school—constructing the credentialized individual. They underline the commodified and alienating character of schooling
when they write, "Institutionalized education has done to the productive learner
what Marx revealed was done to productive labor: schools have commodified
learning to the point that *every learner must worry more about what others know
than about what might be learned if people worked together*" (2002, 21, emphasis
added). The rubric of alienation allows us to perceive how learners are alienated
from the products of their learning (worksheets, tests, essays), from the practice of learning (why so many kids are "off task" if one takes more than a passing
glance), and from themselves as learners (how many kids say that they "don't
like learning"?). Although they did not elaborate this point, Lave and McDermott shine a light on students' alienation from *one another*. How can students
encounter one another as something more than other objects to which they are
compared and ranked? If the institutional structures and practices of schools

make students subjects within the smart hierarchy, how can they encounter one another as equals, as humans, within it?

For Marxist theorists, the primary cause of alienation is the laborer's absence of control over the labor process. For critical educational theorists, this is embodied in the hierarchical teacher/student relationship and the teacher's control of a curriculum removed from any significance to students' lives. With the conflict predefined in this way, one is disposed to look for ways students attempt to take control over their labor, in other words to resist this manifestation of teacher power. I have countless examples of these forms of resistance.[8] But resistance would overlook or misrepresent the kids' orientation to collaborative practices and would reduce its meaning and significance in their everyday lives.

In contrast, the notion of "escape" (see the introduction) is attuned to the kids' views on their life activities, their desires and struggles, and those impulses that are not simply reactions or negations of the way we understand the oppressive conditions of schooling. Escape orients us to questions such as these: When did the kids experience themselves to be free? When did they not feel the yokes of discipline and control? When did they experience joy? Escape forces us to contend with the kids' energy, enthusiasm, and engagement in cooperative learning activities, and shines a light on otherwise hidden struggles and invisible power relations. It opens up a space to explore how the social relations constructed within them enable kids to relate to one another and experience themselves in more authentically human modes, if only temporarily.

SUBMERGING DISTINCTIONS IN COOPERATION

The submergence of the hierarchy of smartness that enabled these activities encouraged the submergence of other status hierarchies and distinctions. The exception to the kids' enthusiastic participation in cooperative activities supports this point. The two kids in Ms. Lee's class who embodied smartness, Lillian and Nedim, were the only ones who always seemed frustrated with the prospect of group work, their pairings, the process, and the outcomes. Their frustration indicates their belief that they would do better work if allowed to do things by themselves (because they saw themselves as smarter and contributing more than others) *and* that work without evaluation was, for all intents and purposes, pointless. Another notable aspect of cooperative activities was the equal participation of the two kids with the lowest status in the classroom, Assad and Gregory.[9] Assad was quite awkward socially, and I will admit that his behavior was often strange. The kids often puzzled at Assad's behavior, and when he attempted to participate in informal conversations around him, his contributions were often so far out that they were ignored or dismissed. This left him unperturbed; he would enthusiastically wait for his next attempt to contribute. Within the space of cooperative learning activities, Assad's quirky contributions were accepted. In a math activity in which kids were tasked with estimating how many steps it would take to get to a local landmark, Assad, Connor, Lucas, and Abdul worked as a team. Teams were decided through musical chairs, a method in which kids maneuvered as best they could to sit near their friends, but it did not usually work out as they pleased. Lucas and Abdul were best friends who managed to get at the same table, along with Connor and Assad. Connor, a well-liked kid with a readiness to laugh that egged on the comedian in his peers, was agnostic about whom he was partnered with. Assad was thrilled to be near Abdul, whom he admired as someone who was "smart," Muslim, and from a nice family (his mom told him the last part).

When I arrived at the table they had finished with the first part of the task and the boys were marveling at Connor's (erroneous) trivia that Croatia is thirty thousand miles away. I asked him if he had been to Croatia, and he told me that his family is from there. Abdul said, "I'm from Lebanon!" "Really?" I remarked, nodding. He looked at me, tilted his head and asked, pleasantly surprised, "Why, do you know where that it?" Of course, I laughed. Lucas then remarked, "I thought you was from somewhere else." "You've only known me for five years!" Abdul shook his head in feigned exasperation. Lucas smiled sheepishly. At that point, Ms. Lee added a dimension to the task, to figure out how long it would take to get to the destination including any stops that had to be justified. The boys jumped to action, all of them leaning forward so that their heads were practically touching in the center of the table. Abdul first suggested that they would stop to drink water. Lucas smiled at his friend and exclaimed, "That's what I was going to say!" Assad then said that they would have to stop at the hospital to get stitches. To my surprise, the boys accepted this contribution and discussed it earnestly, figuring it would take about forty minutes to do so. Then Lucas offered a scenario of figuring out how long it would take if you forgot something at home. After discussing it for a few turns, Abdul remarked, "Who would do that?" Lucas replied, "I would." Abdul accepted his contribution with a shrug, "All right, whatever." The boys then discussed how long that would take and then moved on to add all of the stops to come to their final answer.

In this interaction, Lucas's and Assad's contributions were treated equally, despite the fact that Assad's was, at least to me, nonsensical. What's more, Abdul did not show favoritism to Lucas's contribution. He even questioned its merit, even though they were best friends and he repeatedly rejected Assad's efforts to be his friend. Within cooperative activities, the temporary collaborative bond was equal to the more enduring bond of friendship. I was consistently surprised to see the bonds of collaboration trumping the loyalties of friendship. Lucas was always generous with sharing the products of his individual labors. He didn't care who copied from him, even offering his answers to his friends and neighbors who did not want to work so they wouldn't get in trouble. During the Family Feud activities, Lucas's friend Oscar asked him to verify his team's answer. Lucas patently refused, his loyalty to the group momentarily stronger than his bond with Oscar.

Collaborative activities generated a unique interactive space. In addition to the submersion of relevant distinctions, they provided opportunities for kids to chat informally and get to know one another on their own terms. Connor performing himself as Croatian and Abdul as Lebanese are such examples. Admittedly, that occurred during a break in the activity, or "free time." A key feature of "free time" (I include formal instructional time during which kids usurped freedom) was that kids interacted with their friends. Collaborations provided opportunities for kids who were not friends, even who "hated" one another, to engage in an interactive structure where friendship was not the key relation. This meant that there was great potential for transformation when race inevitably materialized as it did in any realm of activity. Consider an interaction among Yanely, Mark, Hakeem, and Connor during an activity in which the kids had to devise a fully functioning community. Although it was a bit more raucous than usual because a special guest, Mr. Torres, a marine biologist from the NYC Department of Environmental Protection, directed it, it is still typical of the informal talk during extended cooperation.

A recurring drama in the classroom was Yanely either fighting with or complaining about the boys at her table: Mark, Connor, and particularly Hakeem. During individual instruction, these conflicts stalled the activity at hand. In contrast, conflicts during cooperative activities did not. In the beginning of the task, Yanely behaved in her usual style, challenging everything the boys did, grabbing a marker from Hakeem, pushing Mark aside, and relishing her performance of exasperated girl. She soon found a comfortable groove by playing the straight girl who ignored them because she had something better to do, which egged the boys further. When Connor suddenly pointed out that Hakeem's mom, little sister in tow, was at the door conferring with Ms. Lee, Yanely paused her role, looked at her with interest and asked, "Is she Spanish?"

HAKEEM: *Nooo!*
YANELY: She looks Spanish.
HAKEEM: Filipino.
MR. TORRES: Yeah?
YANELY: Where are *you* from?
MR. TORRES: The Bronx.
MARK: Really? I'm from Brooklyn, son! I'm from BK!
CONNOR: BK! I'm from Burger King!

As Mr. Torres started working with another group, Yanely considered Hakeem as if for the first time and asked with a kindness that was uncharacteristic of her, "Do you like your sister?" Hakeem was nervous that his teacher and mother were watching him, so he pretended to be concentrating on the task. Connor informed him, "She's staring at you. She's gonna strike in two minutes!" Yanely went back to taunting, "Trouble! Trouble!" although lacking her usual wicked glee. Connor turned to answer Yanely's question about Hakeem's sister: "She knows everything about wrestling!" "She *does*?" Yanely replied sincerely. Connor affirmed approvingly. Yanely's interest in Hakeem and her first acts of kindness toward him involved learning about family and his Filipino background in this relaxed learning environment. Although Yanely was ambivalent about her own Mexicanness and treated it as an irrelevant aspect of her identity (for example, she rejected the romantic interests of a boy because he was "ugly and too Mexican," and said she didn't like her previous school because "it was only Mexicans there"), she obsessively tried to place people and demanded they make their belongings clear. Hakeem for his part was even more ambivalent about his identity than Yanely. With a Filipino Catholic mother and a Pakistani Muslim father, Hakeem often had trouble making his belongings fit with the school's multicultural discourse. He was uncomfortable when forced to put himself into a recognizable category. He often patently refused multicultural activities or answering peers' questions like "What are you?" even when part of an attempt to bridge with him.

Yanely for her part was trying to bridge their differences, constructing a similarity through his mom "looking" Spanish. For her, it was a transformative moment of racial learning. Her pause and her change in style and tone signaled a shift of received racial knowledge. Yanely was learning that there is more to people than meets the eye, that making assumptions about someone based on the individual's bodily markers is even less assured than she previously thought. It it's not just hard to place *some* people into racial categories, there's trouble even with those people whom you thought you had pegged. Yanely previously assumed Hakeem was solely Pakistani. Although still concerned with placing him, Yanely now put this practice to work in different ways. She established a fictive kin relation with Hakeem through his mother's appearance. She forged a temporary alliance across racial lines by using bodily traits such as skin, hair, and eyes, the prominent markers of race. In the process, Yanely complicated the categorical basis of race, the meanings of bodies, and the very certitude with which racial knowledge presents itself.

The participation structure of cooperative learning also provided opportunities for kids to implicitly teach one another moral and ethical lessons about race. As this same activity was drawing to a close, I returned to the kids as Yanely stepped back to inspect their collaboration. She demanded of Connor, "What the heck is that?" and flatly declared to Mark, "You drew everything ugly." Mark said, "The only ugly thing is you! Woo Woo!" Connor continued his beat, "Hoot hoot! Hoot hoot!" "Idiot," Yanely rolled her eyes and continued drawing. Mark asked, "Yanely, why you drawing so ugly?" Not glancing up, she retorted, "I'm not drawing ugly, look at your face." Soon Mark began singing, "We are the lazy generation!" "Stop!" Yanely yelled. Mark modified the lyrics and sang, "She is the lazy generation!" "Yeah right," she said. Connor joined in: "*Yeah!* Right!" Mark now sang, "Oh! We gonna rock out today, party today, we party all night." Yanely said to Mark, "Sing a song, dedicate it to our class." Ms. Lee was still with Hakeem's mother, and the class was quite wild so I tried to calm them down. I stood in front of Mark to interrupt his singing and dancing: "Excuse me, Justin Timberlake," using a pop singer whom many kids liked, incidentally a white one. Yanely objected loudly, "He's not white!" Mark paused, turned his head to look at her, then turned back and continued singing. Yanely realized her blunder and said, "I'm not being racist or nothing." Mark heard and continued singing, still not looking her way. Yanely again repaired herself and said directly to Mark, "Sing 'What Goes Around Comes Back Around,'" a single by Justin Timberlake that was currently popular. Mark turned his body and belted out an impassioned rendition of the chorus.

The sequence that began with Yanely ascribing Mark's race represents a moment of authentic teaching and learning about race—where kids were learning how to be with and against race, when bodies are important and when and why they are not. Yanely violated the established cosmopolitan ethos by implicitly claiming that Mark's racial ascription was more important than his artistic portrayal, indeed that his racialized body was the most important performative feature of the context. Mark's subtle shift in tone and body language let Yanely know she had erred. In case it is not obvious, I should emphasize that Yanely was hardly the type to apologize, even when she was in the wrong. Neither did she did care to uphold any arbitrary notions of politeness. Her repair work was her way to make an apology. Her first attempt ("I'm not being racist or nothing") was not enough, because in the contemporary color-blind era, it can be easily interpreted as violating the taboo about naming race. Realizing this, she continued her repair work by telling Mark to sing the song. Mark's tacit acceptance was symbolized by his singing. This is not to say that these moments completely shifted Yanely's racial worldview. Even flashes of insight must accrete, be absorbed, and be reinforced. But the unique interactive space of collaboration provided multiple opportunities for kids to acquire the skills and capacities of navigating multiracial milieus, creating an inclusive ethic and transforming race.

Despite their fleeting character, laboring in shared tasks constructed a relationship between kids that was unique. This relationship did not lie on the continuum from friend to stranger or from friend to enemy, nor was it characterized by the positive affects associated with friendship. This is what made these activities so important in the construction of conviviality—they forged relations between kids who would not ordinarily be friends with one another. While the development of friendships was somewhat unpredictable, they were often based on some similar interests and registers of style that drew on and transformed race through the creation of affective sentiments (chapter 2). The bonds created out of shared tasks, while making no pretense to love or mutual admiration, were as important as those formed through affinities. Ignoring the dense web of relationships created through these routine classroom activities would tell a partial story, and a dismal one at that, for putting all our efforts toward destroying race in friendships is an impossible task. Friendships cannot be engineered, nor do I think we should wish to even if it were possible. Collaborative activities are a way to form bonds of civility between students without the need for affinity and affection. The sloughing off of the weight of hierarchies of smartness and status hierarchies of popularity or coolness and the favoritism of friendships redoubles the humanizing potential at stake in collaborative practices.

THE COLLABORATIVE BOND: NEITHER STRANGER NOR FRIEND

The cumulative effects of the shifts, ever so slight and imperceptible, in the way kids perceived one another increased the density of kids' interactional networks by bringing together those who simply would not meet. In theory, schools provide a meeting place for kids to experience the same activities and rituals in a relatively small space over long durations of time. In reality, many kids either remain strangers or interact on an unequal field because of friendship, smartness, coolness, or race. I devote considerable space in the paragraphs to follow to discussing the relation between Keisha and Lucas because these are two kids who, absent these collaborative activities, would not have developed a working respect or a relationship. They would remain strangers. Keisha and Lucas were not friends before they entered fifth grade, nor did they become friends throughout the year. Living in the same neighborhood but at different ends, they perhaps would have given one another a passing glance at one of the many parks between their homes, or grazed shoulders on a crowded bus or subway. The racial, spatial, and gendered divide in social relations, as well as the divergence in consumption and style that are partly related to them, practically ensured that Lucas's and Keisha's social networks and experiences significantly diverge. Again I insist that the point is not to suggest that adults should intervene in the way kids form attachments and how relationalities become meaningful aspects of their lives. Rather I highlight the potential of collaborative activities in giving kids opportunities for meaningful encounters with those with whom they occupy the same space but often do not truly meet.

Keisha was proud of her roots and belongings. A Black girl from the projects, she derived immense pleasure by expressing her identity as being from "the hood." Feared by most kids and respected by all, her no-nonsense, tougher-than-leather exterior masked her sweet personality. Her friendship network was grounded in her residence in the projects. She counted Steven, Mark, and Darryl as her best friends and Jacinta as one of her good friends; these were all the fifth-grade kids who lived in the projects. She cultivated her "ghetto" persona as she called it and quietly functioned as the guardian of its authenticity. Lucas's outer orientation was as uncultivated as Keisha's was guarded and reserved. To know Lucas is to know that he did not love anything more than he loved Mexico, a love that he expressed at any opportunity. Sometimes he interjected his love for Mexico out of the blue, as when he sat there sighing until someone asked him what was wrong. He sadly remarked that he was ineligible for the Mexican presidency because he wasn't born there. Lucas had a few other affections. He loved watching soccer but not so much playing it, to his father's chagrin, and playing wrestling but not so much watching it. Besides his family, Lucas's only other expression of tenderness revolved around his best friend Abdul. He never named any other friends, only amiably remarking that he liked and was friends with everyone. Lucas was the kid who would valiantly comfort a crying kid, or help a humiliated kid who had tripped up off the floor. Although I had a great rapport with Lucas, my adult status meant more to him than my participants. He was the only one of my boy participants who was visibly flustered when anything remotely sexual came up around me. One time Sebastian relayed to me a dirty joke that originated with Lucas. Lucas was devastated and avoided my gaze the rest of the afternoon. He was also sheepish when I expressed my shock upon finding him engaged in a rather violent-looking wrestling contortion one day in the park.

Whether you consider their differences superficial, deep, or somewhere in between, Keisha and Lucas had few things in common. But collaborative activities allowed them to recognize their transcendent commonalities, beyond their various "differences," social networks, pop culture consumption patterns, and all those other things that "matter" to kids or analysts. Consider one of their earliest collaborations. It was the first activity of the day in the meeting area at the front of the classroom, a writing "mini-lesson" on revising leads. The kids sat on the floor in a loose huddle next to their writing partners as Ms. Lee read an example of a simple lead that needed revision. After modeling examples, she gave another example and asked the kids to think of a revision with their partners. Instantly, all the kids oriented their bodies to their partners and the room began to buzz with life. Even kids who had not been paying attention knew to team up with their partner. Keisha and Lucas began immediately. There was no warm-up chitchat, no discussion or disagreement about who should go first, no procrastinating by clarifying the task. Keisha simply began, "I think they should change the action and how they said it." Lucas wasted no time either and replied, "I think they should change the setting or talk more about the setting." Those were the only words exchanged. They looked at each other and nodded for a few seconds. Then they both cracked a smile and burst into giggles. They surveyed the room with their gazes synchronized—Lucas with a crooked smile and Keisha nodding in satisfaction at their efficiency. Ms. Lee waited another minute for more partners to finish, reiterated her point, and sent the kids back to their seats with the task of spicing up the lead on their writing pieces in progress.

That instant when both Keisha and Lucas's smiles were turning to laughter, their heads tilting back while their gazes met to confirm that the other was experiencing something similar, they experienced a flash of perception. In this instant, Keisha and Lucas saw one another simply as they were right then and there—as collaborators or co-conspirators. Their collective action stretched beyond the task as they surveyed the room in unison, with the same mixture of satisfaction and delight. Through their collaborative task they discovered common ground beyond their differences. Most relevant would be their orientation to school, one that notwithstanding appearances was at core indistinguishable. Both of them seemed to be saying, "Let's just get this business over with! I'm not thrilled about this but it takes less energy to do it than to resist!" Perhaps it was moments like this that led Keisha and Lucas to realize later that they also shared an orientation toward the dramas that punctuated classroom life. Neither of them liked to "start shit." Lucas actively defused tension, and Keisha refused to escalate drama, although she seemed to enjoy taking it all in. There were many occasions when a dispute erupted between their peers and Keisha and Lucas would glance at one another to gauge their assessment of the situation.

On another level, Keisha and Lucas remained opaque to one another. They knew little of one another's family, out-of-school activities, and experiences, and only a vague idea of one another's attachments and belongings. Decades of mainstream multicultural discourse in schools have convinced us that kids must "know" about one another and understand their differences in order to "get along." I am suggesting precisely the opposite. Keisha and Lucas did not need to know about one another or their respective "differences" to encounter one another as humans. A human encounter is one in which kids did not view one another as inferior or superior, or as competitors, or as another body in space, but one with which purposeful action in the world can be accomplished. The specific character of Keisha and Lucas's encounters, or any kids' for that matter, overturns the conventional scholarly and commonsense relationship between collaboration and affective propensities.

THE RELATIONALITY OF MULTIRACIAL CONVIVIALITIES

The current phase of informational capitalism has generated research asking the very same question that generations of scholars have asked of schools: How can we cultivate positive affective states so that knowledge can be generated (so that learning can occur)? Geographer Ash Amin (2012) has refocused attention on "collaborating strangers," arguing that they are one of the ways civilities are generated in hybrid and plural living conditions. Such scholarship illuminates the humanizing potential of collaboration by demonstrating how bonds formed within working communities generate embodied empathetic and ethical understandings, where "people simultaneously learn about, learn how and learn *to be*" (Duguid 2008, cited in Amin 2012, 40, emphasis added). These insights are culled from empirical work in various workplaces or "communities of practice": from craft- and task-based sites of artisans and insurance processors to the highly creative sectors of scientists, software developers, and performance artists.[10] Amin asks us to rethink the nature of conviviality by reversing the causal arrow conventionally drawn between practice, relationships, and affective stance. This perspective is extremely productive for thinking about the unrealized possibilities for conviviality in schools.

The conventional understanding that guides multiculturalism within and outside schools is that individuals are divided by ethno-racial differences that must be reconciled through recognition and then tolerated. Once this process is achieved, individuals can develop trust, and *then* can work together on shared goals like an academic inquiry, designing a workplace innovation or getting a traffic sign installed in the neighborhood. "Multicultural" knowledge and affective states like civility, reciprocity, and trust are thought to be crucial *prerequisites* to collaboration. The kids' collaborations propose the contrary: the kids didn't need to know about the foods and festivals of one another's "cultures," and furthermore, kids don't need to be friends. Some kids disliked one another, and collaborative practices did nothing to change that. The kids' collaborative encounters were chock full of conflict. Disagreements, frustration, an elbow in the ribs or poke in the back were part and parcel of extended collaborations. But expressions of conflict were always secondary to accomplishing the defined task: they were ephemeral and did not extend into any other arena. For these kids, conflict and cooperation were not dichotomies, nor were they analogous to stranger and friend. Contrary to popular belief and scholarship, we don't need multiculturalism to build a community in an idealized Kumbaya sense for kids to learn together!

I suggest that the relative dearth of insights from schools on this matter stems from the conceptual legacy on which educational scholarship is built. Despite the robust literature on cooperative learning in schools, this scholarship is rooted in social psychology, with its attendant faulty assumptions of race. Although well-meaning, this work conceives of differences as naturally repulsive and antagonistic. If trust or distrust is assumed to arise from some original sin of difference as it were, scholars are unlikely to explore how trust can be an "acquisition(s) of practice, with all its qualifications" (Amin 2012, 55). Furthermore, these assumptions discourage scholars to explore how local hierarchies play out in classrooms to produce antagonism, racial or otherwise.

A significant source of antagonism in PS AV stemmed from the school's structuring of smartness. The fact that sorting students is the preeminent function of schooling highlights the incompatibility but not *impossibility* of collaboration. Collaborative practices could not have been humanizing if embodied distinctions of intelligence were as operative as they were in Ms. Anastasia's classroom. Teachers' uneven use of cooperative learning strategies may very well be linked to students' refusal, coupled with teachers' sense that they do not serve the larger purpose of individually defined success.[11] The practices in Ms. Lee's class had such profound effects because they were regular and recurring features of the class. Sporadic and irregular practices do not create embodied habits and dispositions, nor do they change the affective structure of a classroom. Recent educational reforms have only ramped up the instrumental and credentializing function of schools. Research has shown that even caring, experienced, and skilled teachers shift from social and engaging pedagogies to more rote, individualized, and outcome-oriented methods when faced with the high stakes of assessment (Valli and Chambliss 2007; Valli, Croninger, and Buese 2012). Because the current stress and pressures on teaching and learning are disproportionately inflicted on struggling students and schools, further research is needed to document if such students have already withdrawn their assent to participate, even in activities that are outside the current toxic structure of schooling.

Finally, these practices could not contribute to incipient cosmopolitanisms if the neighborhood did not provide a catchment area for the meeting of such diverse kids. That much may seem obvious, but when we consider the segregated nature of our nation's schools and neighborhoods, it bears repeating. Of course, demographics alone do not produce convivial social relations. In fact, the alienating conditions of schools may exacerbate already-existing tensions among different groups. In Ms. Lee's classroom, collaboration contributed to the kids' antiracist sociabilities by providing opportunities for kids to interact in ways that they would not otherwise. Collaboration constructed relationships that ran counter to dehumanizing racial types, essentialized meanings, and the dictum that we need to stick to our own kind. Such practices hold much potential for realizing the promises of diversity. We claim diversity in schools is important, but we flounder when it comes to articulating what it helps us achieve. My argument illuminates how diversity can help develop antiracist praxes and more human ways to be. Diversity is an important prerequisite, but it is not by itself enough. The conditions under which students encounter one another are crucial. At the same time that we advocate for diversity, we need to advocate for institutional policies that bring students together in communities of practice. We need to unabashedly champion schools as sites of humanization and insist that it is only our entangled relationalities that make us human. This is part of the tragedy of schools—they are our first public, one with tremendous potential. Many students not only are denied the learning opportunities that arise from exploring together, but also miss out on the humanizing effect of collective inquiry.

4 ◆ RACIST OR FAIR?

I was casually participating in a conversation with Jacinta and Mark in the art studio as we worked on our projects. In the midst of their reminiscing about the previous academic year, Mark abruptly turned to me and said, "Last year our teacher was a racist. She didn't like Blacks or Puerto Ricans." Jacinta immediately countered him. "Ms. DeAngelo was *not* a racist!" Mr. Freidrich asked for all eyes on him to announce the next steps. Mark quickly whispered to me, "Yes she was," before turning toward the teacher. I was jolted out of my participant role. When the kids called someone a racist, it was a rare and serious charge, one where the threat of violence lurked. Normally, kids warned or censured others with a statement like, "You're *being* mad racist right now," implying a lack of awareness that is mutable. Otherwise, accusing someone of being a racist was a source of humor among the kids. They enjoyed exploiting such comedic opportunities, as when Selena asked Lillian for a marker and specified "the black one." Joseph quickly called out, "Ooh, that's so racist!" to the embarrassment of Selena and the laughter of kids in the vicinity. Such comments could elicit laughter because of the mixture of confusion and taboo surrounding contemporary discussions of racism.[1] Humor often points to unresolved dilemmas, and the debate about Ms. DeAngelo was one particular manifestation of the larger one that continually plays out in the US public sphere. Indeed, "Is this racist?" veritably encapsulates our "sprawling, unwieldy and often maddening . . . national conversation on race" (Hartigan 2010b). As the kids debated Ms. DeAngelo, they articulated the key themes and conventions evident in the broader sphere. Akin to these public disputes, the DeAngelo drama became a site of racial transformation because learning *racism* is a key aspect of learning race. As in other spheres, kids actively interpreted and brought disparate elements together to apprehend and make meaning of a germane issue in their lives. In their struggles to make sense of racism on the local scene, they contended with issues of truth and fairness, as well as how racism operates in the world beyond this particular drama. It was a site where kids were shaped as racial subjects in unpredictable ways.

That the issue of racism emerged within the conglomeration of practices of discipline was, however, utterly predictable. The theme of discipline haunts conversations about racialized inequality and education. Social-scientific research has convincingly demonstrated that discipline is a premier site for the production of racialized inequalities, and the "school-to-prison pipeline" is a well-mapped phenomenon (Gregory, Bell, and Pollock 2014; Losen 2014; Noguera 2014). Black and brown students, especially boys, are more severely punished than white or Asian boys. Poor Black and brown boys even more so, and poor Black and brown boys with learning or physical disabilities are at the receiving end of our most inhumane and punitive disciplinary measures. This is a straightforward example of how institutional racism operates: zero-tolerance policies and increased police presence in schools "push out" and "funnel" Black and brown boys into the juvenile or criminal justice system, leading to large-scale inequalities. In her highly textured and nuanced ethnography of "bad boys," Ann Annett Ferguson (2001) convincingly demonstrates the destructive way routinized punishments stunt the possibilities of boys so identified. Perhaps better than any school ethnography, her book shows how boys craft and negotiate their subjectivities as Black and male in their interactions with school practices, and the dignity that is ultimately at stake for them. In this chapter, I explore effects that go beyond the bad boys and the straight and narrow path of the pipeline. I argue that the site of discipline is one powerful way that schools subject kids to race, although with more ambiguous and contradictory meanings than we have come to expect.

To understand how discipline becomes a site of racial formation, we need to recognize that discipline is not just or primarily about race, nor does it pertain only to "bad" kids, schools, or neighborhoods. Discipline is a fundamental concern within virtually every educational institution, as it was in PS AV, a good public school (according to students, parents, teachers, official designations based on test scores, local reputation, and my own estimation). There was no police presence, metal detectors, or threat of juvenile detention. Suspensions and other disciplinary measures did not disproportionately fall on racially minoritized kids. But yet discipline became an active site for racial formation not only because discipline is such an obsession in schools, but also because the central categories of "good" and "bad" that we employ to make sense of it are entangled with race. These central categories guided the way kids and teachers interpreted one another's actions (Hartigan 2010a).[2] In this chapter, I explore how the register of discipline guided the interpretive ways that kids made sense of this drama, the surprising lessons kids learned, and how this meaning making contributed to racial transformation on the ground. I conclude by putting insights from the kids' experiences to work in a way that inspires us to think anew about discipline, fairness, and justice.

THE STICKINESS OF DISCIPLINE CATEGORIES

Nothing that goes on in schools can be understood without taking discipline into account. To appreciate its pervasiveness, we need to consider not only the compulsory nature of mass schooling, but also the fact that any teacher's agenda is often in direct opposition to a student's agenda.[3] The kids' fundamental struggle revolved around the desire for "free time," or as some kids expressed it more radically, "free time all the time!" or "no work for a whoooooole year!" Kids were always ready to seize "free time" and employed any method at their disposal to do so. As soon as a teacher stepped out into the hallway, kids immediately sprang to life in a flurry of interaction. There was no telling what fascinating occurrence would transpire in those few moments. Most of the spectacular performances and forging of friendships, reputations, romances, and identities occurred during free time. It was the time to enact and create the curriculum of everyday life, a living and constantly evolving subject matter of which the kids' critical cosmopolitanism was but one aspect. If we also consider that kids willingly and pleasurably engaged in certain kinds of schoolwork, such as cooperative learning activities (see chapter 3), the kids' demands start to appear less ridiculous, unrealistic, or idealistic.[4] Rather, their desires underscore the arbitrary, excessive, and even unjust nature of control, and allow us to approach kids' perspectives on discipline with an open mind.

How did kids view discipline? They viewed it all the time, experiencing it as a constant obstacle to their bodily autonomy.[5] Kids related to and evaluated teachers chiefly through the constraints and categories provided by the ever-present requirements of control. Besides their classroom teacher, the kids had six other teachers they met on a weekly basis for the better part of an hour. The kids' attitude toward this time had very little to do with the subject matter and everything to do with whether teachers were "nice" or "mean." "Nice" teachers gave kids more free time, did not exercise as many controls over kids' bodies and labor during work time, and did not use humiliation to punish infractions.[6] Although there has been a shift in the ideal of a productive classroom, from kids silently working at their own desks to the loud buzz of kids actively at work, even "nice" teachers have to exercise extraordinary control over kids in this more "relaxed" classroom organization.[7] However, there were significant differences depending on whether a mean or nice teacher was at the helm, an effect that was immediately palpable. Some teachers were so oppressive and demeaning that I could not resist the urge to escape. For instance, Ms. Mathews, the math specialist, who thankfully came in only monthly rather than weekly, would regularly humiliate multiple kids upon arrival in order to signal the change in authority and to achieve her version of order. On a day when I missed her arrival, I entered the room as she was interrogating Eliza and accusing her of lying about her work. She stopped only when she noticed James was out of his seat and yelled at him, "Where do you think you're going?" Eliza's trial then ended with a terrifying "Get back to your seat!" Sabrina walked in from the bathroom and froze at the scene. She was then blindsided by her own humiliation. Ms. Mathews noticed her entrance and barked, "Where were you?" Sabrina replied, "Bathroom." Mathews asked menacingly, "Did you ask permission to go?" Sabrina simply answered, "I didn't need to." Infuriated and incredulous, Mathews yelled, "Your teacher lets you go to the bathroom without asking?" Sabrina nodded, as did other kids in support. "Do I look like Ms. Lee?" she barked as she took a few steps toward her. Sabrina shook her head, and Ms. Mathews turned to the class to announce, "When *I'm* here, you don't do whatever you want." I found such scenes hard to bear. As much as I would prepare myself to be around teachers such as Ms. Mathews, it was rare that I lasted more than a few minutes. I would get up and roam around the school or neighborhood. Some kids even got in trouble when their eyes longingly followed me to the door. "Eliza, where are your eyes?! . . . Is there something more interesting, Lucas?!"

Much as kids related to teachers through discipline, the reverse was just as true. The categories of "good" and "bad" were central for teachers, guiding how they treated and thought about kids. Obtaining their force through the school's system of punishments and rewards, "good" and "bad" categories are just as salient as or more salient than measures of supposed intelligence, ostensibly the categories for which schools are tasked to sort.[8] From the perspective of school personnel, "good" kids make it easy to enact control—they submit and appear to do so willingly. As you may suspect, all kids regularly enacted interests that were opposed to teachers' rules, regulations, and expectations. That is, *all* kids acted "bad" to some extent. *No* kid willingly complied with every teacher's demands. The pertinent questions become: How do some kids acquire the "bad" label? Is it a matter of quantity of bad acts? And what's this got to do with race?

The job of a cultural analysis of race is to illuminate the processes through which "sticky" categories of good and bad graft on to categories of race. Appearances and interpretations were key to this process, but not in a straightforwardly racialized way. A racial analysis would draw a straight line between the criminalization of Black and Latino males in society at large and teachers categorizing Black and Latino boys as bad. This perspective omits teachers' active interpretation of kids' practices, movements, and internal states in the real time of everyday life in classrooms, interpretations that are based on more ambiguous criteria than a racial analysis suggests. It would also ignore how kids' perspectives on questions of fairness and justice shaped their interpretations of racism, and how these interpretations became part of their racial subjectivities. In short, this closed-circuit analysis eliminates how this drama of interpreting racism (and others) was an important site for racial meaning making and transformation.

RACIST OR FAIR?

Fairness is how we evaluate discipline. It's the central theme when we debate whether something is racist in the public sphere. If someone is punished for behaving badly, this is indisputably considered fair. Things are rarely so straightforward with charges of racism, because what looks and feels like racism to one person could be seen as fair treatment by another. The DeAngelo debate pivoted around fairness. Before I was privy to the deliberation about whether she was racist, I had already heard the kids dispute her fairness. During a loosely structured classroom activity, Ms. DeAngelo's name came up and Steven, one of Mark's best friends, dismissed her with "she's mean." Eliza, one of Jacinta's best friends, was just as immediate and adamant as Jacinta in her defense, "No she's *not!*" Jacob, overhearing at the next table, nodded, "Yes she is." Steven began to recount why he "left" her class, more accurately how he transferred classrooms in an agreement that pleased his father, the principal, Ms. DeAngelo, and himself. He explained how Ms. DeAngelo kept telling him to shut up, and that at first he would "ignore it." He told his dad, who told Steven to "stay cool, she doesn't know you yet." Then one day she told him to shut up "for no reason and I told her 'make me, you can't tell me that.'" At that, Jacob walked over to tell his own tale. He recounted how Ms. DeAngelo had kicked his mom out of the classroom on the day when parents came to observe the class, a theoretically open invitation formalized once or twice during the school year. Jacob walked back to his table, satisfied with the reaction to his story, Steven shaking his head in disapproval and Eliza struck silent.

Although Ms. DeAngelo was not characterized in racist terms, Steven established her irrational, undeserved, and *unfair* treatment of him. Mark expressed this in an explicitly racial register when talking to Hakeem and me a few days after the initial accusation in the art studio. The boys were discussing especially fun times with nice teachers when Hakeem mentioned that his brother thought Ms. DeAngelo was fun.

MARK: He said she was fun?

HAKEEM: Yeah.

MARK: We only had free time two times the whooole year.

HAKEEM: So did we [in another teacher's classroom].

MARK: Stop lying son! Y'all had free time every thirty-seven and a half minutes [extended day]. . . . She don't like Black people, she racist.

MK: Why do you say that?

MARK: Because. She don't like Dominican people, she don't like Puerto Ricans, she don't like Blacks.

MK: You think that's true?

MARK: I *know* that's true.

MK: Did she like you?

MARK: ((so-so face)) And Darryl, you know that boy Darryl? She hated him.

MK: Yeah?

MARK: That's why, that's why I ain't go to summer school. My mother told the principal.

Mark, with the help of his mother, was able to challenge the teacher's evaluation of his academic standing, and by implication her fairness and professional legitimacy. This is not a precedent most teachers appreciate. It partly explains Ms. Lee's emphatic defense of Ms. DeAngelo, a position that stood in contrast to her own disciplinary style, explored later in the chapter.[9]

It was the end of the day during the casual hubbub of activity when kids were writing down their assigned homework, gathering their things, and tying up loose ends. Mark was joking about possible responses to a homework prompt to write about a "lucky moment" when Ms. Lee walked by. Steven playfully pretended not to see her and exclaimed, "My first lucky moment is when . . . I came to fifth grade." Ms. Lee and the boys bantered about humorously until mention of Ms. DeAngelo's name quickly deteriorated the encounter. Mark shook his head and said, "That teacher did *not* like him!" Steven added, "She was mean!" Ms. Lee defended her by saying that she could have sent Steven to summer school if she wished. "Why would she send me to summer school if I passed all my stuff? And Ms. DeAngelo was racist," Steven declared. "She *was*," Mark affirmed. This turned into a heated exchange where Ms. Lee vehemently denied the charge while Mark and Steven passionately avowed it with statements such as "She didn't like Blacks," "She didn't like Puerto Ricans," and "My whole family said it!" Although Steven tried to defuse the tension and change the subject by asking Mark an unrelated question, Ms. Lee warned the boys about "throwing the race card around, you know a lot of people do that 'oh, you don't like me? You're a racist.' Come on!" After Mark's denial, "No! We don't say that!" Ms. Lee asked how they could be sure that "Ms. DeAngelo didn't like you because you didn't behave?" At this, Steven was indignant: "No she didn't! I always behaved! Every time I turned around, she accused me of talking, and then she goes in my face and tells me I'm stupid. That's why I had to talk back to her." When Ms. Lee questioned the veracity of his account, Steven added, "*Yo!* She told me to shut up!" After bringing up another instance where Steven was not telling the truth, Ms. Lee said, "At the same time, Steven, don't you think sometimes you should shut it up?" This remark does sound quite harsh (Mark even exclaimed "Ohh!"), but Steven and Ms. Lee's warm relationship (explored in the pages to follow) softened what could have been a severe blow to Steven's "face" in the classroom. It was clear that the conversation had run its course; the kids lurking around to hear cemented this fact. Steven added his finale, "I speak the truth! And only the truth!" He then turned his attention to me. "Iww, Maria!" he said laughing while looking into my teacup. "It's black dots in there! Oh look, it looks like a piece of hair!" "That's just from the tea bag," I explained. Steven glanced to make sure Ms. Lee was gone, raised his eyebrows and said, "You drink tea bags?" Not acknowledging the sexual reference that was currently in vogue, I flatly noted, "You need tea bags to make tea, right?" He put his arm around Mark's shoulder and laughed, humor working to pierce the tension and restore balance in the room.

With its multiple breaches of the classroom order, this two-minute interaction became a spectacle in the classroom. The first breach was Ms. Lee's public censuring of Steven, something that rarely occurred in their delicate relationship. Furthermore, Mark and Steven breached the taboo of maligning a teacher's character in the most serious way barring sexual impropriety. And finally, they broke the color-blind taboo by mentioning racism in the present within the school. While kids openly talked (and joked) about race and racism among one another, they never did so with an agent of the school. Within the school's formal curriculum, racism existed only in the past—firmly tucked away in social studies textbooks and historical fiction. If kids tried to pierce this taboo during formal discourse, Ms. Lee censured them, telling them to "stick to the text" or directed the conversation back to the past. Within formal school talk and curricular materials, color blindness holds a discursive monopoly.

Color blindness is simply our official talk about race in the United States.[10] If one tries to articulate race in any other register, one is struck by its dominance in the public sphere by getting invalidated, silenced, or ridiculed. Color blindness structures this debate so rigidly that most debates appear ritualized. Ms. Lee marshaled the tools of color blindness predictably. She denied the kids' truth claims by accusing them of "pulling the race card," the principal way of discrediting accusations of racism (Jackson 2008). She then evoked the meritocratic playing field, the all-purpose weapon in the color-blind arsenal. As Eduardo Bonilla-Silva (2013) points out, abstract liberalism (individualism, universalism, egalitarianism) is one of color blindness's central frames, allowing what appears to be racism to be simply the result of reasoned action. It very well may be the case, as Ms. Lee argued, "that Ms. DeAngelo didn't like you because you didn't behave." What appears to be racism is, from the color-blind perspective, fair and ultimately deserved.

My interest in this debate is its pedagogical nature—how kids learned about race as they improvised and interpreted their way through it. It was not just the principal participants who did so. Bystanders were also parties to this classroom drama and had to interpret what was going on. It is instructive to delve into how "good girls" like Jacinta and Eliza articulated their views on discipline, fairness, and racism. We discussed Ms. DeAngelo during an interview after we had walked by her classroom upon their request. The girls were giddy about snooping, and they started reminiscing about the numerous ways Ms. DeAngelo favored them and gave them special freedoms. I was surprised, considering her generally humorless expression, what I had heard, and her well-known reputation as "strict." I asked if she really was one of their favorite teachers. Eliza gushed, "I just loved her, she is so *so* nice." Jacinta affirmed longingly, "I miss her."

MK: I didn't know you guys liked her so much; that's nice.
JACINTA: They say she's racist but she's not.
ELIZA: She's not.
JACINTA: Just because, you know they say people hate Black people, but it's not true, they're being critical and saying stuff like, saying stuff like "Oh you guys hate us" but sometimes they be like talking about the white people or the Spanish people. So anyways, they said she's racist just because um, she send Mark to summer school and you know how Mark says "Oh she's racist because she sent Black people to [summer school]." Yeah, but it's not, she's not racist 'cause maybe she's putting you there because you *need* it.

After a momentary interruption, the girls got back to the conversation, something that rarely occurred in the frenetic pace of group interviews:

ELIZA: She is like the nicest old lady I ever had.
JACINTA: ((laughs)) Old lady! She's nice though.
ELIZA: But, I'm not saying it in a mean way but Darryl says she's racist because um she always says shut up to Darryl in the middle of class, 'cause he's always the one talking, every single hour, and she goes "Shut *up* Darryl" and he starts saying "f you" and stuff like that. Right in front of her! And she sent him down to the principal but the principal won't even do anything.
JACINTA: I feel bad 'cause she would always get the hardest class. She got Darryl and Steven. Steven was in the class too, for a little bit of days. . . . But the other teacher, I'm not trying to be mean to the other teacher that Steven and Keisha had. That teacher didn't care how they acted or anything. She would be like "Oh that's fine, they're throwing chairs and everything, oh that's fine." ((leans back and throws her head back, swirling a wine glass with one arm and delivers in a lazy voice)) "Who cares, they're throwing paper, that's fine."
ELIZA: She's a first-grade teacher now.
JACINTA: She doesn't care, she doesn't put her mind to it, she doesn't care if they do something wrong. So I think Ms. DeAngelo was actually a better teacher 'cause

she would actually pay attention, she would be like "Okay, if you do this, you're in big trouble." Ms. Kotsou would be like "Oh who cares?"

Eliza and Jacinta also evoked the meritocratic playing field as the key to their argument. Ms. DeAngelo was only being fair and treating all children equally, and Steven, Mark, and Darryl did not measure up to her standards. Her fair, balanced, and indeed righteous persona is constructed against her polar opposite—a teacher without these standards whose class effectively became a zoo. By the girls' calculation, Ms. DeAngelo established rules for one and all. Jacinta and Eliza played the game better and were rewarded. The boys did not. This was fair, just, and good.

From my experiences discussing this particular drama with my own undergraduate students, many of them aspiring teachers, I have learned how interpretations of Ms. Lee and Ms. DeAngelo are shaped by their adherence to color blindness, which encapsulates their racial worldview and does not necessarily fall on predictable racial lines—that is, white students defending DeAngelo, Black students defending the kids. Those who subscribe to color blindness assume Ms. Lee's defense of Ms. DeAngelo is true. Sniffing out Steven's boisterousness, they conclude he deserved to be disciplined, although not so harshly. Those students critical of color blindness and its shoring up of white supremacy assume Ms. DeAngelo is a racist, as is Ms. Lee for her complicity and defense of Ms. DeAngelo.

I would like to shift attention to the legalistic frame that structures this interpretation. The perpetrator model of racism ensures that, preoccupied with reaching a verdict on Ms. DeAngelo, any outcome, guilty or innocent as it were, will be impotent. Critical race scholars have demonstrated how judicial focus on the intensions of the "perpetrator" effectively maintains racial discrimination by making it nearly impossible to prosecute racism. Perhaps more insidiously, this framework serves to legitimize all forms of racism that do not fit the wrongful action, person wronged, and wrongdoer model (Young 2012, 506–507). Mica Pollock (2008) found as much to be true in her analysis of the everyday workings of the Department of Education's Office for Civil Rights, the institution charged with investigating and resolving disputes concerning racial discrimination in schools. She argues that centering intent and fixation on *causes* rather than *effects* of discrimination obfuscates the workings of racism, leaving "victims" of discrimination ignored. Furthermore, color blindness places those who make claims on trial, suspected of playing the race card and, ironically, marking *them* as racists for making race relevant when it is not.

I raise this point to say that Ms. Lee's inability to at least acknowledge the kids' perspectives is not a personal or professional failing. Teachers' avoidance of race talk has been well documented by researchers working in US schools at the primary, secondary, and even tertiary levels (Michie 2012; Pollock 2004; 2008). Educators (among others) are ill equipped to deal with such issues that regularly erupt in schools, and they fear where this kind of talk may lead and the emotions it might bring forth. In this specific instance, engaging with this talk might have led to acknowledging the kids' embodied knowing of race, with all the complexity that this phrase suggests. As Ferguson (2001) explained in her ethnography, the "bad boys" experienced and understood the arbitrary and unjust nature of school policies through their bodies and emotions. In the same way, Steven knew that there was something amiss with Ms. DeAngelo's treatment of him, her suspicion of him, her singling him out. It was similar to Mark's response when I asked him if he thought his claim was true. "I *know* that's true," he responded. This "knowing" was lodged in his body, and the manner in which he said it suggested it held more weight than the other evidence that he elaborated. It was a knowing that was however discounted, implicitly by my playing devil's advocate, by Jacinta and Eliza, and by Ms. Lee. This knowing was not based on a rational calculus of evidence, whereby I behave *plus* she suspects me of misbehaving *plus* she does the same to my Black friend Darryl *equals* DeAngelo is racist, although it was partly based on that too. Rather, both Steven and Mark *felt* something that they could keep articulating only as "she didn't like Blacks or Latinos," an explanation that faltered when they tried to elaborate further. What "proof" would the boys need to convince their peers, teachers, or others? They could not claim "I know because I felt it," because we do not consider feelings valid, subjective as they are. The only valid knowledge is that within the rational frame, one that kids are not assumed to fully possess in any case. Add to this the fact that it is virtually impossible to prove someone acted in a racist way, barring some confession of racist intentions, and all this practically ensures that claims of racism will be dismissed. Steven's emphatic "I speak the truth and only the truth" was his refusal to be discounted, and points to his awareness that there was more at stake than the particulars of this argument and the public persona of those involved. What was at stake was a certain vision of the social order, the relevance of race, and the authority to name racialized experience as such. The boys' inability to account for what they experienced in a way that honors what they both felt alerts us to a critical moment of dissonance. These moments must be explained if we are to disrupt them and their troubling repercussions.

HOW FAIRNESS PERPETUATES RACISM

What did happen between Ms. DeAngelo and the boys? Institutional theories of racism and critical race accounts leave a gap in our understanding of how disturbing racialized effects are perpetuated in day-to-day interactions in classrooms and further afield. Is the question of whether something is racist completely unknowable? While I agree on some level that the question is misleading, the obsession with the question allows us to exploit the opportunity to offer a more complex answer than a verdict of "guilty/innocent." Understanding how so-called color-blind racism operates can allow us to address the troubling repercussions that some kids face, to say nothing of the countless others who face harsher consequences. A cultural analysis dives into the waters left uncharted in so-called structural accounts. In this case it provides the tools to explore how the broad and omnipresent register of discipline creates such struggles. These tools can provide an account of how Ms. DeAngelo *unwittingly* produced harm because of her ideas of good and bad students, and the way these categories stick to race in complex and indirect ways.

Ms. DeAngelo represents the familiar "strict" teacher, universally admired among her colleagues for not taking any "bullshit." Although I did not observe or interview Ms. DeAngelo, my formal observations of over a dozen teachers' disciplinary styles in this research, informal observations of dozens of other teachers and substitutes during trips, assemblies, and library time and in the hallways, and dozens of other experiences in my other research and as a teacher have shown me how, despite internal variation, strict and not strict teachers are prototypes that operate with similar general principles. From my analysis, I can safely assume that Ms. DeAngelo, like other strict teachers, had very clear ideas of how a good student looks and acts and that she held all students to these standards, a common enough definition of fair. However, the conception of fairness as sameness ignores the racially saturated nature of our evaluations: of beauty, intelligence, and, most relevant here, "goodness" and "badness." I give Ms. DeAngelo the benefit of the doubt and assume, again I would wager safely, she is not an "old-fashioned racist," discriminating and treating people based on their skin color or other bodily markings. Her dislike of Steven was *not* because of his skin, ancestry, or last name. I am just as certain that, like other strict teachers, she *did* dislike him because of the way he talked and dressed, his overall attitude and stance, and, yes, his "behavior." As Ferguson (2001, 92) notes, students are marked as inappropriate "through the very configuration of self that school rules regulate: bodies, language, presentation of self." Steven's speech style, his gold chain, the name brand of his clothes, the cocked angle he wore his baseball hat when he was not in class, the tempo with which he walked, the manner in which he gesticulated and held his body were indirectly yet potently shot through with racial meanings. Her distinctions of "good" and "bad" were based on these intermediary objects and postures and space (here, the public housing projects where Mark, Steven, Darryl, and Jacinta lived). These objects and spaces do not have a skin, but they are nevertheless mapped onto racialized bodies. These distinctions form the filter for "the broad latitude for interpretation and cultural framing of events" whereby one boy's "fooling around" is another boy's disruptive behavior (Ferguson 2001, 92). And because they are not apparently racialized, they produce harmful effects that persistently appear to be fair.

Fairness and justice, the foundational myths that govern the national collective consciousness, are always already entangled with the issue of inequality. Racial, class, and gender inequalities, to the extent that they cannot be denied, must be explained *away*. They must be explained as the result of a fair and just system that discriminates different levels of ability, intelligence, hard work, willingness to play by the rules, and good ol' character. American culture exerts an inexorable pressure to uphold the meritocratic myth. Even some who know it is a myth publicly uphold it, for challenging it involves questioning the legitimacy of the nation's institutions, as well as one's own professional status and position within them. This may be why some teachers continue to uphold these myths to their students, to protect their own professional legitimacy and because they fear students' reactions to laying bare our deepest social conundrums. Despite the commonsense assumption that all hell would break loose if teachers and students engaged in frank discussions of racial inequality, small-scale exploratory studies have shown that in fact the striking opposite occurs. Students, especially those who are most "at risk"—left behind several times, forgotten, or "pushed out," thrive when presented with a critical curriculum of everyday life (Akom 2009; Cammarota 2014; Ramos-Zayas 2003). In this particular case, sorting through the conundrums of the Ms. DeAngelo drama with the kids would have validated their experiences and knowing, a knowing that is virtually impossible to name through our racial baggage or the impoverished language of color blindness, or even the scholarly discourse of institutional racism.

INTERPRETING RACISM

Schools inculcate the official view of race in various unpredictable ways outside of the formal curriculum. Some of these episodes will be quite spectacular, such as Steven and Mark's disputing with their teacher. Other less remarkable events occur as kids try to make sense of the occurrences in their everyday lives, as when a kid silently wonders if a teacher's preferential treatment of a student has to do with him being "like" her. The dispute between Ms. Lee and the boys represents a dramatic moment of racial learning that left more debris for Mark, Steven, and the kids who participated as audience members. The way these lessons became part of kids' racial subjectivities cannot be read off an analysis of the event alone. Any racial "lesson" is incorporated within the multitude of other lessons that kids have learned, their subjective apprehension of the world, and their network of relations. The kids who were directly or indirectly involved in the Ms. DeAngelo drama did not understand it in a singular manner. Nor could we predict the way they understood it from their racialized positioning. Even kids whose racial worldview was most similar to the official version did not simply buy it hook, line, and sinker because the school authorized it. They had to interpret these events and reconcile them with their situated stance on race and the larger world, their view of fairness and justness, and their sense of the trustworthiness of social institutions like school.

Eliza's rejection of the racist charge against Ms. DeAngelo, for instance, must be understood in terms of her racial worldview. As we saw in chapter 2, Eliza practiced and expressed cosmopolitanism in her friendships, pop cultural consumptions, and crossing, bridging, and displaying her worldliness. Like other kids, Eliza often performed herself as Albanian and expressed excesses of belonging, at times claiming she was part Australian because she had kin there or called herself American/Albania/Australian. Despite her participation in the local cosmopolitan ethos, her racial worldview was at times hegemonic and her celebration of diversity ambivalent, especially in the stark line she drew at interracial mixing in romantic relations (explored in chapter 5). Eliza's rejection of Ms. DeAngelo's racism must be situated in terms of her sense of self (classed, raced, and gendered) and dignity. This drama simply did not chafe her enduring self. In fact, it validated it. From her standpoint, Steven, Mark, and Darryl pulled the race card to contest the treatment they deserved: getting sent to the principal for being bad and summer school for not being smart. For some "good" kids like Eliza, it is simply easier to think about the world in the way that it is officially narrated, protecting them from having to challenge a whole set of truths to arrive at a reality that can be disorienting.

Although Jacinta narrated the same position as Eliza, she did not apprehend the events in the same way, nor did her interpretation entail the same embodied meanings. Jacinta had to sort through a mess of conflicting information and understand it through her contradictory subject locations as a poor Dominican kid from the projects who was considered a good girl with a scholastic orientation, middle-class aspirations, and white middle-class best friends. As she sorted through these things, meritocracy and fairness were perhaps more urgent for her than they were for Eliza. She had to reconcile her position with her parents' talk about the deserving versus the undeserving poor, as well as her stance that it was unfair that Blacks could make fun of Dominicans and other Latinos and not be considered racists. Furthermore, as someone who was often interested in school subjects, Jacinta was impatient with "bad" kids' disruptions wasting her time. On the other hand, Jacinta also belonged with Steven, Mark, and Darryl on a concrete level. They were her friends, they lived in the same building, they knew one another's families, they relied on one another in emergencies. Jacinta was not naïve. She was well aware that racism existed and wrestled with these issues. At times she was willing and able to critically apprehend the world and pierce its contradictions because the official narration of the world chafed her experiences and dignity. In this particular instance, Jacinta's improvised and embodied calculus guided her to ultimately stand by her position that the game is fair and you have to play by its rules. This was not an easy stance to take considering the multiple perspectives she inhabited. First and foremost, Jacinta had to validate her perspective, experiences, and aspirations. She had earned Ms. DeAngelo's favoritism through her own efforts, duplicitous as they may have been, and her skin color did not work against her. Her position was a part of the crafting of her own subject position, and how she fit into the world. While all the kids' racial worldviews are open-ended, Jacinta's contradictory subject positions made her perspective more vociferous and fragile. As she hopefully gets exposed to critical perspectives (after all, her favorite subject was social studies, and she liked learning about "slavery and racism and stuff like that"), we could imagine Jacinta making connections and revising and complicating her stance.

In contrast to Jacinta's ambivalence, Steven's racial learning was decisive. He felt Ms. DeAngelo's aversion firsthand. Although I argued that her aversion was not directed at Steven's body, it was nevertheless *felt* on his body. However terrible this was, Steven (as well as Mark and Darryl) did not go home crying, nor was his self-worth destroyed as some liberal social science would have us believe. Although Steven did not have the language to articulate it, he had one of his first explicit lessons in the hypocrisy of our official truths and the illegitimacy of our institutions. While Ms. Lee treated him with care and love and he liked her and thought she was "cool," he saw that her position as teacher aligned her with the official view of race. For kids hanging on to school by a few threads as multiple factors push them out, piercing the school's illegitimacy can highlight the school's exit. This was not the case for Steven. For him, it was an affirmation of the superiority of his critical knowledge of everyday life that regularly pierced adults' hypocrisy.

Eliza, Jacinta, and Steven learned different things in distinct ways. This is to say nothing about the other kids who overheard, wondered, discussed among themselves, and made meaning of this dramatic story. For instance, when I asked Joseph later what he thought of the dispute since he was so carefully spying, he wrote it off quite simply, "All teachers are racist." I purposefully troubled this simplification by asking if he thought Ms. Lee was a racist. When he said no, I raised my eyebrow to point out his logical fallacy. He qualified that it was the "oldies." His overall critical stance on race (see chapter 1) structured his interpretation. Perhaps his overdetermined interpretations would make him cautious of placing trust or experiencing warmth with "old" teachers.

Another troublesome repercussion of this event involved other bystanders' interpretations. For a kid like Juan, this drama reinforced what was, for him, the fact that Black people falsely cry racism and that Blackness (and Black culture-oriented Latinos) was equated with badness and criminality. This was such an uncontroversial matter of fact for Juan that he didn't even feel self-conscious expressing it in conversations with Black kids. There were more than a few awkward moments during an interview with Juan and Keisha when Juan talked about how bad some high school was because "all the Black people go there." He did not even sense Keisha's warning, nor did he understand my questioning of his stereotypes. Juan was making connections that incorporated his experiences of race. This drama served to support his feeling that it wasn't fair that Black people get to act bad and call racism when punished. Juan's lessons have to be understood in light of the local culture of masculine cool, one to which he had very little access and often felt alienated by, as well as his protective parents who were fearful of urban gangs and what they might do to a small and soft-spoken boy like their son. It is possible that as Juan goes off to junior high, makes new friends, gains more spatial freedom in his neighborhood, and begins to participate in various multiracial consumption-based subcultures, he will have experiential evidence and the will to challenge problematic constructions of Blackness and criminality. But at that point and time, his interpretation was what made sense. Juan's lessons about what race is and means proceeded by learning about racism.

To underscore the unpredictable nature of how such lessons will be incorporated, I cannot help but include a story of one ambiguously white girl in a "smart" fourth-grade classroom in 1984. I will never forget the bodily feeling, my eyes almost blinded and my face, ears, and skin burning with embarrassment as my teacher abruptly and viciously screamed at my classmate Andrew to "get that dirty necklace out of your mouth!" This incident did not instantly change me, but it has been packed in my racial baggage ever since, influencing my journey in ways that I can only surmise. What I know now and knew then is that this incident had much to do with the fact that Andrew was Black. A rational calculus would suggest otherwise; the teacher liked all the Black girls in the class well enough, to the extent that she liked any of us. But I knew otherwise because I felt it, like Steven and Mark. The phantom pain from that incident activates any time I witness a kid spoken to with maliciousness, whether or not race has something to do with it. It has taken me many intervening years to explain how race operated in that fourth-grade classroom, and I hope this account provides an opportunity to do something different.

REIMAGINING DISCIPLINE

Recent scholarship provides compelling normative accounts of what discipline "should be": caring, compassionate, and directed toward (re)engaging students in the learning process (Noguera 2008). It is hard to imagine what enacting these principles looks like in practice; scholarship has yet to provide any descriptive account. How can teachers manage to keep a classroom in "order" while embodying the deep principles of caring? How can they prevent the bad apples from spoiling the bunch, without exclusion, humiliation, or fear? Do any models exist between or beyond the military and the zoo? And perhaps even more difficult, can any of these ways be fair? The way my college students express their fears of chaos and disrespect with a hard-line attitude and the way Jacinta and Eliza contrasted Ms. DeAngelo with Ms. Kotsou suggest that these are the only options. But Ms. Lee and Ms. DeAngelo provide a more productive comparison, and allow us to get beyond categories of "good" and "bad" and simplistic narratives of fairness.

Despite her official sanctioning of color blindness, Ms. Lee practiced a style of discipline that disrupted the way ubiquitous good/bad categories adhere to race and racialized styles. She understood that "good" students do not all look, sound, or act in a specific way. Steven for his part was not a conventional model student. But Ms. Lee did not disparage him for using Black English varieties or dressing in hip-hop style: she never told him to pull up his pants or to leave his gold chain at home, as other teachers did. She was not disgusted at his pop cultural tastes that many teachers consider vulgar. As we saw, she even used these as a resource in her teaching. She did not save her affections for kids who were the most visibly pro-school or who immediately complied with her every request and aimed to please her at every turn. She understood why some kids might be bored during lessons and tried to get them engaged in creative ways that often created more work for her, as discussed in chapter 3. She did not treat uneducated parents patronizingly, nor did she constantly complain about some parents' lack of visible engagement in their kids' schooling. This is in precise contrast to how many "strict" teachers think and act toward kids and their parents who don't look, act, sound like "good" students or parents. They sometimes show a level of polite disgust or exasperation, but more often they apply their "impartial" criteria to them and their behavior, a fairness that works to push some kids away from school.

Although I urge us to rethink "badness," I will admit that Steven was one of those kids who was capable of being bad. I have seen him exhibit his full calamitous power in the face of inept teachers or substitutes, teachers whose classroom management skills were so poor that they could not mete out disciplinary consequences, nor would they want to draw attention to their ineffectiveness by asking for administrative assistance. Steven was primarily interested in making the classroom a fun and funny place, chiefly by injecting humorous commentary to the activity at hand. He could read "nice" teachers' limits and was skilled at toeing the line and breaking rules in a way that didn't raise their ire. He had learned to do so because his larger agenda forced him to walk the tightrope of being well liked by teachers and admired by his peers. Ms. Lee often allowed Steven to "call out" when other kids were censured. She sometimes allowed herself to enjoy his wit, other times rolled her eyes in slight disapproval that did not embarrass him but let him know she was eager to pursue the matter at hand without interruption. Other times she simply ignored him and proceeded with her agenda, so that he was allowed his quip and she did not waste time responding to it. It was a perfect balancing act on her part, producing a symbiotic truce whereby she co-opted Steven into the classroom order. And he was absolutely hyperalert and focused on everything Ms. Lee said, much more so than the most conventional pro-school students. If Ms. Lee was annoyed because she could not be heard over the classroom chatter, it was Steven who would invariably yell at his peers to shut up. Steven was so attentive that if Ms. Lee forgot what or if she had said something, she would ask Steven because she knew he could recall. Ms. Lee kept Steven engaged by disrupting the sticky assemblage of badness with race and style.

Keisha, the tougher-than-leather girl, was if not completely engaged, then voluntarily complicit in the classroom order out of sheer emotional attachment to Ms. Lee. Keisha could also be "bad," and the most repeated tale in the field involved Keisha punching a kid in the face so hard that he spun around and fell to the floor. Incidentally, Keisha decked the boy because he finally revealed their suspicions that he was racist with a patently bigoted comment. The story had legendary status, and no kid omitted the details of Keisha gingerly holding onto her apple in the other hand, and nonchalantly taking a bite after the punch heard round the playground. The kid was South Asian, although that detail was not as often repeated as the fact that he was in the accelerated or "smart" class. Keisha did not have a bad label because she did not disrupt the order of the classroom. However, it was clear that Keisha had the potential to delegitimize any teacher's authority. Her compliance was tenuous at best. I have seen her challenge teachers simply by looking at them dead in the face, or position her body so that she seemed either ready to pounce or willing to move only by force. In all cases, teachers backed down and let her have her way. Mostly she was subtler, muttering comments under her breath to show how much she begrudged the enterprise of schooling. And that was only because Keisha was methodically economical in the expenditure of her efforts and it was simply easier to get school tasks over and done with.

I immediately liked Keisha not only because she was funny and warm, but because I am instinctively attracted to kids who reluctantly play the school game. Ms. Lee was the same way, as are many of the teachers I have bonded with over the years. Ms. Lee deliberately began applying her magic on Keisha on the first weeks of school: she positively reinforced any of Keisha's actions within reason, established private jokes with her, called her "my little cookie," and nominated her for classroom tasks that teachers usually reserve for "good" kids, like carrying messages to the main office. Keisha was too tough to lap it up in any obvious way, but not tough enough to be impervious. By mid-October, Keisha even allowed herself to be enthusiastic about some learning activities, primarily cooperative ones. This attitude did not extend to her dealings with other teachers. As soon as another teacher took control, Keisha instantly put on her game face, one that unambiguously said, "Don't mistake my cooperation here for submission. And don't push it." This was her default attitude when I met her. On a hot September afternoon on the second week of school, Ms. Lee interrupted an activity to admonish the kids on their sluggishness. She asked, "Can you imagine if we were in a school without AC?" Keisha muttered loud enough for the kids around her to hear, "I would have left the school." Keisha seemed to be saying to her teachers, "For your own sake, don't push me." I don't think I can emphasize Ms. Lee's effect on Keisha any better than by recounting her mother's reaction at graduation. After the ceremony, Keisha's mom hugged Ms. Lee tightly with tears in her eyes, thanking her for loving her daughter. Another time, Keisha's mom told me how much she admired Ms. Lee, explaining how she was the first teacher who liked her daughter and made her daughter like school. These things still resonate for me emotionally, and highlight the extraordinarily delicate improvisational dance that good discipline involves, and what discipline means. Discipline is a method to achieve the impossible task of engaging all kids in the learning process.

Ms. Lee was tangoing not just with Keisha and Steven, but with over twenty more kids at the same time. She disrupted the predictable good/bad assemblage with Eliza and Jacinta, although in opposing ways. The girls successfully occupied the good label and played the game so well that Ms. DeAngelo was convinced. Ms. Lee, because she did not subscribe to the conventional categories, was not so easily deceived. As Ms. Lee watched them too enthusiastically skip away to bring the attendance to the main office early in the school year, she turned to me and said, "I'm watching those two. I don't buy the act, at *all*." Her intuition was correct. They regaled me with tales of exactly what they were up to when Ms. DeAngelo, or more rarely Ms. Lee, gave them spatial privileges together. They roamed to unauthorized areas of the school, climbed on sinks to spy on girls, and stuffed toilet paper in the toilets. So convincing was their act that they were occasionally able to escape the impenetrable lunch ladies to roam the halls. I became worried when, in the midst of laughing about their adventures, they told me how they had an excuse at the ready if accosted: "We would just say we're going on an interview with Maria." They did think they were clever.

Although Ms. Lee was "onto" them, she dealt with them differently. I have seen her embarrass Eliza for relatively minor things. On one occasion Eliza was sneaking to her closet to get something she should have taken out in the morning; Ms. Lee harshly told her to sit down. It was severe enough to catch many kids' attention, and Eliza was beet red as she skulked back to her desk. Ms. Lee always maintained a calm demeanor. Thus any slight deviation stung, and she had a few working levels of sting. She never embarrassed Jacinta, not even the few times when Jacinta disappointed her. Admittedly, Jacinta was quicker to follow rules, but this is not why Ms. Lee treated her differently. Rather, Ms. Lee's calculus made her sensitive to each kid's personality, background, and possible futures. At some not-quite-conscious level, Ms. Lee knew that a few embarrassing moments might help Eliza understand that she was not as slick as she imaged herself, and that it would be better to follow the rules. Ms. Lee knew Eliza's temporary crimson cheeks would not be a part of an impending downward spiral. Her middle-class privilege and doting parents would ensure that she would be reproducing her middle-class status and would most certainly go on to college. Ms. Lee knew that Jacinta's path was not paved in stone, that things could go many ways. Although she clearly enjoyed school and had professional aspirations, chance circumstances could pull her away. Ms. Lee appreciated that Jacinta was sincere about school and had a genuine interest in scholarly learning that is independent of parents' social class. I recall one enjoyable experience when I helped her reorganize the social studies books in the classroom library (she was the library monitor). We were so caught up in the task that Jacinta begged me to ask Ms. Lee if we could continue instead of going to science. Knowing as well as I did that science consisted of listening to an uninspired teacher's canned lecture and completing a manufactured worksheet, Ms. Lee acquiesced. Jacinta and I talked as we sorted, about history, religion, the politics of multiculturalism, the follies of George W. Bush, and more. She earnestly expressed a wish to know more about the past and how it affects the present. I told her that this was one of my interests in college, in my own way subtly reinforcing the path toward her aspirations. This is what Ms. Lee was doing. She wanted to be the one of the forces that helped Jacinta achieve her aspirations amid uncertainties and obstacles.

In the conventional understanding that equates fairness with same exact treatment, Ms. Lee appears inherently unfair. Some might even claim that she is just as unfair as Ms. DeAngelo. Some kids occasionally thought this way, but it was a fleeting feeling that she would quickly soothe. For instance, on one occasion Omar tried to continue the humorous breach in the classroom business by calling out a funny remark right after Steven made one. Ms. Lee censured Omar although she had not censured Steven. Ms. Lee picked up on Omar's bad feeling and within a minute called on him to come to the blackboard amid an enthusiastic sea of waving hands. Scowl off, good feeling restored. However exhausting this sounds, Ms. Lee was improvising, guided by an embodied ethic of caring and, I would argue, fairness. It is a more compelling conception of fairness that is relative to ends rather than means. Should we be satisfied with a goal for discipline, or education even, that "everyone be treated exactly the same way"?

The politics of race in schools, indeed the politics of education, require that we debate questions about the ultimate values and goals of education. In response to cries of "that's not fair!" we must argue the difficult position that, while entrenched inequalities exist, we must be "unfair," that is, treat some differently to be fair (Brayboy, Castagno, and Maughan 2007). We must insist that there are worthier goals than same treatment. In my estimation, Ms. Lee's disruption of the good/bad, race/gender assemblage was worthwhile in its repercussions for racial learning and transformation.

To disrupt the disciplinary assemblage of skin and style, we must understand how conventional notions and obsessions of discipline continually produce the sticky categories of good and bad, how they grab hold of racial meanings, become part of racialized subjectivities, and contribute to large-scale racialized inequalities. I hope that the Ms. DeAngelo drama demonstrates that blunt analytical tools contribute to some of these troubling effects by providing a language that obscures how race operates. An analysis that remains at the level of race and considers people only as racial beings ensures that we will continue to go in interpretive circles about whether an act was racist or fair, waiting in vain for the incriminating evidence that will never arrive.[11] All the while, people's felt experiences continue to be invalidated; troubling racial meanings, like those that equate racialized minorities with badness and criminality, are reproduced, and with racialized inequalities perpetuated and explained away by neat packages of meritocracy and fairness.

Despite the dreadfulness of racial learning within the site of discipline in schools, surprising and transformative possibilities lurk. Some kids exploit fissures within stagnant assemblages of race to derive at more critical understandings of the world. Steven, Mark, Keisha, and Joseph may not have had the conceptual arsenal of critical race scholars, but that did not prevent them from knowing what racism entails. Their critical knowledge highlights a fact often obscured in academic discourse: "old-fashioned" or individualized racism is much more similar to institutional racism than it is different. Both inflict injuries to bodies, deny opportunities, entail culpability by individuals, and are unjust. Concerned scholars and practitioners should begin by listening to students' perspectives and expanding the contradictions in their own and students' views to nourish their critical appraisals of their situated raced realities. Cosmopolitanism is not simply an acceptance, appreciation, or celebration of diversity; it must be antiracist and oriented toward justice. Discipline is a productive site for racial formation, the site where many kids will learn powerful lessons about race and racism. As this chapter demonstrated, kids will understand the processes and outcomes differently, and different contexts will pose their own conundrums and possibilities. If we are to join students on critical journeys, it will necessarily involve unpacking our own racial baggage, as well as our obsessions with order, efficiency, and control that are the hallmark of the way we do school. Ms. Lee, despite her mishaps when the issue of racism inevitably encroached in her classroom, enabled the kids' cosmopolitanism to flourish because her classroom was not a site where kids were known as "good" and "bad," nor a site where these categories grafted onto race. Her classroom was not a space of humiliation and exclusion. Treating all students with the dignity that is their birthright must be considered part of the struggle to consciously shape racial transformation toward a more just present and future.

5 ◆ ENACTING SEX ED

The way Oscar beamed when I told him how cute his girlfriend Jessie was, you would have thought I just complimented his newborn baby. My off-hand quip was an unintentional icebreaker, and from then on Oscar did not hold back recounting his romantic ups and downs to me. I quickly began to see that Oscar, quiet and reserved in the classroom, was a bona fide Lothario—always in love and enjoying every part of it, even the inevitable heartbreaks. His perfor-mances of the boyfriend role surprised me in their intensity and the way they challenged gendered stereotypes. When kids made fun of his declarations of love, he unapologetically affirmed his truth with head held high. Throughout the academic year, Oscar had been in love at least three times, four or five times if the unrequited ones are included. Jessie was his first real girlfriend in the fifth grade; their attraction was mutual and publicly acknowledged, the only required elements for an official couple. Soon after it became official, Oscar celebrated by decorating his binder with a bold "Oscar loves Jessie" surrounded by hearts. His online profile was full of romantic quotes, poems, and graphics—a silhouetted couple, lovebirds kissing, and simply the word "love" flashing at a dizzying pace. Jessie publicly displayed her affections on her profile with these manufactured declarations of love as well. Her friends monitored Oscar's feelings and brokered the couple's exchanges of messages in the schoolyard. Oscar and Jessie would wait with anxious anticipation, the unease morphing to glee with the delivery of good news. I suspected that one day the friends would carry a hurtful message to Oscar. My prediction turned out to be right soon enough, literally and figu-ratively. After her friends announced that Jessie didn't want to be his girlfriend anymore, Jessie herself arrived to slap him in the face for dramatic flourish.

There was not one obvious reason that led me to believe that Oscar would eventually be dumped. It was not because of imbalance in their affections or social standing, two of the usual predictors. Nor was it because Oscar was too nice or sweet, which is what some of the girls suspected post facto. Despite the impression the slap may have given, Jessie was also a nice, sweet kid who was well liked and had many friends. A girl's girl, she expressed love for her friends as enthusiastically as she did Oscar or any of her other subsequent boyfriends. Although I normally roll my eyes at commercial invocations of girl power, Jessie was one girl for whom the distinction was not just a slogan on her T-shirt. She had confidence, charisma, and a unique style that drew many admirers, boys and girls. She was one of the few girls in the English Language Learners class whose social network extended beyond kids who were currently or previously in ELL, like Oscar. My premonition was due to Oscar's steady adoption of a hip-hop cultural orientation and his crossing into Puerto Ricanness, interrelated processes that began with and well outlasted his six-week relationship with Jessie. My key interest in Oscar's relationship and the kids' romantic desires in general is the way they were entangled with race. Indeed, my argument is that sexuality is the site where race as embodied type materialized most forcefully in the kids' lives. Because the potential for racial reproduction and transformation is heightened within sexuality, the risks are higher and the urgency is palpable. Indeed, within the domain of sexuality it was imperative that kids become proper racial subjects. As this chapter explores, learning race is interwoven with learning sex.

In this chapter, I explore how kids navigated the core of our racial baggage—the assumption that there are distinct types of people and that people belong with their type—that consistently emerged in the sexual arena. Within sexuality, individuals had to "fit," "make sense," "be good for each other," or "make a good couple" in the sense of being of the "right type." Much as the heterosexual matrix operates pervasively and constructs sexual attraction to the "opposite sex" as the normal state of affairs, race operates through the discourse of "right type" that figures sexual attraction to the "same kind" as a natural matter of fact. These two discourses depend on one another, for types can persist only if they are reproduced through heterosexual procreation. Thus, developing into a proper racial subject is interwoven with becoming a proper sexual subject. Kids learned that couples must "fit" together in a variety of domains: parents' wishes for cultural, ethnic, or racial continuity as well as the racial common sense that suffuses the media, popular culture, and the public sphere in the United States. These pervasive discourses compel kids to reproduce them through their desires and practices. Without exception, when kids expressed sexual desires or discussed those of their peers, they had to contend with the "right type" notion. Kids had to acknowledge it even when couples or sexual attractions were of the same socially defined racial, ethnic, or cultural group. However, these discourses did not completely regulate desire. Just as often as not, kids' desires exceeded the boundaries of their "type." In these cases, kids had to mediate the "right type" obstacle through creative interpretive and interactional work. Oscar's crossings into Puerto Ricanness represent how he reconciled his desire with the "right type" requirement, practices that were also entangled with the crafting of his gendered and other spiritual belongings.

IT'S NOT ONLY ABOUT ROMANCE: SEXUAL ENTANGLEMENTS

On the surface, Oscar's crossings and refiguring of difference look similar to crossings within friendship explored in chapter 2. Like many of his peers, Oscar wanted to claim belongings that included his spiritual, social, and sexual desires and relations in addition to his blood, body, or place of birth. But crossings within sexuality were often missing the exuberance of those within friendship. In contrast, they were strained and coerced. It seemed that Oscar had something to prove, even though there were some aspects of truth to his crossings. Although Oscar was born in Ecuador to Ecuadorian parents and spent the first few years of his life there, he did have actual claims to Puerto Rico. His mother was living in Puerto Rico at that time with her partner, and Oscar had stayed with his mother there the previous summer. However, he began to claim Puerto Ricanness soon after he began dating Jessie, sometimes alongside his claims to Ecuador, sometimes in place of them. I first observed Oscar crossing in a space safe from the risks of his peers' evaluation. It was a writing assignment titled "All About Me," with one-page chapters on different aspects of the kids' lives (see chapter 2). Oscar described himself in his chapter "cultures": "I'm half Puerto Rican and half Ecuadorian. I like being Puerto Rican because over there it's much hotter than colder. In Ecuador it's a lot colder than Puerto Rico but the best thing is I'm proud to be myself. Every summer I go to both my countries. One month I go to Ecuador and another month I go to PR. They both have hot temperatures. I go a lot more to Puerto Rico than Ecuador. My mom is Puerto Rican and my dad is Ecuadorian." Oscar's writing piece showcases his creative crafting of self, and his concern to convince the reader about the primacy of his Puerto Ricanness. His visits to Puerto Rico were not recurring as he wrote in this piece, nor was his mom Puerto Rican in the conventional sense. Like all "deep crossings," Oscar's Puerto Ricanness was fictional, overturning the conventional way identity and belonging are figured.

Soon after this initial crossing, Oscar created and placed a graphic on his online profile in a prominent position that announced "Puerto Rican and Ecuadorian 4 Life" in graffiti-style letters. It replaced an earlier graphic celebrating his Ecuadorianness, a cloud of smoke in the background with "ECUADOR" in block letters seemingly exploding in the foreground. Oscar made his claims in compressed form with the graphic, in line with the visual nature of the medium. Unlike the old graphic of Ecuador, the new one included the phrase "4 Life," so that Oscar could emphasize the seriousness of his claim. The graphic remained on his profile for some time, perpetually performing his Puerto Ricanness until it was eventually replaced with a photograph of Oscar wearing a doo-rag and clutching a spanking new Nike sneaker near his face.

Oscar's opportunistic crossings, say when Puerto Rico or Puerto Ricans were brought up, were somewhat tense, and I often looked away just in case he would be challenged and embarrassed. As a somewhat quiet kid, he wasn't the most charismatic performer after all. I was especially uneasy during the spectacle of the classroom Multicultural Day when I found out Oscar was presenting Puerto Rico. Multicultural Day was an all-day classroom affair where kids were required to make public presentations on "their countries or cultures," that ubiquitous and familiar school ritual whereby schools invoke multiculturalism (see Kromidas 2011b for an extended account of the event). This was in the spring, well after his romance with Jessie was over. He was spared any humiliation at the expense of his friend Mark, who had asked Oscar to join his presentation since he was unprepared. The boys had planned the previous night on the telephone to take turns reading sentences that Oscar wrote to accompany his poster. Mark, you may recall, is African American by established standards that include the visible body and his own claims. Ms. Lee and his peers roundly humiliated Mark for defying the fundamental rules of multiculturalism that require that you must "look" like your claim. For instance, after the class corrected him for mispronouncing the dessert *flan*, Jacinta rolled her eyes and dismissively said, "He swears he's Puerto Rican," as his classmates laughed or snickered. As this was proceeding, Oscar nervously kept trying to move the performance along, not so much to spare his friend, but lest his number was called next. Although it wasn't, Oscar realized that like with all strategic crossings, the risk lurked. This raises two questions: Why would Oscar subject himself to the potential humiliation? And what's this got to do with sex?

It is true that we must understand Oscar's crossings in the context of his relationship with Jessie. But Oscar's romance was also bound up with his "growing up," and his attempts to claim a more masculine identity. Claiming Puerto Ricanness along with wearing the latest name brands associated with commercial hip-hop culture were, through the twisting circuit of Americanness, a way for him to look tougher and more mature and to effect an urban cool. "American" in the conventional sense was not his goal in any way. Oscar claimed Puerto Ricanness to overcome the foreignness that being Ecuadorian entailed, for the American male is more virile and tougher than the immigrant male. In the local context, ELL status was equated with an undifferentiated foreignness that was more threatening to boys' gendered requirements of cool. Despite the solid equation of ELL and "forever foreigner" status, Jessie's style, savoir faire, and Puerto Ricanness ensured that she was not locked into this category. Her Puerto Ricanness mediated a Latinidad without associations of foreignness, an urbanness without association of Blackness or delinquency, as it does for other Latin American youth in the United States (see Ramos-Zayas 2007).

I am not claiming that Oscar's desire to be "cool" or Puerto Rican was greater than his attraction to Jessie, nor does it make sense to think in these terms. Rather, I argue that these processes are irreducibly entangled. That is, becoming racial, becoming gendered, becoming classed, and becoming sexual are simultaneously operative processes, themselves entangled with everyday practices that are part of childhood—growing up, attaining greater spatial freedom, consuming pop culture, making friends, learning about the world and one's fellow humans. Like many of these processes, sexuality was a site where kids actively crafted their selves, often in ways that had to defy racial ideologies that prescribed what they should be, prescriptions that were often at odds with how they imagined themselves as being. But racial baggage emerged most forcefully here, exaggerating the regular anxieties and uncertainties of sexuality and of being a kid in general.

I am arguing that Oscar was compelled to claim his Puerto Ricanness, and his crossings did not proceed in the spontaneous, cheerful, devil-may-care manner with which friends crossed differences. Indeed, I never heard any mention of two friends not making sense because of their racial, ethnic, or cultural difference, although kids sometimes expressed good-natured perplexity if friendships crossed style boundaries. Within the sexual realm, crossing boundaries was risky and mediating difference became obligatory and characterized by angst. It is true that parents affected some of this angst, and not surprisingly, many parents hoped that their kids would maintain their language, religion, culture, and race. But to chalk up all the kids' creative mediations of difference within their sexual desires to some "cultural thing" or to racist parents would too readily mystify the larger sociopolitical and historical force of racial ideologies in structuring everyday life, and especially our most intimate sentiments. In the next section, I delve into the cultural dynamics of sexuality that make it an active site for racial transformation.

THE PANIC OVER CHILD SEXUALITY AS SYMPTOM

Public discourse on child sexuality is in a perpetual state of moral panic, compressing social and psychological fears and inciting increased surveillance and regulation of young people (Herdt 2004; see also Cohen 1972). Constantly bombarded by media tales of sexting, rainbow parties, and thongs for tweens, it would be difficult to *not* be concerned (Best and Bogle 2014). However, like all moral panics, the frenzy of child sexuality is out of proportion with the reality of threats to social and moral life. As Danielle R. Egan (2013) demonstrates in her summary of empirical research from the United States, United Kingdom, and Australia, children's purported hypersexualization is not nearly as salacious as the current discourse implies. Egan and Gail Hawkes's (2010) pathbreaking analysis of the foundational discourses concerning sexuality in modernity explains why the discourse of child sexuality in the Anglophone West is so fraught with angst. They argue that discourses on child sexuality rarely are or have been about children themselves. Rather, "childhood sexuality and the desire to bring it under control provided an avenue for addressing other cultural anxieties (e.g., racial purity, affirming the institution of marriage, and constructing more rigid gender boundaries)" (155). Indeed, the taboo nature of children's sexuality and their presumed innocence amplify many of the general anxieties surrounding sexuality, particularly the vexed concerns about the sanctity of marriage and maintenance of gendered differences and of childhood itself. Sexuality is such a charged site for the learning of race because intimacy (and related processes of marriage and reproduction) has been the premier site for racial formation in the United States at all levels (federal, state, and local), throughout the country (North, South, Southwest, West), throughout its history, and involving various sectors (economic, political, legal, educational). Sexuality has been one of the key ways to maintain the so-called racial purity on which white supremacy depends. Sex in the United States is always saturated with race, for sex reproduces race, and can threaten its very existence. The local manifestation of urgently subjecting kids to race in the domain of sexuality is born out of a much broader and tragic history.

Threatening the caste-like boundaries of race and white supremacy, interracial relations were, until quite recently, too dangerous to be controlled by mere social norms. Interracial boundaries were encoded and enforced by the so-called justice system, and their claims thoroughly woven throughout society. "Anti-miscegenation" laws have a deep history in the United States, with efforts to prevent the "abominable mixture" of whites appearing as early as 1692 in Virginia. While much scholarship has rightfully focused on the violence and terror inflicted on Black men in the South through these laws, Peggy Pascoe's (2009, 6) work demonstrates the "national scale and multiracial breadth" of these laws, their embeddedness in the fabric of US law and society, and their continuing pernicious significance in structuring the present day. When the US Supreme Court ended school segregation through the landmark *Brown v. Board of Education* ruling in 1954, interracial unions were still illegal in many states, until the Supreme Court's declaration of them as unconstitutional in 1967.[1] Hannah Arendt (1959, 49) pointed out the hypocrisy, arguing that the "right to marry whoever one wishes is an elementary human right" to which "political rights, like the right to vote, and nearly all other rights enumerated in the Constitution, are secondary."[2] This reveals the flash point in public opinion. While many northern whites supported integration of public spaces like schools, they reserved this enthusiasm when it came to intimate matters. A public opinion poll in 1958 showed that 79 percent of northern whites thought Black-white marriage "would hurt in solving the negro-white problem" (cited in Pascoe 2009, 296). It is true that there have been dramatic changes in these attitudes. It is also true that anti-miscegenation laws and systematic violence are no longer operative. This makes it easy to assume that interracial relations are, if not enthusiastically accepted, at least neutral territory.

Today, interracial relations are structured, that is, discouraged, by "softer" cultural rather than legal means: by ideologies that naturalize differences of race and culture. This makes them no less powerful. At their core, these ideologies of difference normalize the notion that there are indeed different "types" of people, that it is necessary to "stick to your own kind" and naturalize notions that people just "prefer their own" (Ahmed 2004, 195). It is productive to consider Pascoe's central argument about anti-miscegenation laws and public opposition to interracial intimacy—that these laws were seen as encoding "*nature* rather than politics" (2009, 1, emphasis added). What is striking is how, despite the dramatic changes in the form of appearance of our thinking, the fundamental core remains unchanged. Common sense dictates that people belong with their own race, as "natural" as elementary molecules attracted to one another. This core assumption is reproduced and legitimated everywhere the discourses of race or multiculturalism are active, that is, throughout the public and private spheres in the United States. And although these discourses operate more subtly, occasional flare-ups in the media showcase people's visceral reactions to the "unnatural" fact of interracial intimacy. For instance, when NYC's mayor Bill de Blasio was a candidate in 2013, a journalist in the mainstream press commented that many had to suppress their "gag reflex" when considering the mayor's mixed-race union (Cobb 2013). The extreme backlash and vitriol directed against the widely distributed Cheerios commercial in 2013 featuring a mixed-race family illustrates the fundamental role the child plays in this national drama. Protecting the innocent interracial child, who would be confused and belong to no place without a race, is perceived as a legitimate and impassioned concern.[3] Indeed, the figure of the child always haunts the future, and its entanglement with race and sexuality has not been theorized until quite recently.

In *Racial Innocence*, Robin Bernstein (2011) persuasively demonstrates how childhood and, more specifically, dolls and the play they scripted were historically important sites of racial formation in the United States, allowing these racial projects to appear natural and inevitable. Asking how the notion of "childhood innocence" became a "crucial element of contests over race and rights," Bernstein also finds the root of these answers in the anti-miscegenation laws of the nineteenth century (2). Thus the seemingly unbreakable crucible between childhood, race, and innocence is in many ways crucially melded with sex, and shapes large-scale racial projects and racial formation on the ground in a variety of ways. If part of the more exciting work in sexuality studies in the past twenty years has been to break down the separate spheres model and argue for the "contradictory and conflictual ways" (McClintock 1995, 5) in which sexuality, race, gender, and class are related, my work here insists that childhood is also critical aspect of this relation. My research demonstrates how kids are burdened with the heavy weight that we place on child sexuality—the purity of children and their psychological well-being, the sanctity of marriage, the reproduction of community, and the structures of racial and economic power.

WHAT AND WHERE IS CHILD SEXUALITY?

Even a little over a decade ago, Gil Herdt (2004, 40) remarked that little had changed since (in)famous sexologist John Money declared that childhood sexuality was the last taboo in sexuality research in 1967. Fortunately since then, researchers have begun to incorporate children's own perceptions of sexuality and their understandings of themselves as sexual subjects into reconceptualizations of sexuality (Allen 2005; Bhana 2007; Renold 2005; 2013; Renold, Ringrose, and Egan 2015).[4] These researchers not only insist that children are sexual subjects,[5] but also demonstrate how dominant notions of childhood innocence, the moral panics about child sexuality, and the regulation of child sexuality that they incite significantly inform how children experience sexuality in their everyday lives.

Being a child today means being entangled in a frenzied thicket of discourses, regulations, and controls of sexuality from multiple sources on multiple scales. These in turn are inscribed on children's bodies and become expressed through language and forms of affect. The affective lens becomes exceptionally useful in the study of sexuality, particularly child sexuality, for it frees sexuality from the realm of instinct and connects it with the totality of social and cultural facts (Herdt 2004; Lyons and Lyons 2011; Vance 2005). Thus the kids' desires become available to analysis, however much they may evade representation (Stewart 2007). That is how I read the kids' sexual desires and practices, as partly a matter of crafting of the self and partly a matter of interpellation. But there are always slippages in "the education of desire" (Stoler 1995; 2001). Sexuality is equally a matter of spontaneous emergence, out of kids' conscious control and out of the reach of the various institutions and ideologies that try to regulate it. This perspective illuminates the tensions *and* the pleasures my participants experienced within sexuality. Despite all the risks of rejection, humiliation, uncertainty, and the heightened marking of the body, kids derived much pleasure from experiencing, acting on, observing, and interpreting sexual desire. Enabled by recent literature that insists children are indeed sexual subjects, I continue on a rarely trodden path of asking how becoming a racial subject informs sexual desires and experiences. I explore what it felt like to experience desire within these raced, classed, gendered structures, the affective states they produced, and the interactional responses they obliged.

Although I was not looking for or asking about kids' sexualities, it did not take long to figure out that school was the premier space where kids enacted and formed their sexual subjectivities and sexual cultures. Sexuality was enacted and expressed everywhere and at all times, during math lessons, while sharpening a pencil, while walking down the stairs. It was a chief concern of my participants—the dramas, comedies, and tragedies that occupied much of their attention. It was thoroughly public, subject to observation, analysis, scrutiny, and debate. The large bulk of time and energy spent doing sexuality included expressing sexual desire by finding ways to get physically near to someone, joking, teasing, play; talking and speculating about who likes whom; imputing others' sexual desires from observed behavior; and obliging others to make their desires public. The kids went through elaborate methods of questioning to force confessions, simply because they derived pleasure out of the admission, not because they needed confirmation of their suspicion. In fact, the kids were especially astute readers of the signs of sexual attraction. These signs were not linguistically or behaviorally based, but it was nevertheless obvious to the kids (and to me) when snatching a piece of paper from someone was an enactment and expression of sexuality and when it was not. The body mechanics may have been identical, but the kids could read differences in energy as clearly as they could interpret any more obvious signs.

Indeed, the kids' sexuality exuded a kinetic energy that was tangible. From an adult perspective, the interactions surrounding sexuality appear rather mundane, even formulaic. For instance, the interactions between two kids who were "going out" were mostly short and heavily scrutinized, as seen in Oscar and Jessie's interactions. It was similarly so with talk about who was "cute" or "hot" or who made a good couple. Disregarding the other side of adult perceptions of child sexuality—that they are meaningless—the kids deeply felt their sexual interactions and their observations, talk, and analysis of their peers' sexuality were deeply meaningful to them. Sexuality was made more resonant because it was always imbricated with race, as well as gender and class, in the kids' lives. It was within desires, talk, and interactions surrounding sexuality that kids experienced their racial subjectivities most palpably.

PRESENT DESIRES AND REPRODUCTIVE FUTURES

Lee Edelman's (2004) notion of reproductive futurism is a crucial concept that helps illuminate how race is entangled in the regulation of child sexuality. He argues that this logic and absolute value lie at the core of our political discourse, organizing our collective life toward the good of the future child. The child functions as the emblem of futurity's unquestioned value and the figure through which the burdens of this discourse are represented.[6] Always imagined as adults in the making or in terms of their "becoming" (James and Prout 2015 [1998]), kids incorporated this reproductive futurism into their experiences of sexuality. That is, their present desires were weighed down with the imperative that one day they would marry someone of the "right type" and reproduce kids of their own. Reproductive futurism and the imperatives of race often manifested in kids' talk and anxieties about future spouses. These discourses structured kids' experiences and expressions of sexuality, and how they negotiated within and sometimes beyond them. This is not to say that kids deferred their desires to the future. Rather, they creatively negotiated them in a way that made them speak to their experiences in the present and their making of themselves as racial, gendered, and (hetero)sexualized subjects experiencing desire, pleasure, as well as anxiety and frustration in the here and now.

I was hanging out in the cafeteria with eleven-year-old Carly (white, self-described as "just American") and eleven-year-old Izel, conventionally Mexican American. Lunch was over and the girls were talking about boys, their "favorite subject," as they gleefully watched and evaluated each boy as he walked across the cafeteria to throw out the food on his tray. The excerpt shows how future concerns came into play with present desires, themselves both entangled with discourses of race and difference.

MK: So, who are the cutest [boys]?

CARLY: [Jack! Not in our class, in Ms. Z's. Oh my god! Oh my god! ((fanning her face))

IZEL: [Andy! A little bit MJ, a little bit Blake, and a lot of bit Andy!

CARLY: He's cute—for Izel.

IZEL: The good thing is we're both Mexican. I saw him wearing one of these the other day ((shows her bracelet that read "I (heart) Mexico on it")).

MK: So Izel, you want to be with someone that's Mexican?

IZEL: ((smiles widely and nods vigorously))

CARLY: Isn't that your culture that you have to marry a Mexican?

IZEL: I don't want to marry someone who's white, or who's American. 'Cause if I marry someone who was born here that would make me 100 percent American, because now I'm 50 percent Mexican and 50 percent American.

CARLY: I can marry someone Bangladeshi. I don't have a culture. I'm just American. It's so boring.

IZEL: Like what are you, English or something?

CARLY: If I was English, I would talk like this [inaudible, in a British accent]. I'm like half Irish, half British, half German.

At first glance, this interaction seems to point to the reproduction of hegemonic norms surrounding race and sex. Izel, a Mexican American, is properly attracted to a boy of the same "type." Her friend Carly approves and constructs this as a proper fit—"He's cute–for Izel," pointing to the suitability of the match in terms of what was understood to be the most important criterion. Izel immediately understood and agreed by explicitly elaborating the meaning to me, the outsider, "the good thing is that we're both Mexican." However, there are also counterhegemonic claims and meaning making involved in this interaction, as Izel's attraction to Andy was not just a direct adherence to having to "stick with your own kind." Rather, her comment ("I don't want to marry someone who's white") suggests an undermining of multiculturalist ideology and its centering of whiteness, an assumption just expressed by Carly's normalizing of herself as "just American." Her attraction to Andy has much to do with the making and crafting of her self and her future cultural orientation. Izel viewed her Mexican and American cultural identity, rather than static and essentialized, as fluid, open-ended, and of her own making—a state of being *and* becoming. To understand Izel's excitement while looking and talking about Andy, we must understand it as an aspect of both her desire for Andy as well as her excitement in the realization of her self-making and refusal to be made by others. In her own way, Izel understood the imbrication of sexual and racial subject making but negotiated them in a way that disrupted her positioning as a future sexual subject—one continually in the making, and unsettled static figurations of race and nation.

The way difference is always already embedded in kids' experiences of sexuality is also evident in the dialogue to follow, recorded during an interview with Jacinta, a ten-year-old girl of Dominican descent, and one of her best friends, Sabrina, a ten-year-old girl of Albanian descent. The talk is emblematic of the informal pedagogical manner in which interactions concerning sex and race transpired, and how this talk became embodied in affective states. It also highlights how reproductive futurism only compounded the general anxieties surrounding sexual desire. At this point, Jacinta was telling me about her then current boyfriend.

MK: What's his name?

JACINTA: Raffi. He has a lot of things in common with me.

MK: Like?

JACINTA: Because um, well we're both not divorced child but uh, we're both from Dominican Republic; we both look great okay? ((laughs))

SABRINA: ((laughs))

JACINTA: Aaaand, I guess that's it.

SABRINA: Wow! ((sarcastic))

JACINTA: Wait wait and, he's not close to my age. . . .

MK: How old is he? He's older?

JACINTA: Yeah, he's eleven.

MK: Oh!

JACINTA: No, but/

SABRINA: So! He's supposed to be older!

JACINTA: Not that old! [. . . ..] He's *not* smart.

MK: How do you know that?

JACINTA: 'Cause every time I be telling him a problem, like just kidding you're stupid anyways, he's like "No I'm not, tell me a problem, watch I could get it" and I would say something and he be like "What?" and I'm like "Oh you got to be kidding me."

MK: So intelligence isn't very important to you, looks are more important?

JACINTA: Well no/

SABRINA: Oh god! That's always what older people say/

JACINTA: Well not really because, because I don't know how like, it's not like I'm gonna spend the future with him, I'm not. . . .

MK: Okay, so you just think he's cute.

JACINTA: Yeah.

MK: So you like him 'cause one, you're both from DR.

JACINTA: For some reason, um, I'm gonna tell you, all the boys from the Dominican Republic, um, they really don't, don't like working, and so they're lazy/

SABRINA: Your dad is lazy?

JACINTA: Well my dad is not lazy, some of them, most of them ((laughs)), they just like to hang out with friends, have girlfriend

MK: Who told you this?

JACINTA: Well everyone I know that's Dominican, except me, ((laughs)) I'm not like that, I would like to work and get a nice future, 'cause then if I don't I'm just gonna end up outside without a house with like five hundred kids and ((laughs))

MK: So you don't want to get pregnant at fifteen and

JACINTA: [*No!* I don't like that.

SABRINA: [No! I don't like that either.

JACINTA: I know my cousin that she, she had a baby when she was sixteen/

SABRINA: ((gasp))

JACINTA: [. . .]And the thing I didn't like is I could tell my cousin was going to get pregnant fast, 'cause she was always be hanging out with her boyfriend, she would always get piercing everywhere, every single day she would come with something new, let's say a tattoo here, a tattoo on the back/

SABRINA: Oh my god, I hate that.

JACINTA: Some things on her ears, and things like that whatever, and she likes gothic music and then one day. . . .

MK: So the gothic music got her pregnant?

JACINTA: ((laughs)) Noooo.

SABRINA: Her boyfriend got her pregnant.

JACINTA: And also, you could tell that her boyfriend was trouble 'cause he would always like, he would always come in like he didn't care what anyone else thinks. You're not supposed to care what everyone else thinks but....

MK: A little bit.

JACINTA: Yeah, a little bit ... [...]

MK: So what kind of person do you see yourself with?

JACINTA: For some reason ... I don't know.

SABRINA: I don't know.

JACINTA: No?

SABRINA: Because my cousin, my mom's cousin married someone that was Arabic but we're Albanian and I don't know now.

JACINTA: ((pause)) I don't know like, I don't, it's not like I really care 'cause it could be like any country that's good, 'cause I don't like being racist, like let's say it's Arabic, if he works if he's good and he treats my kids right ... then it's good.

SABRINA: My mom's cousin which is my far far cousin, she got married and she got divorced because she like, her husband was bringing her [...] to her sister's house and the husband just left her like thirty blocks, like one mile away in the rain, with no cell phone, no umbrella, nothing. And she was just walking and she didn't have no money either, and he just keeps on like smacking her/

JACINTA: What?

SABRINA: And screaming at her.

JACINTA: If a man hits me, it's over. Okay?

SABRINA: They were only married for two months.

JACINTA: I'm not saying I would try to kill them, but I would just, it's like.... Especially if you have a kid, 'cause if it's a boy he would think it's all right to do that to girls.

SABRINA: I know.

MK: Exactly.

JACINTA: My dad doesn't think it's all right to hit girls and neither does my mom, 'cause if you hit girls you're a pussy.

MK: Well you know what happens, you know why some of these women stay/

JACINTA: Sometimes they think like "Oh, how are my children gonna feel?" It's like ((exaggerated exhale)) "How they gonna feel if they see you getting hurt and they have to hide somewhere?!"

While there are many rich meanings and agentive practices involved in this short talk, what concerns me here is how Jacinta's experience of sexuality, like Izel's, was negotiated through the discourse of reproductive futurism. Both girls constructed their own sexualities not through simplistic adherence to the "right type" discourse but in a way that connected their present desires with their future becomings. For Jacinta, this involved her upwardly mobile class aspirations. If anything, Raffi's Dominicanness (and his perceived intelligence!) worked to mollify her excitement and desire toward him as she imagined a future that looked different from many of the girls and women with whom she was intimately familiar. Jacinta's classed subjectivity—as someone whose family was on public assistance—was more salient in the imbrication of sexuality, gender, and race than it was for Izel, whose family was more or less middle class. Jacinta's classed (and raced) subjectivity was also more salient in her performance of academic standing (just as "smart" as her middle-class friends) and in the way she consumed pop culture. For instance, when I asked about her after-school activities, Jacinta described her favorite website that allows her to design a house. She viewed this as training for a future career as an interior decorator and remarked, "I know, I'm such a white girl, right?" Jacinta's making of herself as a classed and raced subject was incorporated into her experience of being a sexual subject. Her ambivalent feelings about her sexuality in the present and future cannot be understood without taking these dynamics into account.

Jacinta's ambivalence about her raced, classed, and sexual future self stands in contrast to her unequivocal irreverence concerning the reproduction of racial/ethnic purity. It is clear that Sabrina disagreed with Jacinta's counterhegemonic pronouncements, as she responded with a cautionary tale about the dangers of sexual crossings. Sabrina's friends understood her position toward this type of boundary crossing. Until the final month of the school year, Sabrina only ever expressed desire for a boy "back in my country," Albania. When her friends would talk about their crushes and relate the details of their flirting, Sabrina would talk longingly about how perfect the Albanian boy was for her, for no other reason really than the fact that he was Albanian. Jacinta interpreted Sabrina's tale much as I do—as a challenge to the moral lesson underlying Jacinta's preceding talk. Jacinta's response reiterated her previous sentiment, claiming "any country" could work and that she doesn't like "being a racist." In light of the presumed natural preference to desire one's own "kind," Jacinta's challenge was a formidable one. She emphasized this point by countering her friend's claim that crossing boundaries was the problem and continued to speak in more general terms about violence within intimate relations.

The two vignettes demonstrate how informal pedagogies of race circulated among the kids, and how sexuality was a site where different behavioral ideologies about race were made explicit. It is important to note how in both interactions, the counterhegemonic pedagogies emerged from racially minoritized girls (Izel and Jacinta) in discussions with their white girlfriends (Carly and Sabrina). This demonstrates how race, class, and gender are simultaneously operative in the kids' experiences and expressions of sexuality, operating in divergent ways for different individuals at different times. This is precisely why sexuality is such an important domain for girls, as well as boys. For within sexuality, the kids opened up these often implicitly racialized discourses, scrutinized them, and subjected them to debate. While the entanglement of sexuality and race produced anxiety and obliged kids to creatively and laboriously mediate differences or legitimize their desires, this did not prevent them from experiencing the pleasures of sexuality as important aspects of their embodied experiences. It is in these fleeting moments of pleasure and frustration that the core of our racial baggage was challenged and transformed.

BRIDGING AND CROSSING DIFFERENCES OF BODY, LANGUAGE, AND BLOOD

Enacting boyfriend/girlfriend subject positions and flirtatious encounters were also important sites to engage the entangled domains of sexuality and race. Besnik and Deirdre's romance illustrates these processes. They were a couple for a few weeks, getting together during the last few weeks of the school year when a "now or never" urgency prevails. They had their own obstacles of difference to overcome. Besnik is biracial—his father is from the Dominican Republic, his mother from Albania. While he considered himself "a mix," his classmates racialized him as Black. This was due to his physical appearance and his performances of Blackness through rapping, clothing, hairstyle, linguistic phrases, postures, and gestures. Deirdre is Latina ("Spanish" in her terms): her mother from the Dominican Republic and her father from Puerto Rico. While they both share parental roots in the Dominican Republic, Besnik's mixedness and his racialization as Black meant that they had to stress this commonality, both among themselves and to their peers, who often remarked that they were a "strange" couple, one that "didn't make sense." Besnik bridged their difference by displaying his knowledge of Spanish (which was extremely elementary), or by speaking in a stylized Spanish accent. He publicly performed these bridges at various times within the classroom and other spaces of the school. His practices illustrate both the necessity of addressing difference in the delicate business of romance and how this proceeded in mundane interactions.

Deirdre also constructed a bridge between their differences. In an interview, Deirdre emphasized a common bond with Besnik. When we were discussing her friends, she mentioned a group of "Spanish" girls in another classroom. I asked her if she spoke Spanish. She replied, "Yeah. I was speaking to Besnik before. We're from the same race, but he has Italian in his blood. Me, I'm Dominican and Puerto Rican." Deirdre made certain to highlight her linguistic bond with Besnik and went even further to say that they are from the same race, an even deeper bond than a linguistic one. By also saying "Besnik has Italian *in* his blood"—an error, as Besnik's mother is Albanian—she suggests that his "blood" is mostly of one race, the one they share. In her efforts to mitigate the difference between

Besnik and herself and the anxiety about this difference from her parents and friends, Deirdre was moved to transfigure the meaning of that material yet mystical substance of "blood."

Deirdre shifted the conversation from friendship to sexuality, and proceeded to talk about how "strict" her father was about boys, and the covert ways she had was forced to communicate with Besnik—borrowing a cousin's cell phone and meeting Besnik at her friends' homes. Deirdre's desire and the pleasure she felt from interacting with Besnik were interwoven with anxiety and frustration at her father's attempts to control her, as well as her family and friends' racialization of Besnik as Black. Deirdre explained to me that her father was suspicious of Besnik because he "looked like a punk" (a term suggesting unruly youth with racialized connotations). From an adult-centric or academic critical race perspective, it would have been more effective, more politically resistant for Deirdre to defy the negative connotations of Blackness rather than reconstruct Besnik's difference. Her statements certainly do not seem as forceful as Jacinta's "I don't like being a racist." But I consider the kids' participation in the everyday politics of race on their particular terms, asking what their interactional goals were at that time and place, how race stood as an obstacle to the realization of those goals, and what tools they had available to them at that time. From this vantage point, Deirdre's meaning making takes on a new level of significance. Deirdre was subverting the meanings of blood as well as flesh, and constructing Besnik's felt and claimed belongings as more important than the signals of his racialized body. She wished to acknowledge and verify Besnik's claims of identity and belonging that racial baggage does not allow. In their talk and actions, both Besnik and Deirdre creatively constructed for themselves a common bond. These imperceptible politics worked to change the lived meaning of race and afforded the kids a way to forge social relations beyond it, if only for a few fleeting moments.

Kids bridged and crossed in more private flirtatious encounters, demonstrating that these practices were not always oriented toward an audience. Since peers could not judge these crossings and bridges, they were not as anxious, even when they had to cross wider chasms of difference. This was so in the romance between Yanely and James. Although they never became an official couple, Yanely and James were the primary focus of one another's attentions for a few weeks. They found numerous ways to be near one another throughout that time, alternately play fighting over a pencil or piece of paper or finding something that they could make fun of together. There were numerous coy actions, such as Yanely's repeated accusations that James liked someone else only so he could deny it. James for his part would cryptically claim that he liked someone, but he wasn't going to tell her who it was. For all their coquettish behavior, it was only a few days before their friends and neighbors caught on. Connor, who sat at

Yanely's table, nudged me in the rib and motioned to them with his chin, "Check out the young love."

Yanely is a second-generation Mexican girl and James is a second-generation Filipino boy. Although they belong to different socially constructed races, both of them belong to "intermediary" races, neither white and Black but defined through reference to them. This meant that race had to be mediated, but not as urgently as would be the case if one of the parties was either white or Black. For instance, during a casual moment in the classroom, I was sitting next to Steven as a flirtatious encounter between James and Yanely unfurled before us. Steven remarked to me, "How come all the Chinese always got to go with the Spanish?" Before I could finish my protest that James is Filipino, Steven was already saying, "Nah, just playing with you, James is all right. Anyway, don't they look like cousins?" After I expressed some confusion, Steven began to describe James and Yanely's physical similarities in terms of skin tone, eye shape, and hair. Steven's comments show how sexuality is at one and the same time a site where racial norms become reinscribed and transformed, where their power and limits are most apparent yet most vulnerable. Outside the domain of sexuality, say if James and Yanely had been merely friends, academic partners, or neighbors, their racialized bodies would not be salient. Indeed, within friendships that crossed gender and race, mostly through kin and neighborly ties or extracurricular activities, I never heard any remarks on the unsuitability or strangeness of these social relations. But within the domain of sexuality, bodies became marked. However, Steven marked the racial inscription of their bodies only to blur racial categories in the next, gesturing toward the absurdity of racial categorization itself.

For their part, both Yanely and James often constructed bridges by creatively and poetically making their differences equivalent. They would accomplish this by speaking about their cultural differences using the generalized term "my country" or by likening various cultural traits of Mexico and the Philippines. For instance, during lunchtime Yanely began talking about the food in Mexico: "The food in my country is so good, everything tastes better there." James immediately responded in kind, "In my country too!" The conversation continued in this vein, both of them paralleling each other's remarks about the various fruits and snacks, the climate, and their ambivalent attachment to "their countries." The juxtaposing of their statements in conversational turn taking constructed parallels between their differences, and made them functionally equivalent. They did this at the same time that they performed their particular identities. These bridges were often the basis of crossing. For example, Yanely had learned a few words of Filipino from James. She displayed her knowledge of these words at various times, thanking James in Filipino (*salamat*) or asking him to repeat something with *ano* (what). James often returned her the favor, calling her across the playground in Spanish with "Yanely, *ven aqui* [come here]!"

Yanely and James's crossings represent playful steps across boundaries of difference. This play was also political, a way for kids to stake claims and declare affiliations across differences. Although it was not their purpose, Yanely and James's crossings, like their peers' practices, helped to de-essentialize difference. In these fleeting moments of pleasure and frustration the core of our racial baggage was made visible, challenged, and transformed.

SEXUALITY AND THE LIMITS OF COSMOPOLITANISM

Some kids drew the limits of their enthusiastic participation in multiracial conviviality at sexuality. Eliza was a participant in the local cosmopolitanism, practicing and expressing it in her friendships, pop cultural consumption, and fandoms, as well as her identifications. She is of Albanian descent, her mom born in the United States to Albanian immigrants and her dad born in Albania. Eliza often and eagerly performed herself as Albanian, and it was an important part of her life. She visited in the summer, anxiously waited for her grandparents to come back and live with her when they were visiting Albania, and frequently communicated with relatives in Albania, typical experiences for kids of the second or 2.5 generation. Like other kids, Eliza also expressed excess of belonging, at times claiming she was part Australian because she had kin there or called herself American/Albanian/Australian. Sometimes Eliza crossed and bridged to display her worldliness and sophistication, and in that sense her brand of cosmopolitanism resembled the elite form much more so than any of her peers.

Eliza's celebration of diversity was ambivalent and stopped abruptly at the point of sexual intimacy. Consider Eliza's reflective writing piece after a read-aloud of Jacqueline Woodson's (2001) picture book *The Other Side*. This story is about two girls in the Jim Crow South, one Black and the other white, who ultimately defy custom and a physical barrier of a fence to become friends. Eliza was one of the few kids who continued to defy the rule of color blindness in her writing after the teacher tried to shut down a conversation about race in the post-read-aloud discussion. Eliza was writing furiously and produced the longest and most passionate response among her peers. She titled it "Different Colored People Separated":

> I really think nobody should be separated by color. Nobody should just care about people's color. A lot of people should also have friends [with] different skin tone. So that's why I really think black and white people should not be separated.
>
> Racisms should not happen. Black and white people should stay like friends. There is no difference between black people and white people. So I really think racisms should not start today.
>
> If racisms starts today I will break the RULES if I want to. The only thing different about people is their personalities. So I would be friends with different color

people. So some people can have just friends their [own] color. But I would have friends [of] different color. But everybody is perfect the way they are.

Eliza's curious use of past tense and hypotheticals is pervasive in school writing assignments, directly related to the school's sanctioning of color blindness as the only legitimate way to talk about race, that is, insisting that it stay safely tucked away in the past. The urgency of her tone suggests otherwise. Eliza was aware and versed in the racial baggage that pervades everyday life. Eliza wrote that friendship is where people *should* have friends "with different skin tone," and indeed her friendship network was multiracial. Jacinta (Dominican) was one of her best friends, and she was chummy with Keisha (African America) and admired her.

Eliza's enthusiasm for interracial friendship was in inverse relationship to her feelings of interracial sexual relationships. I recall the horror and disbelief on Eliza's face when she learned that Ashley, a Bolivian girl, liked Darryl, an African American kid. She reconsidered Ashley, and although they were not close friends, she kept her at arm's length after that point. Most illustrative of her fractured subjectivity is the way Eliza would "correct" herself if her desire managed to slip through the restrictions of our racial baggage. Throughout the whole fifth-grade year, Eliza expressed desire for Alex, a fifth-grade boy in another class who was of Serbian and Albanian descent. In individual and group interviews, Eliza would often change the subject to talk about Alex and recount every (excruciating) detail of every encounter with him. Sometimes Eliza allowed herself to agree with one of her friends that another boy was cute, and a few times even expressed sexual desire that violated the "right type." For instance, in chapter 1 I discussed how the boys admired the "cool" tattooed janitor Ody. Likewise, many girls held him as an object of sexual desire. After passing him in the hallway on our way to an interview, Keisha and Eliza were bubbling with excitement and could not wait to start talking about how "hot" he was. Ody, with ambiguously white physical features but with youthful hip-hop style, teetered on racial boundaries and was attractive to both girls. I was initially surprised that Keisha found him desirable because she often derided the masculinity of white males. The conversation ended with Eliza almost correcting or controlling an improper feeling, literally shaking him off her and bringing up Alex, a much safer object of desire.

Even Alex, "not 100 percent" Albanian, was potentially problematic as Eliza's future spouse. Eliza explained this to me on a few occasions, and went into this issue at length in an individual interview. I had asked if her grandfather was speaking Albanian to Nedim's grandfather when I saw them in the park the other day. She explained to me that the men were speaking Serbian, and that they had known one another since they were children. Eliza then spontaneously brought up intermarriage: "My parents would never let me marry a guy that was Serbian or anything. Has to be Albanian."

MK: So is there, so you can marry someone like/

ELIZA: [Alex?

MK: [Nedim?

ELIZA: Nedim? No, I can't marry Alex or Nedim, stuff like that.

MK: So Alex is, I thought Alex was Albanian.

ELIZA: Alex is Serbian. He talks a little Albanian, 'cause his mom's Albanian, no his dad is Albanian, his mom is Serbian. So. . . .

MK: So he's half.

ELIZA: He's half and half.

MK: So that wouldn't work.

ELIZA: That wouldn't work either. Well maybe that would work, I'd have to ask my mom.

MK: So where are you going to meet someone that's Albanian?

ELIZA: My parents have to find a guy for me and stuff so, and I, I don't know, there's a lot of Albanian people in New York, I never knew that, I just thought it was me and my uncles and stuff, my uncles and aunts ((MK laughs)) but I see people talking on the phone and stuff in Albanian and stuff and I just go "oh, oh" ((mimes nodding in realization)).

MK: ((laughs)) Yeah. So, do you have to marry someone that's Muslim too?

ELIZA: Yeah, he has to be Muslim, but, I don't know, my cousin, she's Catholic and she married a Muslim. It's weird.

MK: Okay.

ELIZA: I see a lot of people with, like I would see a black guy with I don't know, a white girl or something.

MK: Uh huh.

ELIZA: I don't know, I see people like Chinese people or anything with different kind of people, from their culture, from cultures and stuff like that, but, my dad, my mom picked the right guy to marry ((laughs)). I love my daddy, he's so nice.

MK: Hmmm ((smiles))

ELIZA: So yeah, that's kind of weird, *but*, it's what they *choose*, so it's not under my condition and stuff, so they could pick whatever they want, it doesn't seem like I care or anything, yeah. For me, I don't think that's the right thing.

MK: Yeah, that's fine.

Eliza's parents have clearly influenced her thinking on these matters. Sure enough, sexuality was one of the few sites where some parents explicitly taught their kids the rules of our racial baggage through their expectations of a future spouse or spouses who would not be allowed. Other parents certainly taught their kids these rules implicitly, although this resembled the manner in which race was learned in arenas like talking about the neighborhood, "good" and "bad" schools, and the "good" and "bad" kids who attended them. Although I do not want to diminish the role of parents, any analysis that too simplistically draws a connection between parents' and kids' attitudes is unconvincing. For instance, I could easily draw a straight line between Eliza's comments and a story her mom told me about how she had chased a Black boy on his bike and would have beat him down had she caught him because he was looking at Eliza when they were standing outside all dressed up for a wedding and waiting for her husband to get the car. I refuse this interpretation because it would create a false closure and obscure the continuous struggle that characterizes learning race and socialization in general. It would also conceal how the production and learning of race are pervasive processes, entangled with and dependent upon other processes, in this instance how whiteness is protected through the maintenance of proper middle-class and gendered norms that include marriage and procreation.

The most impoverished aspect of emphasizing parents' socializing kids in race through sexuality is that it obscures how these controls often miss their mark. These controls are, depending on one's stance, either dreadfully or hopefully imperfect. I was often surprised at how desire emerged in spite of pervasive inner and outer regulations and controls. For instance, the similarities between Eliza's views and Sabrina's (her friend and fictive kin) expressed earlier in this chapter are obvious (see also Sabrina's discomfort during the visit to the junior high school in chapter 1). Despite the fact that Sabrina had clearly learned race and her racial subjectivity "properly," in the spring of the fifth grade, Sabrina finally allowed herself to express her attraction to Steven, the Puerto Rican boy. I use "allowed" deliberately because her attraction had been obvious to me since my very first day in the classroom early in September. So much had these feelings been repressed that in the last week of school with nothing to lose, she mustered up the courage to boldly ask Steven to the senior dance, friends, teachers, and family be damned! Even though it was a humiliating prospect, she took the risk of rejection because she knew this would be her last chance. Although she and Steven were zoned for the same junior high school, her parents ensured that she would be going to a junior high school without any of these "kind" of kids. It is clear that parents simply knew the point I have been belaboring—desire is slippery and cannot be fully controlled, not even for white middle-class girls, despite the abundance of cautionary tales of abandonment, poverty, and abuse they would face at the hands of men of a different "type." Knowing they could not trust ideational forces of control, they did what other parents did with the will and means to "protect" their daughters—they changed the space itself. Eliza was off to an all-girls school and Sabrina to the school without any project kids and virtually no Black kids.

CONCLUDING THOUGHTS

Despite my best intentions to resist thinking about the kids' experiences in the present as a foreshadowing of their adult futures, I must admit that it is hard to do when considering this material. For sexuality highlights the temporal fact that this was a critical biocultural juncture for the kids: the end of elementary school marks the end of childhood and the point at which sexual development switches into high gear. Race and the regulations of sexuality become only more frenzied as the kids become teenagers. It is easy to become melancholy when considering their futures. For some kids, graduating elementary school marks the end of their integrated social networks. It's not just that middle-class girls like Eliza and Sabrina and upwardly mobile working-class girls like Lillian are sent to schools to avoid "bad kids." Gifted and talented or accelerated programs that separate kids according to their so-called abilities, but are just as much based on their parents' cultural capital, also segregate kids within schools. Local school segregation and within-school segregation policies only partly explain the seemingly natural phenomenon of drifting apart.

Many kids were aware and understood that they would be drifting apart from some of their friends. On the last week of school, every kid in Ms. Lee's classroom was full of emotion and shedding or holding back tears. It was not just the dramatic ones like Ashley or the sensitive ones like Gregory and Sabrina, but tough ones like Keisha and Yanely, cool ones like Steven and James, and ambivalent ones like Sebastian and Hakeem. On the last day I saw the kids as a whole class, I ran out because I could not handle the scene of them hugging, crying, and clutching one another with this knowing, and taking comfort at their anxiety of the unknown. Who and how were they going to *be* in their futures was at the center of this emotional outpouring, questions that had much to do with their future social relations: friends, boyfriends, and girlfriends. My melancholia takes its cue from the kids and my own analysis that illuminates that sex is one of the primary reasons for the "drifting apart" of these multiracial social networks. We segregate young people, if not physically then ideologically, with the fear of sex. And racial anxieties partly explain the controls of sexuality. Sexuality was where the limits of cosmopolitanism were found and the site where race emerged most starkly. It was here that kids felt and experienced their raced subjectivities, and where kids also revealed it to others. Could Izel and Carly's friendship be sustained, even though they would be attending the same school and cocooned within their gifted and talented program, as sexuality became an ever more important part of the crafting of their selves? Would Izel brush aside Carly's statements, "He's cute, for *her*," that signified that Carly saw her as essentially a different type? Would Carly become alienated by Izel's more exuberant claims of belonging that could not include her? Could Jacinta ignore what would surely be her friends' distaste for her sexual attractions? And would Jacinta be willing to be a party to Eliza's and Sabrina's relationships once they concretized?

If these particular kids have taught us anything, it's not only that we are all knotted in the deep historical entanglement of sex, race, and class, but that critical transformations always lurk as a possibility. In an ironic twist of regulatory controls of sexuality, the hypervisible emergence of the bare bones of race compelled some kids to push and question boundaries of race, twist and shift its logic, challenge or refuse some of its most fundamental assumptions, and refigure it in unruly ways. While graduation marking the "end of childhood" signals the end of these unruly processes for some kids, these imperceptible politics may be prefigurative for a good many others. For these kids, the racial baggage they inherited will not weigh as heavily, nor will it take them on a singular journey of reproducing dreadful types and kinds of humans. Rather, they will take it on journeys in the making of their own present and future life experiences.

CONCLUSION
Out of the Heart of Whiteness

White supremacy's greatest trick is that it has convinced people that, if it exists at all, it exists always in other people, never in us.

—Junot Diaz, "On Decolonial Love"

In the introduction to this book, I articulated the ethico-political goals of this project within a specific set of academic-intellectual and disciplinary conventions. I wanted to demonstrate precisely *how* kids learn race because I was unsatisfied with the way the dominant strand of research analytically euphemizes this answer with vague connections to "larger sociopolitical dynamics, structures, or settings." By not tracing precisely where, when, and how race materializes in everyday life, and just as crucially how it is often refused and transformed, I argued that accounts of race in childhood function as sites where race is naturalized and made real. I told my story of these cosmopolitan kids to emphasize the absurdity of this social fiction and gesture toward actually existing alternatives. Across these pages I have dutifully followed the genre-specific constraints of the social science monograph, with its burdens of proof, evidence, contextualizing, and authority-claiming references. Yet there still linger loose strings that are difficult to tie within these conventions. For accounts of race in childhood are not just intellectual endeavors. These accounts serve deeply emotional and psychic functions. They affect us. They exert a powerful force on us. They form us as racial subjects. As we interact with these narratives, we perform and figure what race is, what it does, and what it means. I have earned a few pages to speak if not free from the way I have been disciplined, at least to be inspired by "childish" things—my felt experiences, my informal critical studies of every-day life, my imaginative musings, and my gut feelings about what's happening in these affectively loaded spaces where we learn about race *from* the child.

Reader, would you be shocked to hear that five-, seven-, and ten-year-olds knew, in their own various ways, that a dime was different from a nickel? That it had greater value? If currency did not have the meaning we will it to have, those two small round shiny pieces of metal would be as similar as two rocks etched with men. Currency too is an elaborate social fiction that structures all aspects of our lives, an abstraction that conceals and distorts social relations, creates inequalities, and alienates humans. But would you take in your breath and ask, "But where do they get it from?" Let's imagine someone did pose this question when presented with social-scientific evidence of such currency-discerning chil-dren. Perhaps the researcher would let out a sigh before dismissing the question by saying the research was not designed to address this, or summarily respond that kids learn a lot about money in the home, and many parents even give kids an allowance to teach them about money. It is likely that the audience's eyes would dart across the room and roll, brows would raise, mouths would smirk. The question would seem naïve, ridiculous even. But that is not what happens when this question is ritually asked about children's racial knowledge.

I have been presenting research on children and race to various audiences for over a dozen years. I have been paying close attention to reactions to my work, and other research that circulates in the public sphere throughout this time. And there's something about the question "Where do they get it from?" that strikes a raw nerve. A flash of terror and white-hot anger engulf my body. But it is not just the regular asking of this question, the murmurs of agreement, and support of its importance. It's the emotions and the tone that accompany this ritualized utterance—the sharp intakes of breath or deep sighs, the shock, despair, dis-approval, and discomfort, from the resigned shaking of heads to the pleading faces that intone that "something must be done!" This is my proverbial loose string—to identify, name, and target this spectacle as an elaborate performance of white racial innocence.

The seeming necessity of this performance and the gusto with which its per-formed suggest that it does very important things for whites. My conception is informed by Eve Tuck and K. Wayne Yang's (2012) argument of how current social justice scholars' easy adoptions of "decolonizing" metaphors function as "settler moves to innocence." They extend Janet Mawhinney's (1998) ideas about specific white "moves to innocence" in antiracist talk that try to relieve feelings of guilt from racism. On one level, I see the performances accompanying the "Where do they get it from?" in much the same way. Like all claims to inno-cence, they absolve all who participate from responsibility in any wrongdoing.

White hands are suddenly clean. In the contemporary era when white privilege has become a commonplace term and more and more whites freely acknowledge their own privilege, the performance disconnects and transforms privilege from its mooring in white supremacy. But there is something more to this performance of white racial innocence that surrounds the race-discerning child. Although present in the "Where do they get it from?" utterance, it becomes much starker, although still amorphous and hard to pin down, when the actors improvise using the social-scientific portrait-prop of the damaged Black child.

I assume you are somewhat familiar with the famous doll research conducted by Mamie and Kenneth Clark between 1939 and 1947. It is one of the most influential pieces of social science ever conducted, notably used as evidence to strike down the legality of segregation in the Supreme Court's *Brown v. Board of Education* decision. The Clarks presented over two hundred African American children with two dolls, one representing "white" and another "black," and asked a series of questions about which doll they prefer, which was nice, which was bad, and which "looks like you." If you don't know the results, I bet you can guess them—Black children overwhelmingly preferred white dolls. You know this because this research is ritually replicated and dramatized in published studies, unpublished master's theses, supervised psychology undergraduate projects, and concerned teenagers. Even CNN's Anderson Cooper conducted his own version of it in 2010. The results proliferate throughout the public sphere; the CNN study alone was picked up everywhere from every major news outlet to the "mommy blogs." I have had students show one of the countless videos available on the web in their end-of-semester presentations on antiracist strategies in schools. And while my students have watched the videos, I have watched them. I have sat there in stiff nervous agitation, wanting to duck for cover or run. I've considered pulling a fire alarm, something, anything to distract from and prevent what was to come.

My terror at knowing what was to come when this research is shared, discussed, emoted over is redoubled by my powerlessness, my inability to counter that hard visual evidence. While I know it in my bones, I can't just shout "bullshit!" But this is just what Robin Bernstein does to the Clarks' research, albeit in much calmer, carefully argued, and convincing prose. She demonstrates that the experiments were not "transparent revelations of black children's damaged self-esteem" but that the Clarks "carefully structured their experiments as a dramatic arc that ensured that most children would prefer the white doll" (Bernstein 2011, 236). The Clarks knew that asking their questions in a different order produced drastically different results, with Black children identifying with and preferring the black doll. In the question sequence the Clarks preferred, the child was first asked to "give me the doll that you like to play with/like best." Bernstein explains how this question framed the doll as plaything, not a symbolic representation of a person. Throughout her book, she shows how pervasive were scripts of abusive play with black dolls from mid-nineteenth-century to early-twentieth-century America. African American children of the 1930s, 1940s, and 1950s were just as well versed in these scripts as white children. After establishing dolls as playthings, the experiment took a sharp turn and asked kids to equate the doll with persons in the climactic "give me the doll that looks like you." After rejecting the script of "violence and servitude" that the doll represented, the Clarks forced the kids to identify *themselves* with this thing. Thus, this denoted not the kids' psychological damage, nor their deluded fantasies of being white, but what Bernstein calls the "impossible choice" of an "epistemological trap": "liken yourself dangerously to a black doll or appear to reject your own racial identity" (240).

Bernstein is able to mount this critique because she does not see experiments as transparently revealing the deep interiority of innocent children or representations of truth. She recognizes historically located children who are experts in their own culture interacting with other human-researchers in a particular setting with its own narrative arc. We need to bring this kind of scrutiny to current iterations of the doll research. I am decidedly not calling for more doll research that serves as a scene of racial subjection for both white and Black children but the urgent need to propose other interpretations and other narratives. Perhaps some of the Black children were being polite to Anderson Cooper when saying the white doll looked nice. Perhaps they all had black dolls and wanted to play with a white one. I'm not sure. But I am sure that there's more to say about these kids. Just like I know that there are plenty of experimental conditions where I, and any other woman I know, could be coaxed to prefer manhood. But this does not represent a deep inner desire to be a man! What would be the purpose of such an experiment anyway? To show that sexism still exists? Is that really the purpose of doll experiments today? The Clarks' experiments were intentionally wrought to achieve a specific goal in a specific context, one that I think was admirable and worthy—to show the pain of African American children in a context when only white children were allowed to hurt, where only white children were thought as innocent, where only white children were properly seen as children. My critique is from another time when this research is doing very different things.

What do these videos of one Black child after another pointing at the white doll playing in a seemingly endless loop *do*? The emotions and anguish do not solely provide a stage for whites to absolve their responsibility in racism. The spectacle surrounding the consumption of this research provides a platform for another crucial psychic move. In the singular focus on Black children, in the anguished pity for them, whites locate the terrors of racism in racial Others. Even when white children are figured in this research (albeit less frequently), they are seen to be merely expressing a preference for their own group. And, just as critical, white children's neutral and "natural" (read: innocent) inclinations are understood to damage and deform Black children. Whites' emotional performances allow them to become innocent once again, but this is a different kind of innocence. This racial innocence is structured not from the guilty/innocent binary but in the corrupted/innocent binary. In the elaborate performances of shock and despair, whites figure their own selves as undamaged and unscathed by race. Race is figured as contaminating Others, but not perverting and deforming the white psyche. What makes me want to run from these performances is my sense that they are moments when whiteness is inhabited and incorporated into subjectivities; when identities in whiteness are confirmed, sedimented, and made normative. These scenes are, much like the moments I narrated in this book, sites of profound racial learning, if more dreadfully predictable. And I detect a tiny glimmer of glee in these performances, not a "phew I'm so lucky I'm white." But some feeling, which may be below any level of coherence, tells whites that people of color, in their heart of hearts, in the very core of their being, want to be white. And this is, I think, where we can discern the heart of whiteness.

Where do we go if whites do not recognize that race perverts and deforms the white psyche? How do we draw attention to the fact that whites, provided with so many material and symbolic advantages, are less likely to question and reject racial ideology, their psyches thus *more* twisted and warped? And that's one of the problems with the dominance of the "white privilege" trope for talking about whiteness—it makes whiteness seem like a great thing! Where can we enact spectacles of pity for whites whom W.E.B. Du Bois figured as "imprisoned and enthralled, hampered and made miserable" in the fantasy of white supremacy (quoted in Roediger 1998, 14)? How can we help whites realize that their inhabiting of whiteness is not bliss but deranged? To be clear, I may be a race traitor, but I am not imagining a fantasy of revenge. Just the opposite. James Baldwin argued that "if you're white there's no hope for you," but he made clear that whiteness is "absolutely a moral choice" (1984, 92). I want my white students to realize that there is a choice outside the guilty/innocent and contaminated/innocent binaries, to develop identities outside this false cloak of superiority, this will to dominate, this cipher of terror. I want them to see and understand that their humanization is also at stake in destroying race and take up antiracist subjectivities. To do this, we must all struggle to move out of the heart of whiteness.

Because whiteness has been such a powerful force in structuring our world, our knowledge, our truth, our values, our sense of beauty, our sense of goodness, our very notion of what it means to be human, moving out of its heart is an enormous undertaking that requires us to turn the world upside down and inside out. As Jason R. Ambroise and Sabine Broeck (2015, 4) write about the critical role of Black knowledges in Black struggles for emancipation, "these counter-assertions and counter-formulations necessarily open up the possibility for new modes of 'thought,' new modes of 'being' human, and/or new conceptions of human 'free-dom.'" Our search for other truths, other ways of knowing, other values, other ways of being in this world must necessarily include children. Their status as the antipode of this particular genre of the human makes childhood studies, one that includes children as makers of knowledge, as potentially radical as Black, feminist, postcolonial, queer, and Indigenous studies. We cannot face the dire circumstances of our current world situation—from ecological destruction to pervasive war, mounting global inequalities, the carceral and security state, the regular extrajudicial killing of Black and brown people—with our racial baggage. My contribution to this struggle in this book is modest. I cannot make those videos disappear. What I can do is alert you that other stories of children's racial lives exist, stories that center their improvised talk, their interactions with other humans, objects, and texts, their debates, their sense of fairness, their critical knowledge of everyday life, their way of living together. What I can do is produce such stories, stories of kids, Black, Latino, Asian, Arab, and, yes, white, rejecting that heart of whiteness with a gravity-defying impulse to escape race's ordering of our world. What I can do is urge and inspire others to produce more stories. Then this will have been a meaningful project.

NOTES

INTRODUCTION

1 Sacrificing orthographic conformity for racial politics, "Black" and "Blackness" are capitalized throughout the text while "white" and "whiteness" are not (see De Genova 2005, 255). "Black" refers to and represents counterhegemonic acts of self-definition, and the capitalization denotes respect, while "white" does not. It appears in uppercase in white supremacist texts or when style guides privilege uniformity in document design.

2 The resounding consensus from the social and natural sciences is that race is an arbitrary social category constructed in relatively recent history. Yet race is one of the major axes of the global distribution of power, property, and prestige. Race was integral to the white power consolidation at the global scale of colonialism, imperialism, slavery, and conquest that gave rise to the capitalist world system. Race was never simply about categorizing people in the name of science, but was and remains about power, domination, and subordination. In the United States, race structures all aspects of life from birth to death and the quality of life one experiences in between. The profound racial inequalities in health reveal most starkly how race is so perniciously real that it *becomes* biology, manifesting in significant disparities in every conceivable realm of health (Gravlee 2009). Yet racial categories are based not on biology or genetics but on social factors. Race does not have the valid biological status of subspecies or breed. Humanity cannot be divided into types, not "back then" before globalization supposedly mixed everyone up, and not now. Although it is based on biologically based traits like skin, hair, eyes, lips, and nose, race is simply not a valid biological grouping. The resounding consensus from those who study human diversity at all levels—historically and contemporaneously, globally and locally, from the level of population to that of the genome—is that human diversity is riotous, continuous, messy, slippery, and nonconcordant, not distinct types or kinds of humans. The only valid ways to construct biological/genetic types would be either one race encompassing all humans or humanity split into thousands of overlapping races.

3 See Ali (2002), Connolly (2002), Lewis (2003), Mac Naughton and Davis (2009), Moore (2002), Pacini-Ketchabaw, Nxumalo, and Rowan (2011), and Winkler (2012). Also see the excellent overview of qualitative research on children and race provided by the Una Qualitative Methods Learning Group (2010).

4 Virginia Dominguez's (1997) critique of Lawrence Hirschfeld's (1997) attempts to synthesize a theory of why race is so pervasive using experimental work on children and race is trenchant. In response to his main claim that our cognitive architecture and race's visuality makes race "easy to think," Dominguez writes, "What system of racial classification is he referring to when he makes such a claim? There is not one system of racial classification, one system of racial nomenclature, or one set of differentiating principles by which racial categories are constituted. There are several, and they coexist sometimes even in one society, state or region. . . . Biologists, physical anthropologists, and geneticists have never even agreed on how many different 'races of mankind' there are, nor what criteria of classification to use. Official U.S.

censuses have never agreed either. . . . Who, then, thinks that 'race' is easy to learn?" (Domin-guez 1997, 97).

5 The neighborhood, school, and all kids and teachers were given pseudonyms to protect the confidentiality of participants.

6 These two periods of research in the school, May to June 2006 and September 2006 to June 2007, were supplemented with two months of fieldwork in the surrounding neighborhood of Augursville as well as archival research on the historical dynamics of the area.

7 I use the term "racial baggage" to refer to our racial common sense, opting for this term because I appreciate how it conjures something tangible, weighty, yet pliable and unpredictable in its destination. My understanding of racial common sense is most similar to Gilroy's (2000; 2005) term "raciology," which he employs to index the historically situated common-sense certainties about race, a conceptual field he sees as one of the major discourses in the modern episteme. Gilroy's delineation emphasizes race's historically specific character and continuously shifting elements along with the general features that stay rather stable through time. Gilroy's mapping of raciology relies on Gramsci's (1971, 324) conception of all ideology as a mosaic of historically specific fragments that exist in tension with elements from previous moments and grounded in the particular social conditions of various groups.

8 Genomics's clumsy translations into popular and public discourse (Lehrman 2008), its proliferation in the market for personal genetic histories (Shriver and Kittles 2008), and its expansion into medical research and medicine (Feldman and Lewontin 2008; Fullwiley 2008; Montoya 2011) are all currently powerful yet unnoticed ways that race as natural type is repro-duced. Most scholars discussing the effects of the new genomic age on US and global racial formations would agree with this stance. However, Abu El-Haj (2007), for instance, argues that genes are increasingly read as neutral markers of geographical origin and "ancestry" and have cast off their essential traits or qualities.

9 Gordon Allport's (1954) *The Nature of Prejudice* is the explicit theoretical treatise of this canon. Its continued extraordinary influence in the field of social and cognitive psychology can be quickly assessed via a Google Scholar search of citations, with over two thousand pieces of scholarship per year that emphasize the so-called nature of prejudice or in-group favoritism, despite critical work within the field of social psychology for over thirty years (Bil-lig 1985; see also Augoustinos 2016; Tileagă 2016).

10 See James and Prout's (2015 [1998]) most recent edition of the now-classic text that put childhood studies on the map for an overview of the deeply embedded roots of seeing chil-dren as representatives of nature.

11 This framework explores how everyday meanings and categories are dialectically linked to the racialized social structure in the process of racial formation, as "race is situated where meaning meets social structure, where identity frames inequality" (Winant 2000, 171). Racial projects are at the center of racial formation, joining social structure and cultural represen-tation. Omi and Winant explain, "Society is suffused with racial projects, large and small, to which all are subjected. This racial 'subjection' is quintessentially ideological. Everybody learns some combination, some version, of the rules of racial classification, and of her own racial identity, often without obvious teaching or conscious inculcation" (1994, 60).

12 The most important ethnographies of race formation that emphasize how race is made in concrete settings amid the processes of everyday life include De Genova (2003), Gregory (1998), Hartigan (2005), Jackson (2001; 2005), and Sanjek (1998).

13 Historians, engaged in the same general goals of understanding what it feels like to live in a particular place and time, have worked equally well as ethnographers in this regard. Thomp-son's work best exemplifies this "people's history" approach.

14 This is not a so-called micro approach but one that dissolves the false distinction between micro and macro.

15 Consider how Hartigan reinterpreted McIntyre's work among white women in antiracist workshops. Where McIntyre analyzed the hems and haws, lack of clarity, and confusion animating the women's "waitress stories" as evidence of racism, he instead sees hope that "the certainty of racial logic is breaking down" (2010a, 52).

16 Notably, Benjamin inverted the traditional hierarchy through which consciousness is conceived, so that it is in childhood that this "higher function" more typically resides. Benjamin conceptualized development outside the unidirectional trajectory of mainstream psychology wherein kids lose these "irrational" characteristics and become "rational." For Benjamin, the eclipse of children's revolutionary consciousness is a direct result of embourgeoisement by the ideological apparatus of the school; however, the revolutionary potential lies more or less dormant or subdued within adults (Buck-Morss 1989, cited in Katz 2004, 98–100).

17 While posthumanist thought has been limited within anthropology (Pyyhtinen and Tamminen's [2011] theorization and the ethnographic studies of Whitehead [2009] and Boellstorf [2010] are notable exceptions), posthumanists' negative critique of the autonomous, rational, and intentional subject and their positive contributions to conceptualizations of subjectivity as relational and embodied (Blackman et al. 2008; Callus and Herbrechter 2011) intersect with current trends of emphasizing embodiment, materiality, and relationality with nonhuman others in the discipline.

18 My first encounter with PS AV was a great relief after being met with apprehension and trepidation in the eight other schools that captured Augursville's superdiverse demographics. Although two other schools eventually granted me permission, I got the sense that they did so with apprehension.

19 See Roediger's (1998) edited collection of Black writers on whiteness, and Ignatiev and Garvey's (1996) edited collection on how "treason to whiteness is loyalty to humanity."

20 This resonates with De Genova's (2005) forceful argument that, citing Paulo Freire (1990 [1968]) as inspiration, the only legitimate way to conduct ethnography is not to study people, but study with them.

21 Practically, this meant that I sat around waiting for race to "happen." Although it would have been seemingly easier to find out what kids knew by asking them about race, this would have defied my intellectual goals of seeing when, where, and how race materialized. Race was indeed an important issue in the kids' lives, but it was not always *the* most important issue. Surrender ensured that I did not confuse my interest with theirs and that this remained clear in the representation of the research. Only when race materialized either plainly or obliquely did I discuss it, employing the idioms with which it was expressed rather than superimposing racial language. This ensured that I was not an agent of racial subjection myself, one of my premier ethical concerns.

22 Superdiversity can connote a social fact, narrative, or policy (see Berg and Sigona 2013).

23 Cosmopolitanism is marshaled in two distinct fields: the first in political theory where scholars articulate the possibilities for normative notions of justice and ethics beyond the nation-state (see Archibugi 2014; Benhabib and Post 2006) and the second in the social sciences and humanities to denote the structure of feeling that I am gesturing toward here. The genealogy of the cosmopolitan "structure of feeling" is more directly tied to Diogenes's formulation, while the cosmopolitanism of normative justice and liberalism is tied to the philosophy of the Roman Stoics like Musonius Rufus and elaborately theorized in Kant's foundational "Perpetual Peace" (1991 [1795]). In many contemporary discussions that deploy Kant's notion, difference is reified and essentialized in a way that has been criticized throughout this work. For instance, Nussbaum's prescriptions for cosmopolitan education advocate the teaching of the Stoics to "address the cognitive roots of those passions" such as the "hatred of members of other races and religions." She believes that the Stoics can teach us to "regard the alien . . . as one from whom they might actually learn something" (1997, 22).

24 The initial resurgence of cosmopolitanism in anthropology, sociology, political science, and cultural and postcolonial studies echoed the detached formulation: one is enlightened by not being bogged down by the baggage of tribe, creed, or nation. This suggests that one has to shed local attachments to become a citizen of the world, producing a vision of the rootless cosmopolitan. Detractors immediately critiqued this position as a mask worn by Eurocentric elites, one that evinces a classed and often raced parochialism (Calhoun 2002; van der Veer 2004). In fact, convivial forms are just as likely, if not more likely, to occur among the working class, migrants, and refugees. Using the example of labor migrants that are "rooted" in various ways but open to other forms of difference, Werbner (1999) best excoriates the elitism of the detached cosmopolitan, arguing that its advocates are socially and culturally encapsulated in their own "cocktail sipping worlds" and more often than not blind to the realities of the working class outside and inside their doors. This echoes Appiah's (2007) argument that "rootedness" does not negate openness to difference nor a universal consciousness, a position most notably taken up by Bhabha (1996), Hall (2002), Gilroy (2005), and Nava (2007). Van der Veer (2004) critiques the "rootless" or universalist conceptions of cosmopolitanism as a trope of colonial modernity, based on the West's engagement with the rest of the world, a type in which he includes colonial officers, missionaries, *and* anthropologists. Kaldor (2006) underscores this by pointing out that the uneducated villagers in Bosnia hid and saved refugees while the most militant nationalists were often elites educated in foreign universities. On a related note, Sichone (2006) argues the people most open and accepting of difference in South Africa are those who never left their homes, for example, the Xhosa "mamas"—women in remote villages who greet strangers with trays of food and as fellow human beings, a cosmopolitanism he likens to the principle of *ubuntu*.

25 Diogenes's absurd and humorous irreverence was also directed at power. Legend has it that when Alexander the Great came to pay his respects to the philosopher and asked him what he desired most, Diogenes simply asked the conqueror to stop blocking the sunlight. As Malecka (2011, 502) observes, Diogenes directed his "mocking at all types of persons who consider themselves superior" as well as their "common sense," habits, and laws.

26 Steven chose a well-known dark-skinned rapper, Ol' Dirty Bastard (of the Wu-Tang Clan), who was not conventionally handsome.

27 Although Vološinov's (1973 [1922]) model is formulated to look at language effects and reflects social change, it can be extended to processes not exclusively linguistic.

CHAPTER 1   SENSING URBAN SPACE

1 In addition to giving the neighborhood a pseudonym, I have altered details in the descriptions to ensure that the neighborhood is not identifiable. For example, demographic information is slightly skewed and statues honoring specific explorers in the park are altered, among other changes.

2 Fawwaz's map was produced in the context of my only formal pedagogical activity with the kids. Ms. Anastasia asked if I would like to impart any of my social studies "expertise," so I decided on a lesson about how maps are purposive representations that distort space in order to highlight specific features. After showing them various types of maps, I had the kids construct a map of their neighborhoods to show the important places in their lives.

3 Urban planners define walkability in relation to the five Ds of development—density, design, diversity of land uses, distance to travel, and destination accessibility (Campoli 2012). Geographers have integrated children's perspectives on neighborhood walkability in policy-oriented research promoting physical activity (Wridt 2010).

4 Although these models represent heuristic devices, they exist in real space and time, varying in materiality (some are ephemeral like the sight of bodies interacting while others are durable like a manufactured store sign) and overlapping with and morphing into one another.

5 During my fieldwork, no infrastructure was catered specifically to "yuppies." In 2015 I was surprised to see an ultramodern coffee shop near the school. Its clean lines of glass, steel, and pale wood looked out of place, as were its offerings of soy and almond milk chai lattes for nearly five dollars. It was full on a late weekday morning, its young occupants' attention focused on their MacBooks.

6 The neoliberal restructuring of many cities has turned them into playgrounds for young professionals that exclude children's needs (e.g., schools and public parks), which are more expensive than restaurants and bars.

7 Because this linguistic capital was so valuable, its boundaries of belonging were carefully patrolled. When Sebastian first tried his hand at a New York accent, he fumbled and was immediately dismissed as inauthentic by Steven for sounding like his "grandma." This signals the importance of age, masculinity, and space in accessing this symbolic capital. It is important to note that masculinity was not necessarily tied to maleness, for Keisha was able to mobilize it (see chapter 3). The kids who owned this valuable symbolic capital were not the only ones to police its boundaries. Moments after he was dismissed as inauthentic, Sebastian excoriated Juan for being unable to voice it, throwing in some slang to boot. At that moment, Sebastian was allowed to cross into temporary membership. This highlights how authenticity had to be continually enacted in practice by both the proficient and the "wannabe." The pleasures and risks of crossing into Blackness were perhaps highest. Roediger's sketch of the historical politics of crossing into popular African American forms cautions us to be skeptical of their impact but attuned to the possibility that they "might connect to antiracism and deepen cracks within white identity" (2002, 221–222).

8 Only 10 percent of the kids in PS AV lived in the projects, the majority of which were zoned for another elementary school. That school did not have a great reputation, but parents largely attributed that to poor administration rather than its students, reinforcing the importance of age and sexuality in the racialized fears of Black youth (see chapter 5).

9 I variously employ the terms "hip-hop culture" and "Black youth culture" to capture specific characteristics. "Hip-hop culture" indexes the point of confluence of the stylistic features discussed and where they are represented and mass mediated. Although hip-hop culture is decidedly multiracial, the term "Black youth culture" indexes the ownership and derivation of these forms in African American cultural production (with important contributions by Latino/as) at the same time that it signals their racialized status in the wider sphere. Both terms are necessary to signal the circuitous relation between on-the-ground forms and expression and their mass mediation through music, video, and other commodities. The term also signals how these kids, along with other youth, appropriate these forms to construct their own configurations, which, while somewhat disarticulated from Blackness, are still incipient racial formations.

CHAPTER 2   LOVING FRIENDS AND THINGS

1 Despite the fact that cosmopolitanism was submerged in Ms. Anastasia's class, the friendship groups also crossed racial boundaries. There was one large mixed-gender group that crossed traditional lines of difference, composed of Deirdre (Dominican-Puerto Rican), Anna (Greek), Sangmu (Tibetan), Fatima (Bengali), Blake (Ecuadorian), Besnik (Albanian-Dominican), Malik (Hakeem's brother, Pakistani-Filipino), Luis (Mexican), and Damon (Chinese-Vietnamese). Another group was composed of four girls, Melody (Korean), Salma (Bengali), Amaria (Mexican), and Rahima (Bengali). Nadia, an Egyptian girl, hung around the margins of this group. There was a group of six boys that included Mehul (Bengali), Fawwaz (Bengali), Akil (Pakistani), Mustafa (Algerian), Cody (Honduran-Albanian), and Imran (Albanian), all Muslim except Mehul, who was Hindu. Finally, there was the friend group of Izel, Carly, and Kamilah, respectively Mexican, white, and Algerian, although the first two girls turned against Kamilah in a most vicious way at the end of the year, enlisting the majority of the class in their campaign so that the top girl ended her fifth-grade year as the most reviled student. This was marked by her seat at the middle of the long cafeteria bench, in close physical proximity to other kids but effectively all by herself.

2 Toward the end of the year, Yanely and Jacinta started to become friendly. It began with Yanely complimenting Jacinta's clothing and then paying attention to and laughing at the way Jacinta dissed the boys at her table (they shared the experience of sitting at a table of all boys). By the end of the school year, they were joking about quite often, and both of them expressed admiration for the other to me. This admiration suggested a longing that could not be fulfilled, as their embeddedness in their own networks prevented them from cementing the bond further.

3 By late March, even the queen of cool had gotten into the wrestling game. During a geometry lesson, Keisha was adamant about getting my attention and waved me over. I thought she needed help figuring out the area of a parallelogram, but instead she wanted to show me her graffiti graphic of wrestler Batista's name. Surprised, I asked, "You like wrestling now too?" She explained that she liked it "a little," but she *really* liked Batista because of his "sexy body." She started a new drawing of wrestler John Cena's name. I asked whom she liked better and she said Batista. She thought for a moment and told me that he wasn't wrestling right now because "this girl said he raped her." She rolled her eyes disapprovingly and went back to her drawing.

4 The groups resulting from these bridges were of a different nature than that denoted by the de facto motto of the United States: *e pluribus unum*, out of many, one. For underpinning the usage of this phrase in the US public sphere is a deep suspicion and anxiety concerning difference. Historically, it has been marshaled to signify the original dream of assimilating or integrating Others and at other times to promote national unity and patriotism. For instance, in an essay of the same name, Robert Putnam's (2007) concern is "the challenge of social solidarity posed by diversity." His solution to this problem is problematic, a "more inclusive identity" that is a rather uncritical and at times jingoistic version of an "American" identity. The crux of Putnam's view is that different "types" of people are naturally antagonistic. He sees a correlation between diversity and distrust in communities both within and between groups, with people of all ages "hunkering down" and retreating turtlelike into their shells. While conservative, his views are less Armageddon-like than others in that he sees "feasible" solutions, whereas others do not, using such discourse to justify and maintain white supremacist policies.

5 Many of the girls successfully navigated the "schizoid subjectivities" of sexually innocent or sexually aware on offer to girls (Renold and Ringrose 2011) to construct femininities within and outside these confines. And while some girls in particularly close friendships were called "lesbians" (e.g., Jacinta and Eliza), their casual responses showed that they could not be bothered to prove or defend their heterosexuality.

6 As the end of the year approached, Sabrina also experimented with adopting stylistic elements of hip-hop culture. She began displaying her newfound knowledge about music and incorporated linguistic elements into her speech. This became a source of great annoyance for Eliza and Jacinta, who highlighted the inauthenticity of Sabrina's efforts in their complaints. They reported that Sabrina was "copying Steven," "she tries to act ghetto," and stressed the sudden temporal dimension of her transformation, she "acts all different *now*." The dismissing of the authenticity of Sabrina's efforts was not explicitly linked to her skin color, but resulted from her friends knowing her hegemonic racial stance. They perceived the change, probably correct, to be due to an instrumental purpose revolving around her romantic interest in Steven. During one of their rants, Mark, who had been eavesdropping, finally exclaimed, "And you two changed a lot too since the second grade!" Jacinta defended their developments as a natural branching out, dismissing the accusation laughingly: "How did we change? We grew?!" The girls were still laughing when Mark suggested their hypocrisy: "You should be talking!" See Kromidas (2012) for an extended account of this particular drama.

CHAPTER 3   THE COLLECTIVE LABORS OF CONVIVIALITY

1 We have recognized for decades that schools are premier sites where race is produced. Scholars have extensively documented how teachers' assumptions about race can impact their expectations, treatment, and evaluation of students and contribute to the reproduction of large-scale inequalities. Conventionally, we think about how these processes impact students' academic performances, not how they impact students' sense of self and Other and their social relations. The latter processes may be just as unpredictable as, if not more unpredictable than, the former. For curriculum, like any knowledge or sensory data, is never simply "received" but interpreted and made meaningful in surprising ways.

2 The most depressing moment in my fieldwork was easily when my kids were implicitly declared "not smart" during a performance of the Poetry Project, one with all four classes of the fifth grade present, as well as some fourth-grade classes. The "smart" class had been assigned a complex and sophisticated poem to perform, which they executed with perfection and pizzazz. My kids' poem seemed infantile in comparison. They went from giddy and excited about their performance to quiet and humorless, and the feeling weighed on us the rest of the day.

3 For instance, the school adopted the Teachers College Reading and Writing Project, which prescribes partnered tasks throughout the reading and writing process.

4 These activities often violated the cooperative principle because they were embedded within a larger competitive frame, or because kids were not solving problems collaboratively but were responsible only for the collective. Although theorists of cooperative learning believe structuring collaborative working groups in competition with one another works against the spirit of cooperation (Kohn 1992), these interactions generated the most concentrated efforts and enthusiastic collaborations. For an overview of the variety of cooperative learning strategies and their impact on "ethnic" relations, see Curry, De Amicis, and Gilligan (2011).

5 Marxist critiques of education in the United States begin with Bowles and Gintis's (1976) argument of the school's essential role in the reproduction of the capital/labor relation. For a current overview and debates within Marxist perspectives of schooling, see Collins (2009), Foley (2010), and Weis and Fine (2013).

6 Although Marx used the term only in his earlier writings, some scholars suggest that Marx's later sustained critique of capitalism is informed by the theme of alienation (Ollman 1971; Swain 2012).

7 The organization of labor (whereby the worker has no control over what, when, where, or why something is produced and how it is produced) is a social relation and process that ultimately alienates laborers so that we relate to our life activities, social relations, and things as something not of our own creation, but standing over and above us and imbued with a power in which they ultimately control us. Marx's critique of capitalism via his fourfold concept of alienation (from nature, from themselves, from other humans, and ultimately from their species-being) can be appreciated only by understanding his conception of labor as the constitutive feature of humanity—the creative, irreducibly social form of action in and with the world that connects living beings with their forbearers and descendants. Labor is the practice through which we constitute culture and society and our very selves, the key aspect in the reproduction and transformation of human beingness in the world. Labor is at the center of his conception of human nature, which is not conceived as a transhistorical essence but is variable, grounded in the ensemble of social relations through which people labor within any given mode of production. See De Genova (2012) on the importance of Marx's corpus for a radical anthropology aimed at analysis and change of our current environmental and social crises.

8 No scholarly account of power and domination ignores resistance, for it is always present, if imperceptible, regardless of how totalizing domination appears. Willis's *Learning to Labour* (1977) was a watershed ethnography because he mapped power relations within schools that were before him, barely visible. Cutting class was not aimless resistance but a way to attain physical and symbolic liberation from the excessive control of the school. This work has inspired three generations of educational scholars to document how students do not passively accept the alienating conditions of schooling: from the outright rejection of the value of education by cutting out or dropping out, to the strategic accommodations that obscure a deep distrust of schooling, to the misunderstood or barely visible acts of deliberate slowdowns, feigned misunderstandings, "lost" homework assignments, and daydreaming.

9 Status in the classroom was much more fluid and dynamic than is conventionally portrayed. Hierarchies were not rigid, clear-cut, or frozen. There were overlaps in status ranking, and status rankings changed through time. Status did not depend on any obvious criterion—say attractiveness, material possessions, intelligence, or friendliness. Rather it seemed to be based on some mysterious combination of charisma, social knowledge, calculation, toughness, and luck, and did well with a sprinkling of some of the aforementioned criteria.

10 This concept has its roots in Lave and Wenger's (1991) scathing critique of the inauthentic model of learning employed by schools, one counterposed to the "situated learning" in which people learn outside of schools—a process whereby novices move from peripheral to central participation in communities of practice.

11 Despite being called "an educational psychology success story" (Johnson and Johnson 2009), teachers implement cooperative strategies unevenly. At times, one gets the sense that it is just a shift in seating arrangements from rows of isolated desks facing a teacher to shared tables of kids facing one another.

CHAPTER 4   RACIST OR FAIR?

1 *The Daily Show*, a popular late-night comedy program, featured a segment on this same question of "racist or not racist" on November 13, 2013. After a fast-paced montage from media outlets asking variations of the question, then-host John Stewart set up an "expert" panel to weigh in on four cases. Most examples were baldly racist, such as a photograph of a child dressed up in Ku Klux Klan garb at a rally. The ambiguous case was a clip of Sarah Palin comparing the national debt to slavery. After some deliberation, the panel decided it was "not racist, just stupid." Unintentional ignorance is thus the third option in our national framing of the question "is this racist?," one that ultimately absolves the racist.

2 Hartigan's cultural approach centers the "active interpretive and performative work we do when we encounter or engage the significance of race," a process that centrally involves meaning (2010a, 10). The concept of "interpretive repertoires" (regularized narrative conventions that are linked to particular locales) helps analysts explore how race is embedded in everyday cultural dynamics in which we express our opinions and articulate our experiences.

3 While teachers seemingly have total power over students, dictating how, what, and when any activity can take place, students ultimately must grant or withhold assent in the classroom (see Erickson et al. 2007).

4 Recent research highlighting the importance of play for the health and well-being of young and old supports the kids' demands for more free time (Sicart 2014).

5 As Sidorkin (2009) argues, no intrinsic motivation could stimulate any student to learn the multitude of things that contemporary schooling requires. Here I ask the reader to temporarily disregard the necessity of such force, in order to recognize the irreducible nature of control that is inflicted on students in schools. Larger debates about whether the ends outweigh the means or if the ends themselves are worthwhile are long overdue.

6 "Mean" and "nice" were superimposed over categories of "boring" and "fun." "Fun" teachers often organized learning in a way that incorporated social interaction and went beyond kids' dichotomy of work and free time. "Boring" teachers, of which there were more, divided up a fifty-minute period with lecture and an independent activity to practice, to assess recall or understanding of the material, or to waste time (or so it sometimes seemed to me).

7 Watkins (2012) provides an interesting perspective on the enabling aspects of bodily discipline in the formation of a "scholarly habitus," one that stands in stark contrast to the perspective of discipline in most critical studies of education (see Butchart 1998, for example).

8 The school as sorter of students is understood to be one of the major functions of schooling in a capitalist society with an entrenched division of labor ever since Bowles and Gintis's (1976) foundational work. In their mapping of the intergenerational reproduction of class in the United States, they argued that this sorting function ultimately legitimates inequality.

9 Although the principal eventually overrode the teacher's recommendation, this did not necessarily mean she believed the charge, but it may have been her way to quickly resolve rather than escalate the problem.

10 Briefly, color blindness authorizes the following five claims about race: racial equality was won in the civil rights era; racism is the result of unenlightened folks discriminating against racialized minorities; legislation from the civil rights now protects said minorities from such discrimination; racial equality is now a reality, although a few unenlightened folks continue to discriminate; talking about race in a racially egalitarian society is a racist act, for it calls attention to that which shall not be noticed if we are to continue living in a racially egalitarian society. For well over two decades now, scholars from multiple disciplines have pointed out how color blindness euphemizes, obscures, and denies the current reality of race and racial

inequality. In fact, color blindness has even been referred to as color-blind racism, as critics note how "not noticing race" and obscuring structural racism can function as a mechanism to maintain white supremacy in a racially hierarchical society (Baker 2001; Bonilla-Silva 2013; Delgado and Stefanic 2012; Omi and Winant 1994).

11 In the rare case where "proof" arrives, as it did in the national spectacle of 2014 when Los Angeles Clippers owner Donald Sterling's recording of despicably racist talk emerged, it provides the opportunity to rehearse our ritual of looking for the "real racists." Such events drag us back into the vicious interpretive circle that reinforces the dominant construction of the United States as postracial.

CHAPTER 5   ENACTING SEX ED

1 North Carolina's amendment prohibiting interracial unions persisted until 1971, four years after the Supreme Court invalidated any such laws.

2 So controversial were these remarks that Arendt's publishers withheld the article for a year and then published it with a caveat: "We publish it not because we agree with it—quite the contrary!—but because we believe in freedom of expression even for views that seem to us entirely mistaken." See Morey's (2014) reassessment of Arendt's piece.

3 As Carlos Ball (2012) argues, the concern for the psychological well-being of the child is used as a rationale for banning same-sex marriages, as the child would be confused by lack of proper gender roles and belonging.

4 Anthropologists of childhood in the United States have been late to discover this work, due to disciplinary (very little published work within anthropology) and geographical boundaries (the bulk of English-language research is primarily composed of the work of researchers from the United Kingdom, Australia, and New Zealand). The publication of the first collection of empirical research on children's sexualities (Renold, Ringrose, and Egan, 2015) represents a critical point that punctures the additional layers of anxiety surrounding child sexuality in the United States.

5 While recent scholarly literature has begun to explore how primary schoolchildren navigate discourses of gender, class, age, heteronormativity, and the sanctity of marriage and how they are productive of children's sexualities, very little research has explored how race intersects with sexuality in children's everyday lives (for notable exceptions, see Ali 2003; Bhana 2007; Connolly 2002). The innocent child construct that inhibits our understanding of children's sexualities also plagues our understanding of children's racial subjectivities. Childhood scholars relying on the inherent flexibility and reflexivity of ethnographic methods (Renold 2000, 310) have thus often "discovered" childhood sexualities through their studies of children's friendships and gendered, raced, or classed subjectivities (Ali 2003; Connolly 2002).

6 Edelman (2004) subjects this universalizing discourse to a queer critique that ultimately excoriates liberal activists who buy into family respectability in the quest for LGBTQ justice.

REFERENCES

Abu El-Haj, Nadia. 2007. "Rethinking Genetic Genealogy." *American Ethnologist* 34(2): 223–226.

Ahmed, Sara. 2000. *Strange Encounters: Embodied Others in Post-coloniality*. New York: Routledge.

———. 2004. *The Cultural Politics of Emotion*. Edinburgh: Edinburgh University Press.

Akom, Anti A. 2009. "Critical Hip Hop Pedagogy as a Form of Liberatory Praxis." *Equity and Excellence in Education* 42(1): 52–66.

Ali, Suki. 2002. "Friendship and Fandom: Ethnicity, Power, and Gendering Readings of the Popular." *Discourse: Studies in the Cultural Politics of Education* 23(2): 153–165.

———. 2003. *Mixed-Race, Post-Race: Gender, New Ethnicities and Cultural Practices*. Oxford: Berg.

Allen, Jafari. 2009. "Blackness, Sexuality, and Transnational Desire: Initial Notes toward a New Research Agenda." In *Black Sexualities: Probing Powers, Passions, Practices, and Policies*, edited by Juan Battle and Sandra L Barnes, 82–95. New Brunswick, NJ: Rutgers University Press.

———. 2012. "One Way or Another: Erotic Subjectivity in Cuba." *American Ethnologist* 39(2): 325–338.

Allen, Louisa. 2005. *Sexual Subjects: Young People, Sexuality and Education*. London: Palgrave Macmillan.

Allport, Gordon. 1954. *The Nature of Prejudice*. Cambridge, MA: Addison-Wesley.

Ambroise, Jason R., and Sabine Broeck. 2015. "Black Knowledges/Black Struggles: An Introduction." In *Black Knowledges/Black Struggles: Essays in Critical Epistemology*, edited by Jason R. Ambroise and Sabine Broeck, 1–20. Liverpool: Liverpool University Press.

Amin, Ash. 2012. *Land of Strangers*. Cambridge: Polity.

Appiah, Kwame Anthony. 2007. *Cosmopolitanism: Ethics in a World of Strangers*. New York: Norton.

Archibugi, Daniele. 2014. "Cosmopolitan Democracy: A Restatement." *Cambridge Journal of Education* 42(1): 9–20.

Arendt, Hannah. 1959. "Reflections on Little Rock." *Dissent*, Winter: 45–56.

Ariès, Philippe. 1962. *Centuries of Childhood: A Social History of Family Life*. New York: Vintage.

Aristotle. 1999. *Nicomachean Ethics*. Translated by Terence Irwin. Indianapolis: Hackett.

Augoustinos, Martha. 2016. "Retheorizing Prejudice in Social Psychology." In *Discursive Psychology: Classic and Contemporary Issues*, edited by Cristian Tileagă and Elizabeth Stokoe, 243–256. London: Routledge.

Badmington, Neil. 2011. "Posthumanism." In *The Routledge Companion to Literature and Science*, edited by Bruce Clarke and Manuela Rossini, 374–384. New York: Routledge.

Baker, Lee D. 2001. "The Color Blind Bind." In *Cultural Diversity in the United States*, edited by Ida Susser and Thomas C. Paterson, 103–119. Malden, MA: Blackwell.

Baldwin, James. 1984. "On Being 'White' . . . and Other Lies." *Essence* 14(12): 90–92.

Ball, Carlos. 2012. *The Right to Be Parents: LGBT Families and the Transformation of Parenthood*. New York: New York University Press.

Baudelaire, Charles. 2009. *Paris Spleen: Little Poems in Prose*. Translated by Keith Waldrop. Middleton, CT: Wesleyan University Press.

Benhabib, Seyla, and Robert Post, eds. 2006. *Another Cosmopolitanism*. Oxford: Oxford University Press.

Benjamin, Walter. 1978 [1966]. "On the Mimetic Faculty." In *Reflections*, edited by Peter Demetz, translated by Edmund Jephcott, 333–336. New York: Harcourt.

Berg, Mette Louise, and Nando Sigona. 2013. "Ethnography, Diversity and Urban Space." *Identities: Global Studies in Culture and Power* 20(4): 347–360.

Bernstein, Robin. 2011. *Racial Innocence: Performing American Childhood from Slavery to Civil Rights*. New York: New York University Press.

Best, Joel, and Kathleen A. Bogle. 2014. *Kids Gone Wild: From Rainbow Parties to Sexting, Understanding the Hype over Teen Sex*. New York: New York University Press.

Bhabha, Homi K. 1996. "Unsatisfied: Notes on Vernacular Cosmopolitanism." In *Text and Narration: Cross Disciplinary Essays on Cultural and National Identities*, edited by Laura García-Moreno and Peter C. Pfeiffer, 39–52. Columbia, SC: Camden House.

Bhana, Deeva. 2007. "Childhood Sexuality and Rights in the Context of HIV/AIDS." *Culture, Health & Sexuality* 9(3): 309–324.

Biesta, Gert. 2012. "No Education without Hesitation: Exploring the Limits of Educational Relations." *Philosophy of Education* 31: 1–13.

Billig, Michael. 1985. "Prejudice, Categorization, and Particularization: From a Perceptual to a Rhetorical Approach." *European Journal of Social Psychology* 15: 79–103.

Bingham, Charles, Alexander M. Sidorkin, et al. 2004. "Manifesto of Relational Pedagogy: Meeting to Learn, Learning to Meet." In *No Education without Relation*, edited by Charles Bingham and Alexander M. Sidorkin, 5–8. New York: Peter Lang.

Blackman, Lisa, John Cromby, Derek Hook, Dimitris Papadopoulos, and Valerie Walkerdine. 2008. "Creating Subjectivities." *Subjectivity* 22: 1–27.

Blommaert, Jan. 2013. *Ethnography, Superdiversity, and Linguistic Landscapes*. Bristol: Multilingual Matters.

Bluebond-Langner, Myra, and Jill E. Korbin. 2007. "Challenges and Opportunities in the Anthropology of Childhoods: An Introduction to 'Children, Childhoods, and Childhood Studies.'" *American Anthropologist* 109(2): 241–246.

Boellstorf, Tom. 2010. *Coming of Age in Second Life: An Anthropologist Explores the Virtually Human*. Princeton, NJ: Princeton University Press.

Bonilla-Silva, Eduardo. 2013. *Racism without Racists: Color-Blind Racism and the Persistence of Racial Inequality in America*. Lanham, MD: Rowman & Littlefield.

Borland, James H. 1997. "The Construct of Giftedness." *Peabody Journal of Education* 72: 6–20.

———. 2005. "Gifted Education without Gifted Children: The Case for No Conception of Giftedness." In *Conceptions of Giftedness*, edited by Robert J. Sternberg and Janet Davidson, 1–19. New York: Cambridge University Press.

Bourdieu, Pierre. 1990. *The Logic of Practice*. Stanford, CA: Stanford University Press.

———. 1999. "Understanding." In *The Weight of the Social World: Social Suffering Contemporary Society*, edited by Pierre Bourdieu et al., 607–626. Palo Alto, CA: Stanford University Press.

Bowles, Samuel, and Herbert Gintis. 1976. *Schooling in Capitalist America: Educational Reform and the Contradictions of Economic Life*. New York: Basic Books.

Braidotti, Rosi. 2002. *Metamorphoses: Towards a Materialist Theory of Becoming*. Cambridge: Polity.

Brayboy, Bryan M. J., Angelina E. Castagno, and Emma Maughan. 2007. "Equality and Justice for All? Examining Race in Educational Scholarship." *Review of Research in Education* 31: 159–194.

Brown, Wendy. 2006. *Regulating Aversion: Tolerance in the Age of Identity and Empire*. Princeton, NJ: Princeton University Press.

Buck-Morss, Susan. 1989. *The Dialectics of Seeing: Walter Benjamin and the Arcades Project*. Cambridge, MA: MIT Press.

Burman, Erica. 1994. *Deconstructing Developmental Psychology*. London: Routledge.

———. 2015. "Fanon's Lacan and the Traumatogenic Child: Psychoanalytic Reflections on the Dynamics of Colonialism and Racism." *Theory, Culture & Society*. doi:10.1177/0263276415598627.

Butchart, Ronald E. 1998. "Punishments, Penalties, Prizes, and Procedures: A History of Discipline in U.S. Schools." In *Classroom Discipline in American Schools: Problems and Possibilities for Democratic Education*, edited by Ronald E. Butchart and Barbara McEwan, 19–49. Albany: State University of New York Press.

Calhoun, Craig J. 2002. "The Class Consciousness of Frequent Travelers: Toward a Critique of Actually Existing Cosmopolitanism." *South Atlantic Quarterly* 101(4): 869–897.

Callus, Ivan, and Stefan Herbrechter. 2011. "Introduction: Posthumanist Subjectivities, or, Coming after the Subject." *Subjectivity* 5: 241–264.

Cammarota, Julio. 2014. "The Social Justice Education Project: Youth Participatory Action Research in Schools." In *Raza Studies: The Public Option for Educational Revolution*, edited by Julio Cammarota and Augustine Romero, 107–121. Tucson: University of Arizona Press.

Campoli, Julie. 2012. *Made for Walking: Density and Neighborhood Form*. Cambridge, MA: Lincoln Institute.

Carlin, Matthew. 2010. "In the Blink of an Eye: The Augenblick of Sudden Change and Transformative Learning in Lukács and Benjamin." *Culture, Theory and Critique* 51(3): 239–256.

Christensen, Pia H. 2004. "Children's Participation in Ethnographic Research: Issues of Power and Representation." *Children & Society* 18(2): 165–176.

Christianakis, Mary. 2010. "'I Don't Need Your Help!' Peer Status, Race, and Gender during Peer Writing Interactions." *Journal of Literacy Research* 42: 418–458.

Cobb, Jelani. 2013. "Who's Still Afraid of Interracial Marriage?" *New Yorker*, November 13. http://www.newyorker.com/online/blogs/newsdesk/2013/11/whos-still-afraid-of-interracial-marriage.html?intcid=obnetwork&mobify=0.

Cohen, Elisabeth, and Rachel A. Lotan. 2014. *Designing Groupwork: Strategies for the Heterogeneous Classroom*. 3rd ed. New York: Teachers College Press.

Cohen, Stanley. 1972. *Folk Devils and Moral Panics*. London: MacGibbon and Key.

Collins, James. 2009. "Social Reproduction in Classrooms and Schools." *Annual Review of Anthropology* 38: 33–48.

Connolly, Paul. 2002. *Racism, Gender Identities, and Young Children: Social Relations in a Multiethnic Inner-City Primary School*. Abingdon: Routledge.

Cox, Oliver C. 1948. *Caste, Class, and Race*. New York: Monthly Review Press.

Curry, Philip, Leyla De Amicis, and Robbie Gilligan. 2011. *Protocol: Effects of Cooperative Learning on Inter Ethnic Relations in School Settings*. Dublin: Campbell Collaboration.

da Silva, Denise Ferreira. 2011. "Notes for a Critique of the 'Metaphysics of Race.'" *Theory, Culture & Society* 28(1): 138–148.

De Genova, Nicholas. 2005. *Working the Boundaries: Race, Space, and "Illegality" in Mexican Chicago*. Durham, NC: Duke University Press.

———. 2012. "Bare Life, Labor-Power, Mobility, and Global Space: Toward a Marxian Anthropology?" *CR: The New Centennial Review* 12(3): 129–152.

Delgado, Richard, and Jean Stefanic. 2012. *Critical Race Theory: An Introduction*. 2nd ed. New York: New York University Press.

Dervin, Fred, and Karen Risager, eds. 2015. *Researching Identity and Interculturality*. New York: Routledge.

Desai, Amit, and Evan Killick, eds. 2013. *Ways of Friendship: Anthropological Perspectives*. New York: Berghahn Books.

Dominguez, Virginia. 1994. "A Taste for 'the Other': Intellectual Complicity in Racializing Practices." *Current Anthropology* 35(4): 333–348.

———. 1997. "The Racialist Politics of Concepts, or Is It the Racialist Concepts of Politics?" *Ethnos* 25(1): 93–100.

Durkheim, Émile. 1984 [1893]. *The Division of Labor in Society*. New York: Free Press.

Edelman, Lee. 2004. *No Future: Queer Theory and the Death Drive*. Durham, NC: Duke University Press.

Egan, Danielle R. 2013. *Becoming Sexual: A Critical Appraisal of the Sexualization of Girls*. Cambridge: Polity.

Egan, Danielle R., and Gail Hawkes. 2010. *Theorizing the Sexual Child in Modernity*. New York: Palgrave Macmillan.

Elwood, Sarah, and Katharyne Mitchell. 2014. "Mapping Children's Politics: Spatial Stories, Dialogic Relations and Political Formation." *Geografiska Annaler: Series B, Human Geography* 94(1): 1–15.

Ensink, Titus. 2003. "The Frame Analysis of Research Interviews: Social Categorization and Footing in Interview Research." In *Analyzing Race Talk: Multidisciplinary Approaches to the Interview*, edited by Harry Van den Berg, Margaret Wetherell, and Hanneke Houtkoop-Steenstra, 156–177. Cambridge: Cambridge University Press.

Epstein, Debbie, Mary Jane Kehily, and Emma Renold. 2012. "Culture, Policy, and the Un/marked Child: Fragments of the Sexualisation Debates." *Gender and Education* 24(3): 249–254.

Erickson, Frederick, Rishi Bagrodia, Alison Cook-Sather, Manuel Espinoza, Susan Jurow, Jeffrey J. Shultz, and Joi Spencer. 2007. "Students' Experience of School Curriculum: The Everyday Circumstances of Granting and Withholding Assent to Learn." In *The Sage Handbook of Curriculum and Instruction*, edited by F. Michael Connelly, Ming Fan He, and JoAnn Phillion, 198–218. Thousand Oaks, CA: Sage.

Evans, Gillian. 2013. "The Value of Friendship: Subject/Object Transformations in the Economy of Becoming a Person." In Desai and Killick, *Ways of Friendship*, 174–196.

Feldman, Marcus S., and Richard C. Lewontin. 2008. "Race, Ancestry, and Medicine." In Koenig, Lee, and Richardson, *Revisiting Race in a Genomic Age*, 89–101.

Ferguson, Ann Annett. 2001. *Bad Boys: Public Schools and the Making of Black Masculinity*. Ann Arbor: University of Michigan Press.

Fields, Barbara J., and Karen E. Fields. 2014. *Racecraft: The Soul of Inequality in American Life*. London: Verso.

Foley, Douglas. 2010. "The Rise of Class Culture Theory in Educational Anthropology." *Anthropology & Education Quarterly* 41(3): 215–227.

Freire, Paulo. 1990 [1968]. *Pedagogy of the Oppressed*. New York: Continuum.

Fullwiley, Duana. 2008. "The Molecularization of Race: U.S. Health Institutions, Pharmaco-genetics Practice, and Public Science." In Koenig, Lee, and Richardson, *Revisiting Race in a Genomic Age*, 149–171.

Gandhi, Leela. 2003. "Friendship and Postmodern Utopianism." *Cultural Studies Review* 9(1): 12–23.

———. 2006. *Affective Communities: Anticolonial Thought, Fin-de-Siècle Radicalism and the Politics of Friendship*. Durham, NC: Duke University Press.

Gilroy, Paul. 2000. *Against Race: Imagining Political Culture beyond the Color Line*. Cambridge, MA: Harvard University Press.

———. 2005. *Postcolonial Melancholia*. New York: Columbia University Press.

Glick Schiller, Nina, Tsympylma Darieva, and Sandra Gruner-Dominic. 2011. "Defining Cosmopolitan Sociability in a Transnational Age: An Introduction." *Ethnic and Racial Studies* 34(3): 399–418.

Gramsci, Antonio. 1971. *The Prison Notebooks*. New York: International.

Gravlee, Clarence. 2009. "How Race Becomes Biology: Embodiment of Social Inequality." *American Journal of Physical Anthropology* 139(1): 47–57.

Gray, Debra, and Rachel Manning. 2014. "'Oh My God, We're Not Doing Nothing': Young People's Experiences of Spatial Regulation." *British Journal of Social Psychology* 53(4): 640–655.

Gregory, Anne, James Bell, and Mica Pollock. 2014. "How Educators Can Eradicate Disparities in School Discipline: A Briefing Paper on School-Based Interventions." Bloomington: Indiana University, Discipline Disparities: A Research-to-Practice Collaborative.

Gregory, Steven. 1998. *Black Corona*. Princeton, NJ: Princeton University Press.

Hall, Stuart. 2002. "Political Belonging in a World of Multiple Identities." In *Conceiving Cosmopolitanism: Theory, Context, and Practice*, edited by Steven Vertovec and Robin Cohen, 25–31. Oxford: Oxford University Press.

Haraway, Donna. 1985. "A Manifesto for Cyborgs: Science, Technology, and Socialist Feminism in the 1980s." *Socialist Review* 80: 65–107.

Hartigan, John, Jr. 2005. *Odd Tribes: Toward a Cultural Analysis of White People*. Durham, NC: Duke University Press.

———. 2010a. *Race in the 21st Century: Ethnographic Approaches*. New York: Oxford University Press.

———. 2010b. *What Can You Say? America's National Conversation on Race*. Stanford, CA: Stanford University Press.

Hatcher, Richard, and Barry Troyna. 1993. "Racialization and Children." In *Race, Identity and Representation in Education*, edited by Cameron McCarthy and Warren Crichlow, 109–125. New York: Routledge.

Hatt, Beth. 2012. "Smartness as a Cultural Practice in Schools." *American Educational Research Journal* 49(3): 438–460.

Herdt, Gil. 2004. "Sexual Development, Social Oppression, and Local Culture." *Sexuality Research & Social Policy* 1(1): 39–62.

Hey, Valerie. 2002. "Horizontal Solidarities and Molten Capitalism: The Subject, Intersubjectivity, Self and Other in Late Modernity." *Discourse: Studies in the Cultural Politics of Education* 23(2): 227–241.

Hirschfeld, Lawrence A. 1997. "The Conceptual Politics of Race: Lessons from Our Children." *Ethos* 25(1): 63–92.

———. 2002. "Why Don't Anthropologists Like Children?" *American Anthropologist* 104(2): 611–627.

Horton, John, Pia Christensen, Peter Kraftl, and Sophie Hadfield-Hill. 2014. "'Walking . . . Just Walking': How Children and Young People's Everyday Pedestrian Practices Matter." *Social & Cultural Geography* 15(1): 94–115.

Ignatiev, Noel, and John Garvey, eds. 1996. *Race Traitor*. New York: Routledge.

Ingold, Tim. 2000. *The Perception of the Environment: Essays on Livelihood, Dwelling and Skill*. Oxon: Routledge.

Jackson, John, Jr. 2001. *Harlemworld: Doing Race and Class in Contemporary Black America*. Chicago: University of Chicago Press.

———. 2005. *Real Black: Adventures in Racial Sincerity*. Chicago: University of Chicago Press.

———. 2008. *Racial Paranoia: The Unintended Consequences of Political Correctness*. New York: Basic Civitas.

James, Allison, and Alan Prout. 2015 [1998]. *Constructing and Reconstructing Childhood: Contemporary Issues in the Sociological Study of Childhood*. Abingdon: Routledge.

Johnson, David W., and Roger T. Johnson. 2009. "An Educational Psychology Success Story: Social Interdependence Theory and Cooperative Learning." *Educational Researcher* 38: 365–379.

———. 2014. "Cooperative Learning in 21st Century." *Anales de Psicología/Annals of Psychology* 30(3): 841–851.

Kaldor, Mary. 2006. "Cosmopolitanism vs. Nationalism: The New Divide?" In *Europe's New Nationalism: States and Minorities in Conflict*, edited by Richard Caplan and John Feffer, 42–58. New York: Oxford University Press.

Kant, Immanuel. 1991 [1795]. *Political Writings*. Cambridge: Cambridge University Press.

Karner, Christian, and David Parker. 2011. "Conviviality and Conflict: Pluralism, Resilience, and Hope in Inner-City Birmingham." *Journal of Ethnic and Migration Studies* 37(3): 355–372.

Katz, Cindi. 2004. *Growing Up Global: Economic Restructuring and Children's Everyday Lives*. Minneapolis: University of Minnesota Press.

———. 2008. "Childhood as Spectacle: Relays of Anxiety and the Reconfiguration of the Child." *Cultural Geographies* 15(1): 5–17.

Kelley, Robin D. G. 2002. *Freedom Dreams: The Black Radical Imagination*. Boston: Beacon.

Killick, Evan, and Amit Desai. 2013. "Introduction: Valuing Friendship." In Desai and Killick, *Ways of Friendship*, 1–19.

King, Michael. 2007. "The Sociology of Childhood as Scientific Communication: Observations from a Social Systems Perspective." *Childhood* 14(2): 193–213.

Koenig, Bonnie, Sandra Soojin Lee, and Sarah S. Richardson, eds. 2008. *Revisiting Race in a Genomic Age*. New Brunswick, NJ: Rutgers University Press.

Kohn, Alfie. 1992. *The Case Against Competition*. Boston: Houghton Mifflin.

Kromidas, Maria. 2010. "Cyberculture, Multiculture, and the Emergent Morality of Critical Cosmopolitanism: Kids (Trans)forming Difference Online." In *Children Under Construction: Play as Curriculum*, edited by Drew Chappell, 233–258. New York: Peter Lang.

———. 2011a. "Elementary Forms of Cosmopolitanism: Beyond Blood, Birth, and Bodies in Immigrant New York City." *Harvard Educational Review* 81(3): 581–605.

———. 2011b. "Troubling Tolerance and Essentialism: The Critical Cosmopolitanism of New York City Schoolchildren." In *Politics of Interculturality*, edited by Anne Lavanchy, Fred Dervin, and Anahy Gajardo, 89–114. London: Cambridge Scholars.

———. 2012. "Affiliation or Appropriation? Crossing and the Politics of Race amongst Children in New York City." *Childhood: A Journal of Global Child Research* 19(3): 317–331.

———. 2014. "The 'Savage' Child and the Nature of Race: Posthuman Interventions from New York City." *Anthropological Theory* 14(4): 422–441.

Lancy, David F. 2012. "Unmasking Children's Agency." *AnthropoChildren* 1(2): 1–20.

———. 2014. *The Anthropology of Children: Cherubs, Chattel, and Changelings.* Cambridge: Cambridge University Press.

Larkin, Brian. 2013. "The Politics and Poetics of Infrastructure." *Annual Review of Anthropology* 42: 327–343.

Lave, Jean, and Ray McDermott. 2002. "Estranged Learning." *Outlines* 1: 19–48.

Lave, Jean, and Etienne Wenger. 1991. *Situated Learning: Legitimate Peripheral Participation.* New York: Cambridge University Press.

Lehrman, Sally. 2008. "Cops, Sports, and Schools: How the News Media Frames Coverage of Genetics and Race." In Koenig, Lee, and Richardson, *Revisiting Race in a Genomic Age*, 285–303.

Lewis, Amanda. 2003. *Race in the Schoolyard.* New Brunswick, NJ: Rutgers University Press.

Lewis, Amanda, John B. Diamond, and Tyrone A. Forman. 2015. "Conundrums of Integration: Desegregation in the Context of Racialized Hierarchy." *Sociology of Race & Ethnicity* 1(1): 22–36.

Losen, Daniel J., ed. 2014. *Closing the School Discipline Gap: Equitable Remedies for Excessive Exclusion, Disability, Equity, and Culture Series.* New York: Teachers College Press.

Lyons, Andrew P., and Harriet D. Lyons. 2011. "Problems in Writing about Sex in Anthropology." In *Sexualities in Anthropology: A Reader*, edited by Andrew P. Lyons and Harriet D. Lyons, 1–6. Sussex: Wiley-Blackwell.

Mac Naughton, Glenda, and Karina Davis, eds. 2009. *"Race" and Early Childhood Education: An International Approach to Identity, Politics and Pedagogy.* New York: Palgrave Macmillan.

Malecka, Anna. 2011. "Humor in the Perspective of Logos." *Analecta Husserliana* 110(1): 495-506.

Marx, Karl. 1964 [1884]. *The Economic and Philosophic Manuscripts of 1844.* Edited by Dirk J. Struik. New York: International.

———. 1970 [1865]. "Theses on Feuerbach." In Karl Marx and Friedrich Engels, *The German Ideology*, 121–123. New York: International.

Massey, Doreen. 2005. *For Space.* Thousand Oaks, CA: Sage.

Mawhinney, Janet. 1998. "'Giving Up the Ghost': Disrupting the (Re)production of White Privilege in Anti-racist Pedagogy and Organizational Change." Master's thesis, Ontario Institute for Studies in Education, University of Toronto.

McClintock, Ann. 1995. *Imperial Leather: Race, Gender, and Sexuality in the Colonial Context.* New York: Routledge.

McFarlane, Colin. 2011. *Learning the City: Knowledge and Translocal Assemblage.* Malden, MA: Wiley-Blackwell.

Meissner, Fran, and Steven Vertovec. 2015. "Comparing Super-diversity." *Ethnic and Racial Studies* 38(4): 541–555.

Meloni, Francesca, Karine Vanthuyne, and Cecile Rousseau. 2015. "Towards a Relational Ethics: Rethinking Ethics, Agency and Dependency in Research with Children." *Anthropological Theory* 15(1): 106–123.

Michie, Gregory. 2012. *We Don't Need Another Hero: Struggle, Hope, and Possibility in the Age of High-Stakes Schooling.* New York: Teachers College Press.

Montoya, Michael. 2011. *Making the Mexican Diabetic: Race, Science, and the Genetics of Inequality.* Berkeley: University of California Press.

Moody, James. 2001. "Race, School Integration, and Friendship Segregation in America." *American Journal of Sociology* 107(3): 679–716.

Moore, Valerie A. 2002. "The Collaborative Emergence of Race in Children's Play: A Case Study of Two Summer Camps." *Social Problems* 49(1): 58–78.

Morey, Maribel. 2014. "Reassessing Hannah Arendt's 'Reflections on Little Rock.'" *Law, Culture, and the Humanities* 10(1): 88–110.

Morrison, Toni. 1993. "On the Backs of Blacks." *Time*, Fall: 57.

Nava, Mica. 2007. *Visceral Cosmopolitanism: Gender, Culture, and the Normalisation of Difference.* Oxford: Berg.

Nespor, Jan. 1997. *Tangled Up in School: Politics, Space, Bodies, and Signs in the Educational Process.* Mahwah, NJ: Lawrence Erlbaum.

Noble, Greg. 2013. "Cosmopolitan Habits: The Capacities and Habitats of Intercultural Conviviality." *Body & Society* 19(2–3): 162–185.

Noguera, Pedro. 2008. "What Discipline Is For: Connecting Students to the Benefits of Learning." In *Everyday Anti-racism: Getting Real about Race in School*, edited by Mica Pollock, 132–138. New York: New Press.

———. 2014. "Urban Schools and the Black Male 'Challenge.'" In *Handbook of Urban Education*, edited by H. Richard Milner and Kofi Lomotey, 114–128. New York: Routledge.

Nowicka, Magdalena, and Steven Vertovec. 2013. "Comparing Convivialities: Dreams and Realities of Living-with-Difference." *European Journal of Cultural Studies* 17(4): 341–356.

Nussbaum, Martha C. 1997. "Kant and Stoic Cosmopolitanism." *Journal of Political Philosophy* 5(1): 1–25.

Oakes, Jeannie. 2005. *Keeping Track: How Schools Structure Inequality.* New Haven, CT: Yale University Press.

Ollman, Bertell. 1971. *Alienation: Marx's Conception of Man in Capitalist Society.* London: Cambridge University Press.

Olsen, Laurie. 1997. *Made in America: Immigrant Students in Our Public Schools.* New York: New Press.

Omi, Michael, and Howard Winant. 1994. *Racial Formation in the United States.* New York: Routledge.

Orfield, Gary, and Chungmei Lee. 2004. *Brown at 50: King's Dream or Plessy's Nightmare?* Cambridge, MA: Civil Rights Project, Harvard University.

Pacini-Ketchabaw, Veronica, Fikile Nxumalo, and Carol Rowan. 2011. "Nomadic Research Practices in Early Childhood: Interrupting Racisms and Colonialisms." *Nomadic Research Practices* 1(1): 19–33.

Papadopoulos, Dimitris. 2010. "Insurgent Posthumanism." *Ephemera: Theory & Politics in Organizations* 10(2): 134–151.

Papadopoulos, Dimitris, Niamh Stephenson, and Vassilis Tsianos. 2008. *Escape Routes: Control and Subversion in the 21st Century.* London: Pluto Press.

Pascoe, C. J. 2011. *"Dude, You're a Fag": Masculinity and Sexuality in High School.* Berkeley: University of California Press.

Pascoe, Peggy. 2009. *What Comes Naturally: Miscegenation Law and the Making of Race in America.* Oxford: Oxford University Press.

Payne, Elizabeth, and Melissa Smith. 2014. "The Big Freak Out: Educator Fear in Response to the Presence of Transgender Elementary School Students." *Journal of Homosexuality* 61(3): 399–418.

Pollock, Mica. 2004. *Colormute: Race Talk Dilemmas in an American School.* Princeton, NJ: Princeton University Press.

———. 2008. *Because of Race: How Americans Debate Harm and Opportunity in Our Schools.* Princeton, NJ: Princeton University Press.

Price, Patricia L. 2013. "Race and Ethnicity II: Skin and Other Intimacies." *Progress in Human Geography* 37: 578–586.

Putnam, Robert D. 2007. "*E pluribus Unum*: Diversity and Community in the Twenty-first Century." *Scandinavian Political Studies* 30(2): 137–174.

Pyyhtinen, Olli, and Sakari Tamminen. 2011. "We Have Never Been Only Human: Foucault and Latour on the Question of the *Anthropos*." *Anthropological Theory* 11(2): 135–152.

Quintana, Stephen M., and Clark McKown, eds. 2008. *Handbook of Race, Racism, and the Developing Child.* Hoboken, NJ: John Wiley.

Ramos-Zayas, Ana. 2003. *National Performances: The Politics of Class, Race, and Space in Puerto Rican Chicago.* Chicago: University of Chicago Press.

———. 2007. "Becoming American, Becoming Black? Urban Competency, Racialized Spaces, and the Politics of Citizenship among Brazilian and Puerto Rican Youth in Newark." *Identities: Global Studies in Culture and Power* 14: 85–109.

Rampton, Ben. 1995. *Crossing: Language and Ethnicity among Adolescents.* London: Longman.

Renold, Emma. 2000. "Coming Out: Gender, (Hetero)sexuality and the Primary School." *Gender and Education* 12(3): 309–326.

———. 2005. *Girls, Boys, and Junior Sexualities: Exploring Children's Gender and Sexual Relations in the Primary School.* New York: Routledge.

———. 2013. *Boys and Girls Speak Out: A Qualitative Study of Children's Gender and Sexual Cultures (Age 10–12).* Cardiff: Cardiff University.

Renold, Emma, and Jessica Ringrose. 2008. "Regulation and Rupture: Mapping Tween Girls' Resistance to the Heterosexual Matrix." *Feminist Theory* 9(3): 313–338.

———. 2011. "Schizoid Subjectivities? Re-theorizing Teen Girls' Sexual Cultures in an Era of 'Sexualization.'" *Journal of Sociology* 47(4): 389–409.

———. 2012. "Phallic Girls? Girls' Negotiation of Phallogocentric Power." In *Queer Masculinities: A Critical Reader in Education,* edited by John Landreau and Nelson Rodriguez, 47–67. Berlin: Springer.

———. 2013. "Feminisms Refiguring 'Sexualisation,' Sexuality, and 'the Girl.'" *Feminist Theory* 14(3): 247–254.

Renold, Emma, Jessica Ringrose, and Danielle Egan, eds. 2015. *Children, Sexuality, and Sexualization.* Basingstoke: Palgrave Macmillan.

Roediger, David, ed. 1998. *Black on White: Black Writers on What It Means to Be White.* New York: Schocken Books.

———. 2002. *Colored White: Transcending the Racial Past.* Berkeley: University of California Press.

Rosen, David M. 2007. "Child Soldiers, International Humanitarian Law, and the Globalization of Childhood." *American Anthropologist* 109(2): 296–306.

Saldhana, Arun. 2010. "Skin, Affect, Aggregation: Guattarian Variations on Fanon." *Environment and Planning A* 42(10): 2410–2427.

Sanjek, Roger. 1998. *The Future of Us All: Race and Neighborhood Politics in New York City.* Ithaca, NY: Cornell University Press.

Sennett, Richard. 2012. *Together: The Rituals, Pleasures, and Politics of Cooperation.* London: Penguin.

Shriver, Mark D., and Rick A. Kittles. 2008. "Genetic Ancestry and the Search for Personalized Genetic Histories." In Koenig, Lee, and Richardson, *Revisiting Race in a Genomic Age,* 201–214.

Sicart, Miguel. 2014. *Play Matters*. Cambridge, MA: MIT Press.

Sichone, Owen B. 2006. "Xenophobia and Xenophilia in South Africa: African Migrants in Cape Town." In *Anthropology and the New Cosmopolitanism: Rooted, Feminist, and Vernacular Perspectives*, edited by Pnina Werbner, 309–324. Oxford: Berg.

Sidorkin, Alexander M. 2009. *Labor of Learning*. Rotterdam: Sense.

Staiger, Annagret. 2004. "Whiteness as Giftedness: Racial Formation at an Urban High School." *Social Problems* 51(2): 161–181.

Stark, Lauren. 2014. "Naming Giftedness: Whiteness and Ability Discourse in US Schools." *International Studies in Sociology of Education* 24(4): 394–414.

Stewart, Kathleen. 2007. *Ordinary Affects*. Durham, NC: Duke University Press.

Stockton, Kathryn. 2009. *The Queer Child, or Growing Sideways in the Twentieth Century*. Durham, NC: Duke University Press.

Stoler, Ann L. 1995. *Race and the Education of Desire: Foucault's History of Sexuality and the Colonial Order of Things*. Durham, NC: Duke University Press.

———. 2001. "Tense and Tender Ties: The Politics of Comparison in North American History and (Post)colonial Studies." *Journal of American History* 88(3): 829–865.

———. 2006. "Intimidations of Empire." In *Haunted by Empire: Geographies of Intimacy in North American History*, edited by Ann L. Stoler, 23–70. Durham, NC: Duke University Press.

Swain, Dan. 2012. *Alienation: An Introduction to Marx's Theory*. London: Bookmarks.

Swanton, Dan. 2010. "Sorting Bodies: Race, Affect, and Everyday Multiculture in a Mill Town in Northern England." *Environment and Planning A* 42: 2332–2350.

Tatum, Beverly. 2003. *"Why Are All the Black Kids Sitting Together in the Cafeteria?" And Other Conversations about Race*. New York: Basic Books.

Thomas, Mary. 2011. *Multicultural Girlhood: Racism, Sexism, and the Conflicted Spaces of American Education*. Philadelphia: Temple University Press.

Thompson, E. P. 1966. *The Making of the English Working Class*. New York: Vintage.

Tileagă, Cristian. 2016. *The Nature of Prejudice: Society, Discrimination, and Moral Exclusion*. London: Routledge.

Toren, Christina. 2012. "Anthropology and Psychology." In *The Sage Handbook of Social Anthropology*, edited by Richard Fardon and Olivia Harris, 27–41. London: Sage.

Treitler, Vilma Bashi. 2013. *The Ethnic Project: Transforming Racial Fiction into Ethnic Factions*. Stanford, CA: Stanford University Press.

Trouillot, Michel. 2003. *Global Transformations: Anthropology and the Modern World*. London: Palgrave Macmillan.

Tuck, Eve. 2012. *Urban Youth and School Pushout: Gateways, Get-aways, and the GED*. New York: Routledge.

Tuck, Eve, and K. Wayne Yang. 2012. "Decolonization Is Not a Metaphor." *Decolonization: Indigeneity, Education & Society* 1(1): 1–40.

———. 2013. "Introduction to Youth Resistance Research and Theories of Change." In *Youth Resistance Research and Theories of Change*, edited by Even Tuck and K. Wayne Wang, 1–24. New York: Routledge.

Una Qualitative Methods Learning Group. 2010. "Researching 'Race' and Ethnicity with Children in the Field: A Critical Appraisal of Qualitative Research Approaches, Methods, and Techniques." Una Working Paper 4, Belfast. http://www.unaglobal.org.

Valli, Linda, and Marilyn Chambliss. 2007. "Creating Classroom Cultures: One Teacher, Two Lessons, and a High-Stakes Test." *Anthropology & Education Quarterly* 38(1): 57–75.

Valli, Linda, Robert Croninger, and Daria Buese. 2012. "Studying High-Quality Teaching in a Highly Charged Policy Environment." *Teachers College Record* 114(4): 1–33.

Vance, Carol. 2005. "Anthropology Rediscovers Sexuality: A Theoretical Comment." In *Same-Sex Cultures and Sexualities: An Anthropological Reader*, edited by Jennifer Robertson, 15–32. Malden, MA: Blackwell.

van der Veer, Peter. 2004. "Cosmopolitan Options." In *Worlds on the Move: Globalization, Migration, and Cultural Security*, edited by Jonathan Friedman and Shalini Randeria, 167–178. New York: Palgrave Macmillan.

Vološinov, Valentin N. 1973 [1922]. *Marxism and the Philosophy of Language*. Cambridge, MA: Harvard University Press.

Watkins, Megan. 2012. "Discipline, Consciousness, and the Formation of a Scholarly Habitus." *Continuum: Journal of Media & Cultural Studies* 19(4): 545–557.

Weis, Lois, and Michelle Fine. 2013. "A Methodological Response from the Field to Douglas Foley: Critical Bifocality and Class Cultural Productions in Anthropology and Education." *Anthropology & Education Quarterly* 44(3): 222–233.

Werbner, Pnina. 1999. "Global Pathways: Working Class Cosmopolitans and the Creation of Transnational Ethnic Worlds." *Social Anthropology* 7(1): 17–35.

Wessendorf, Suzanne. 2013. "Commonplace Diversity and the 'Ethos of Mixing': Perceptions of Difference in a London Neighbourhood." *Identities* 20(4): 407–422.

Whitehead, Neil L. 2009. "Post-human Anthropology." *Identities: Global Studies in Culture and Power* 16(1): 1–32.

Wiegman, Robyn. 1995. *American Anatomies: Theorizing Race and Gender*. Durham, NC: Duke University Press.

Willis, Paul. 1977. *Learning to Labour: How Working Class Kids Get Working Class Jobs*. New York: Columbia University Press.

Winant, Howard. 2000. "Race and Race Theory." *Annual Review of Sociology* 26: 169–185.

———. 2001. *The World Is a Ghetto: Race and Democracy since World War II*. New York: Basic Books.

Winkler, Erin N. 2012. *Learning Race, Learning Place: Shaping Racial Identities and Ideas in African American Childhoods*. New Brunswick, NJ: Rutgers University Press.

Wise, Amanda, and Selvaraj Velayutham. 2009. *Everyday Multiculturalism*. Basingstoke: Palgrave Macmillan.

———. 2013. "Conviviality in Everyday Multiculturalism: Some Brief Comparisons between Singapore and Sydney." *European Journal of Cultural Studies* 17(4): 406–430.

Wodak, Ruth, and Martin Reisigl. 2003. "Discourse and Racism." In *The Handbook of Discourse Analysis*, edited by Deborah Schiffrin, Deborah Tannen, and Heidi E. Hamilton, 372–395. Oxford: Blackwell.

Woodson, Jacqueline. 2001. *The Other Side*. New York: Putnam.

Wridt, Pamela. 2010. "A Qualitative GIS Approach to Mapping Urban Neighborhoods with Children to Promote Physical Activity and Child-Friendly Community Planning." *Environment and Planning B* 37(1): 129–147.

Young, Donna E. 2012. "Post Race Post Haste: Towards an Analytical Convergence of Critical Race Theory and Marxism." *Columbia Journal of Race and Law* 1(3): 499–510.

Žižek, Slavoj. 1994. "The Specter of Ideology." In *Mapping Ideology*, edited by Slavoj Žižek, 1–33. London: Verso.

INDEX

ability grouping, 11, 80–81, 91–92, 101; and
  race, 11, 84–85, 145. *See also* intelligence;
  smartness
aesthetics. *See* style
affective states, 6, 97, 99–101; and friendship,
  58–59, 62–65, 69–70, 76; and relation to
  power, 131, 133, and sexuality, 131–132,
  134
African Americans, 11, 19–20, 30, 42, 47, 75,
  84, 107–108, 127
agency, 5; children and, 7–8, 55–56; of space,
  28
Ahmed, Sara, 30, 130
Albanians, 33, 40, 63, 70, 75, 115, 136–138,
  141, 143
alienation, 91–92, 160nn6–7. *See also*
  humanization
amalgamation, as mode of relationality, 32
American-ness: alternative constructs, 127,
  133–134, 137; as English-speaking, 33; as
  whiteness, 30, 75, 133–134, 158n4
Amin, Ash, 57, 100–101
anti-linear becomings, 56. *See also* subjectivity: poststructuralist accounts
anti-miscegenation laws, 129–130, 162n1
antiracism, 17, 23, 57, 101–102, 122, 157n7
Arabic, 34, 41, 72–74, 136
Arendt, Hannah, 129, 162n2
Aristotle, 54–55
attachments, 18, 40, 57, 75, 98, 140. *See also*
  belonging(s); identity performances
Augursville, 2, 28–33, 101, 157n5. *See also*
  modes of relationality; New York City
authenticity, 15, 45, 62, 65, 66, 77–78, 157n7,
  159n6

"bad" kids: fear of, 46–47; and good kids, 86,
  115, 120; and racial formation, 104, 106,
  110, 112–113, 122; rethinking, 118–121
Baldwin, James, 151
baseball, 57, 67–68

Baudelaire, Charles, 27
becoming other, 64, 70, 73, 76, 78
belonging(s), 9, 18, 126, 128, 141; alternative constructs, 56, 63, 70, 73, 75–76,
  115; and friendship, 55–56; and multiculturalism, 95; and pop cultural objects,
  57, 62, 63, 69, 77–78; spatial, 30, 35, 39,
  45–46
Bengalis, 31–32, 34, 41, 133
Benjamin, Walter, 8, 155n16
Bernstein, Robin, 130, 149–150
bilingual students. *See* English Language
  Learners
Blackness: anti-Black racism, 21, 30, 38, 85,
  116–117, 128; and Black/white binary,
  21–22, 140; counterhegemonic constructs, 20, 35, 45–46, 47–48, 49–50;
  experimental studies and, 1, 149–151; in
  PS AV, 42–43, 127
Black studies, 12, 151–152
Blommaert, Jan, 29, 32–33
bodies, in racial formation, 1, 13–14, 19–21,
  48, 94–95, 96, 138–140
Bonilla-Silva, Eduardo, 109, 161n10
Bourdieu, Pierre, 15
boyhood, 37, 40, 46, 51–52, 64–66, 67–69,
  124, 127, 157n7. *See also* masculinity
Braidotti, Rosi, 56
bridging differences, 13, 70–72, 75, 95,
  138–140
Brown v. Board of Education, 129, 149
Burman, Erica, 7

cafeteria, 43, 51–54, 58, 61, 68, 133, 140; as
  symbol of segregation, 54
childhood, and reification of race, 3–5, 7, 55,
  147–148
childhood studies, 1–3, 14, 26, 56–57, 152,
  153n3, 154n10, 162n4
children: constructions of, 56, 130, 133; and
  essentialism, 3–5, 8, 56, 150, 154n10;

ABOUT THE AUTHOR

MARIA KROMIDAS is an associate professor of anthropology at William Paterson University. Her work revolves around issues of race, posthumanism, and cosmopolitanism, and how they can be rethought with and through the critical lens provided by children and childhood. She has contributed to the journals *Anthropological Theory, Critique of Anthropology, Harvard Educational Review,* and *Childhood: Global Journal of Child Research.* She was born, was bred, and lives in the big city of dreams.

CPSIA information can be obtained
at www.ICGtesting.com
Printed in the USA
LVHW091940091118
596595LV00002B/17/P